FRANCE EN VÉLO

The ultimate cycle journey from the Channel to the Med

Hannah Reynolds and John Walsh

FRANCE EN VELO

CONTENTS

Overview

The Ride

Information

THE ROUTE

This spectacular and beautiful 1,000 mile route across France passes through 19 *départements* taking in the most famous cycling regions, such as the Loire and Provence, as well as lesser-known gems, like the Lot river and the verdant banks of the Vienne.

Passing through a patchwork of subtle and striking changes in terrain and landscape, this is a route of two distinct halves. You begin by hugging the Brittany coastline momentarily, flirting with Normandy and seeing the iconic Mont St-Michel before heading south to the banks of France's longest river, the Loire. After crossing the wheat fields and grazing land of Poitou-Charentes, you reach the rolling hills of the Dordogne.

On leaving the Dordogne you turn a corner. The terrain changes as hills become ever more prominent, slowly giving way to mountainous terrain and steep-sided valleys; and there is also a change in climate and *terroir*.

The route hugs the banks of the Lot river, picking a gentle route into the mountains and occasionally being propelled up its valley sides, before reaching the source and the northern edge of the wild and wooded Cévennes.

The route plunges down into the fruit and vineyard choked Ardèche *département* before following the famous gorge of the same name to the Rhône valley, and the world-renowned wines of Châteauneuf-du-Pape.

Crossing the Rhône announces your arrival in Provence. The towering shape of Mont Ventoux on the skyline, hot sun, lavender fields and blue-shuttered cafés, combine to make you feel as if you are in a separate country entirely.

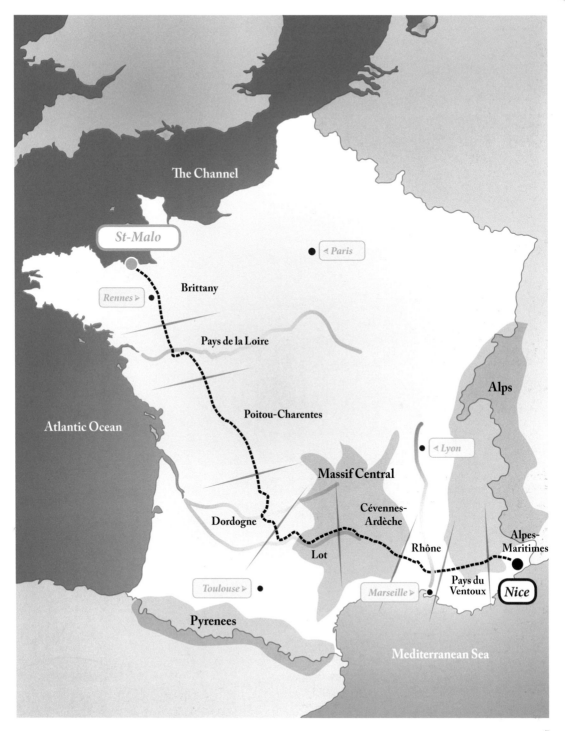

THE REGIONS

Few countries can rival France for the sheer scale of physical diversity. From the rugged coastlines of Brittany, to the gentle hills of the Dordogne; from the wooded mountains of the Cévennes, to lavender covered plateau of Provence, it is an ever changing panorama.

Each region looks, feels and even smells different. It has its own architecture, dialect, traditions, food and culture. The French can be fiercely proud of their own region, referring to it as '*mon pays*' ('my country'), and each has a strong sense of identity.

We have divided the route up into nine regions, not by using the strict boundaries you will find on any map, but as a way of encompassing the changes and characteristics you will feel as a rider passing through these regions.

1 - Brittany

With a strong sense of cultural identity and a feisty attitude, Brittany is one of the most independently minded regions of mainland France. Its wild and beautiful coastline brings in a third of France's total fish catch.

A turbulent history has left Brittany dotted with castles and fortresses, yet today its quiet, narrow, backroads criss-cross the landscape, bordered by rich pastures, grazing cows and orchards.

2 - Pays de la Loire

Languid and graceful, the Loire is France's longest river, following its slow 600-mile course from the Massif Central to the Atlantic. Tree-lined banks and lush green fields create the perfect foil for the stunning architecture of the châteaux for which the Loire is famous. From the sparkle in a cool glass of Saumur *crémant* to the turrets of Château de Brissac, elegance pervades the region.

7 - Rhône

Despite being one of the most industrialised valleys in France, here the Rhône river flows past some of the most beautiful rural villages and vineyards of the route. Make sure you stop to raise a glass in Châteauneuf-du-Pape. Along the Rhône you will see Mont Ventoux drawing closer with every pedal stroke, while the Mistral wind at your back blows you along.

5 - Lot

Despite its beautiful river valley, stunning medieval bridges and wooded hillsides, the Lot valley is virtually undiscovered by tourist traffic. Its many secluded and empty roads take you through unspoilt villages, where life continues in the old, traditional pattern. From Figeac the route follows the river, either low in the valley or climbing its sides, for dramatic views of the river below.

3 - Poitou-Charentes

Cycle through a pastoral idyll where fields of wheat, corn and cattle border the roads. Agriculture is an important part of the economy here, which naturally leads to a pride in the *gastronomie*. Narrow lanes alongside rivers or between high hedgerows and fields take you past Roman ruins, medieval towers and fortified châteaux – reminders that this wasn't always such a settled and bucolic region.

8 - Provence: Pays du Ventoux

Ventoux, often known as the *géant de Provence*, dominates the flat land around it. Sometimes Ventoux stalks you; at other times you are hunting it down. Whilst Ventoux may be the high spot of this region, there is so much more to see. Fields of lavender fill your nostrils with their strong scent and your ears tune in to the persistent buzzing of honey bees.

4 - Dordogne

Rolling hills and wide rivers lead you through three of the four of the old Périgord regions: *blanc* for the outcrops of limestone, home to early man; *vert* for the fertile lands; and *noir* for the tightly wooded hillsides. The Périgord is where many of France's most renowned delicacies can be found. Here you will be able to enjoy truffles and *foie gras*.

6 - Cévennes-Ardèche

The chestnut and pine woods which cloak the hillsides of the Cévennes conceal quiet roads and unspoilt villages. As you descend from the top of the Col du Mas de l'Ayre the landscape changes. Suddenly, laid out beneath, is a patchwork of fruit producers and vineyards. A warm blast of air greets you, a welcome to the south.

9 - Provence: Alpes-Maritimes

From the high *cols*, to the dramatic narrow gorges and the sparkling Côte d'Azur, this is a region with big visual impact and contrast. The road hugs vertiginous cliff edges or plunges into the blackness of tunnels blasted straight through the rock. The route is an exhilarating roller-coaster of climbs and descents on remote mountain roads, with the occasional village perched way up high in the hills.

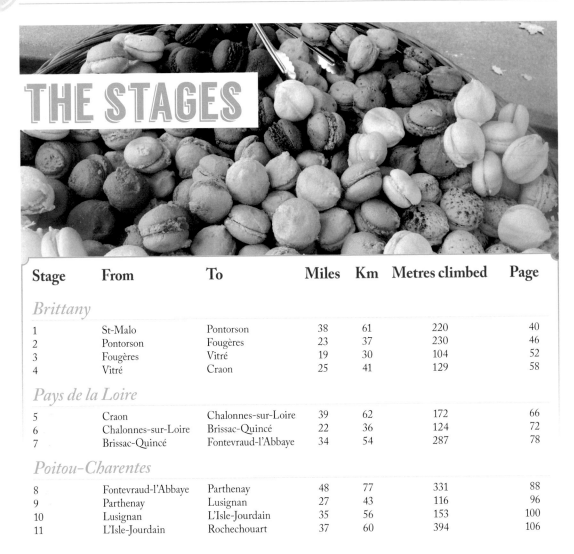

THE STAGES

Stage	From	To	Miles	Km	Metres climbed	Page
Brittany						
1	St-Malo	Pontorson	38	61	220	40
2	Pontorson	Fougères	23	37	230	46
3	Fougères	Vitré	19	30	104	52
4	Vitré	Craon	25	41	129	58
Pays de la Loire						
5	Craon	Chalonnes-sur-Loire	39	62	172	66
6	Chalonnes-sur-Loire	Brissac-Quincé	22	36	124	72
7	Brissac-Quincé	Fontevraud-l'Abbaye	34	54	287	78
Poitou–Charentes						
8	Fontevraud-l'Abbaye	Parthenay	48	77	331	88
9	Parthenay	Lusignan	27	43	116	96
10	Lusignan	L'Isle-Jourdain	35	56	153	100
11	L'Isle-Jourdain	Rochechouart	37	60	394	106
Dordogne						
12	Rochechouart	Brantôme	39	62	409	114
13	Brantôme	Hautefort	32	52	443	120
14	Hautefort	Les Eyzies-de-Tayac	36	58	444	126
15	Les Eyzies-de-Tayac	Souillac	34	54	413	132
16	Souillac	Gramat	28	45	613	138

THE JOURNEY

Why Journey?

"It is good to have an end to journey toward; but it is the
journey that matters, in the end."

Ernest Hemingway

A journey is not just physical but emotional, mental and
educational; a long journey can change the fabric of who you
are. A journey may be undertaken for wandering, relaxing or as
a challenge. Life on the road is a microcosm of life itself; you
have good days and bad days. The differences are important,
with time for reflection and time for action. You need to
experience highs and lows because it is the change of pace that
separates the spectacular from the simply special.

One of the greatest joys of travelling by bike is that you
move at a pace perfect for observation; even without any
deliberate sight-seeing you will experience a vast amount of
what France has to offer. The landscape and rivers, châteaux
and fortresses, all these can be experienced from the saddle,
though of course close inspection can be infinitely rewarding.
Changes in the scents in the air, the gradients you are
pedalling, even the direction of the wind will be constantly
telling you things about the land you are riding through.

When to Journey?

In short, any time between May and October. July
and August provide the best guaranteed weather
in the north though it can be hot in Provence, with
temperatures regularly reaching above 30 degrees.

June and September are pleasant for cycling in the
South, if you don't mind the occasional chilly morning
in the north of the country. France's popularity may
also be a factor in your choice of time. In August it
appears half of Europe is camping near the Ardèche
and it's best to book accommodation in advance in the
more touristy places. However, much of the route is off
the beaten track and the Lot valley remains virtually
deserted even in high season. Cycling while the Tour
de France is on (the first 3 weeks of July) adds a unique
dimension, allowing you to relax in a bar after a day in
the saddle by watching the pros sprint for the line on
the TV. October sees the beginning of autumn, and be
aware that temperatures can dip to just above freezing
towards the end of the month in the higher Lot and
Cévennes regions.

Why France?

"Every man has two countries his own and France"

Thomas Jefferson

France encompasses the finest collection of landscapes in Europe and receives over 80 million international tourists a year from all over the globe; more than any other country on the planet.

At the same time, France is a deeply rural country, one-quarter as densely populated as the UK. It is possible to find yourself off the beaten track with ease even in the height of summer, and the French are passionately proud of their land.

France is also the cultural home of the bicycle and the country most synonymous with cycling. Motorists are more likely to pip their horn in encouragement rather than anger, and shout a supportive *'bon courage'*. The Tour de France may be criticised for its commercialism, but its almost month-long celebration of France and the art of touring through its landscape is as important as who wears yellow in Paris.

The land is as rich and varied as its gastronomy and wines. If you have ridden Lands End to John O'Groats in the UK you will appreciate France's cycling culture– its better wine, its better food and its better weather. France has been designed

for the cyclist and its countryside offers a variety of perfect rural idylls where traditional farming has not been as readily dismantled or as industrialised as its northern European counterparts. It is also a country of contrasts: the rounded hills of the Dordogne are perfect for rolling along whilst the plateaus of Provence assault the senses with strong aromas of lavender and thyme.

Many French villages have a wealth of beauty, history and architecture that would be heavily promoted in other countries. Here the abundance of *monuments historiques* is taken for granted. An 11th-century church will be barely signposted, meandering medieval lanes are often *de rigueur*.

The ride takes you through many places steeped in history, from prehistoric man in Les Eyzies-du-Tayac to the medieval fortress of Fougères; you can cross the route of King Richard the Lionheart in Rochechouart and the paths of pilgrims in Parthenay. Even without an active interest in history you will find yourself absorbing the odd fact or tale almost by osmosis.

Rivers and Gorges
The French Cyclists Best Friends

Rivers shape the geography of France and this epic cycling journey. Each river has its own personality. The first giant is the Loire, France's longest river at over 1,000km.

The Loire is a lazy river, relaxing in a vast open valley that affords gentle cruising through vineyards on its southern banks, and ensures flattish terrain for 100km either side of its braiding, sediment-choked channels.

The Dordogne, on the other hand, cuts deep meanders and encourages rocky headlands on which you'll see some strikingly beautiful châteaux. Its tributaries have been harder at work than those of the Loire, creating a patchwork of rolling valleys and hills.

Climbers shouldn't be discouraged; following rivers still

allows you your fix. The Ardèche's accumulated angry, erosive power has eaten away at its limestone setting. This affords a lung-busting climb to the top of a gorge which surpasses all superlatives, and a fantastic undulating and weaving ridge ride that darts from one breathtaking view of the river below to the next.

The Rhône is an immense channel, some 500m wide in places, and once across it you arrive at the gateway to Provence and the final leg of the journey. From its source high in the icy Alps, the river broadens into a transport route of great importance to the regional economy.

In places along its banks, life continues as it has done for many hundreds of years. Farmers grow peaches by traditional methods and still hand-pick grapes in nearby Châteauneuf-du-Pape.

Why this route?

"Go not by the most common road but the smaller paths"

Pythagoras

There are many ways to cross France. Several different routes would take you from the Channel to the Med, and cycle tourists have their favourites, tried and tested over decades.

Some French cyclists try and complete the *diagonales*. These nine rides criss-cross France to create a six-pointed star shape. Whilst joining up two furthest points is one way of creating a cycling route, there is no guarantee that the line will take you on the most beautiful, most interesting or most enjoyable regional rides.

A straight line across a map is not a route; certainly not a journey. However a quick glance at the map will show you this journey is a *chemin des écoliers*, a winding path that children take to avoid getting to school too quickly.

The route ensures you can discover *la France profonde* on your way to Nice, as it links the two most iconic ports in Brittany and Provence via a sweeping graceful curve.

Your Journey

"Athletes will go the farthest distance: lovers the shortest. But the lovers may be out the longest time."

Stephen Graham, The Gentle Art of Tramping

Whether riding unsupported or guided, whether you plan to ride the 1,000 miles as quick as you can or watch the flowers grow, this book will help. Our repeated visits refined the route, curiosity leading us to explore hillside villages or narrow lanes, and we encourage you to do the same.

The route is described in 32 'stages', the building blocks of your journey, to help you tackle the route over anything from a week to a month, or on multiple holidays.

Let this book be an inspiration as you sit by the fire. Take it with you as your companion on the road and see where it leads. Enjoy your journey.

Hannah and John
hello@franceenvelo.cc

YOUR RIDE
YOUR WAY

Whether you load up your
panniers and revel in the freedom
of the open road, or slip into some
Lycra and get down on the drops,
there are many ways to ride this
route, and each will give you a
unique experience.

The road and the route remain the same but how you tackle them, what you take and what you get out of the experience can vary wildly. Get up early, get in the saddle and get to the end, knocking off the mileage as quickly as you can before spending the afternoon or evening exploring the end-of-stage town.

Alternatively make the same distance last all day by pedalling just a few miles at a time, then getting off your bike to explore whenever you spot something interesting.

When planning your trip there are two key questions – how long have you got to complete the route? Do you want a guided or self-sufficient holiday? Time is obviously an issue. With a three-week tour you can afford to take it at a slower pace, allowing plenty of time for cooling swims in rivers, picnics complete with wine, cheese and indulgent afternoon naps on sun-warmed grassy banks. Alternatively this trip could be a chance to learn a little more about France, visiting museums, seeking out narrow back-streets and taking in snippets of history in the villages you ride through.

With a limited time frame, the emphasis becomes more about covering distance at a pace that allows you to complete the journey in the time you have available. Although if you don't want to compromise your leisurely pace, or lose the time needed to relax or explore, you could choose to do one of the 'Regional Discovery' itineraries and focus your break on just one or two regions of the route.

Another decision is whether to be self-sufficient or supported. The original St-Malo to Nice route was created and developed for Saddle Skedaddle. A guided trip with them has a host of advantages, not least your bags being transported, allowing you to travel further and faster each day with mechanical assistance for your bike, should you need it, giving you peace of mind. A guide will take care of the day-to-day complications of travel, find you the best cafés and restaurants, deal with hotel staff and cover all the details so all you need to do is enjoy riding your bike. Skedaddle will even set up delicious picnics of carefully selected local foods in the most beautiful spots on the route. What could be better than rounding a corner to find a sumptuous picnic already laid on, so all you have to do is park your bike and find the perfect spot in the sun.

One of the other benefits of a guided trip is the chance to share your experiences with other cyclists, and your guide. Sitting around the dinner table in the evening and sharing of your adventures from the day creates a feeling of camaraderie and will give you new perspectives on the things you have seen and done. Skedaddle guides will also bring their own depth of knowledge, interest and passion for France, giving you insight into the route and the culture.

Although riding with panniers will slow you down, cycle touring gives you a sense of complete freedom. You have everything you need with you, and are not reliant on anyone else's time keeping or plans. Travelling this way you are likely to meet lots of people as a fully loaded bike always attracts curious looks. Cycling is a part of French culture and you are likely to be greeted warmly and questioned about your journey along the way.

For the traditionalist, 'proper' touring means carrying all your own gear and being completely self-sufficient. If you are planning on travelling this way and haven't done so before, it is worth doing a few shorter tours before embarking on the full 1,000-mile route, so you can pare down your kit and work out how much you are comfortable carrying, and how many miles a day you will be able to cover.

Tents and sleeping kit are the heaviest items for a touring cyclist to carry. The alternative is 'credit-card' touring where you travel unsupported but stay in hotels or *chambre d'hôtes* along the way, carrying only the bare necessities with you.

Saddle Skedaddle

The UK's largest independent cycling holiday specialist offers highly recommended, quality guided trips from St-Malo to Nice and all around the world.

The Cycle Hub, Quayside,
Newcastle-upon-Tyne,
NE6 1BU
0191 265 1110
www.skedaddle.co.uk

THE CLASSIC:
TWO-WEEK ITINERARY

Fourteen days adds up to just the right amount of time to cover the miles at a pace that doesn't feel as if you are racing against the clock, but still allows you to pack a 1,000-mile journey into two weeks of holiday.

There will be some long days in the saddle, the biggest day is just over 90 miles in total. Pace yourself well and you will arrive at every destination with time to look around and relax over a cold glass of the local tipple in the evening.

The Classic

Day	From	To	Miles	Km	Metres Climbed	Stages
1	St-Malo	Vitré	80	128	554	1, 2, 3
2	Vitré	Brissac-Quincé	86	139	425	4, 5, 6
3	Brissac-Quincé	Parthenay	82	131	618	7, 8
4	Parthenay	L'Isle-Jourdain	62	99	269	9, 10
5	L'Isle-Jourdain	Brantôme	76	122	803	11, 12
6	Brantôme	Les Eyzies-de-Tayac	68	110	887	13, 14
7	Les Eyzies-de-Tayac	Gramat	62	99	1026	15, 16
8	Gramat	Entraygues-sur-Truyère	64	103	634	17, 18
9	Entraygues-sur-Truyère	Mende	74	119	1514	19, 20
10	Mende	Pont d'Arc	75	121	1008	21, 22
11	Pont d'Arc	Sault	93	149	1544	23, 24, 25, 26
12	Sault	Moustiers-Ste-Marie	70	113	939	27, 28
13	Moustiers-Ste-Marie	Castellane	50	81	1293	29, 30
14	Castellane	Nice	57	91	746	31, 32

THE EXPLORER:
THREE-WEEK ITINERARY

Designed to allow plenty of time for getting to know the places you pedal through, this itinerary allows you to look around, savour your environment, properly relax and absorb the experience.

The only **ride covering** over 70 miles comes after a rest day, so you should be feeling refreshed and ready to tackle it.

Shorter rides provide you with the freedom to stop whenever the fancy takes you, and fully embrace the carefree life of the open road.

The Explorer

Day	From	To	Miles	Km	Metres Climbed	Stages
1	St-Malo	Pontorson	38	61	220	1
2	Pontorson	Vitré	42	67	334	2, 3
3	Vitré	Chalonnes-sur-Loire	64	103	301	4, 5
4	Chalonnes-sur-Loire	Fontevraud l'Abbaye	56	90	411	6, 7
5	Fontevraud l'Abbaye	Parthenay	48	77	331	8
6	Parthenay	L'Isle-Jourdain	62	99	269	9, 10
7	L'Isle-Jourdain	Rochechouart	37	60	394	11
8	Rochechouart	Brantôme	39	62	409	12
9	Brantôme	Les Eyzies-de-Tayac	68	110	887	13, 14
10	Les Eyzies-de-Tayac	Gramat	62	99	1026	15, 16
11	Gramat	Entraygues-sur-Truyère	64	103	634	17, 18
12	Rest Day	Rest Day				
13	Entraygues-sur-Truyère	Mende	74	119	1514	19, 20
14	Mende	Villefort	35	57	532	21
15	Villefort	Pont d'Arc	40	64	476	22
16	Pont d'Arc	Châteauneuf-du-Pape	50	81	597	23, 24
17	Châteauneuf-du-Pape	Sault	42	68	947	25, 26
18	Sault	Forcalquier	33	53	310	27
19	Forcalquier	Moustiers-Ste-Marie	37	60	629	28
20	Moustiers-Ste-Marie	Castellane	50	81	1293	29, 30
21	Castellane	Nice	57	91	746	31, 32

THE CHALLENGE:
TEN-DAY ITINERARY

Ten days to cover 1,000 miles is a tough but achievable challenge. A high level of fitness and preparation is needed before taking it on. Long days in the saddle will see the landscape change rapidly as you pedal your way from one region to the next.

Whilst you may not have time to linger in every village you ride through during the day, the overnight stops have been carefully chosen to provide a wide variety of experiences from small villages to medieval towns.

The Challenge

Day	From	To	Miles	Km	Metres Climbed	Stages
1	St-Malo	Vitré	80	128	554	1, 2, 3
2	Vitré	Fontevraud l'Abbaye	120	193	712	4, 5, 6, 7
3	Fontevraud l'Abbaye	L'Isle-Jourdain	109	176	600	8, 9, 10
4	L'Isle-Jourdain	Brantôme	76	122	803	11, 12
5	Brantôme	Souillac	102	164	1300	13, 14, 15
6	Souillac	Entraygues-sur-Truyère	92	148	1247	16, 17, 18
7	Entraygues-sur-Truyère	Villefort	109	176	2046	19, 20, 21
8	Villefort	Villes-sur-Auzon	114	183	1367	22, 23, 24, 25
9	Villes-sur-Auzon	Moustiers-Ste-Marie	89	143	1592	26, 27, 28
10	Moustiers-Ste-Marie	Nice	107	172	2039	29, 30, 31, 32

REGIONAL DISCOVERY HOLIDAYS

Not everyone has the time to spare to take on the full 1,000-mile challenge in one go. These shorter itineraries are designed to allow you to complete the route over the course of several holidays; or you could pick a favourite region or even an unfamiliar one, to explore in more depth.

Shorter distances make great trips for families, as well as those who want an introduction to cycle touring or a more leisurely experience. Equally, if you are a regular rider who wants to delve deeper into a specific region of France, these suggestions are perfect, allowing you time to linger a little longer over coffee or explore myriad market towns and villages along the way.

Brittany and Pays de la Loire

Arrive 🚶 🚢 St Malo ✈ Dinard

Day	From	To	Miles	Km	Metres Climbed	Stages
1	St-Malo	Pontorson	38	61	220	1
2	Pontorson	Vitré	42	67	334	2, 3
3	Vitré	Craon	25	41	129	4
4	Craon	Chalonnes-sur-Loire	39	62	172	5
5	Chalonnes-sur-Loire	Fontevraud l'Abbaye	56	90	411	6,7

Depart 🚶 Saumur 10miles/17 km from Fontevraud l'Abbaye ✈ Angers or Tours

Poitou–Charentes and Dordogne

Arrive 🚶 Saumur 10miles/17 km from Fontevraud l'Abbaye ✈ Angers or Tours

Day	From	To	Miles	Km	Metres Climbed	Stages
1	Fontevraud l'Abbaye	Parthenay	48	77	331	8
2	Parthenay	L'Isle-Jourdain	62	99	269	9, 10
3	L'Isle-Jourdain	Rochechouart	37	60	394	11
4	Rochechouart	Brantôme	39	62	409	12
5	Brantôme	Les Eyzies-de-Tayac	68	110	887	13, 14
6	Les Eyzies-de-Tayac	Souillac	34	54	413	15

Depart 🚶 Souillac ✈ Toulouse

Dordogne and Lot

Arrive ⌂ Souillac ✈ Toulouse

Day	From	To	Miles	Km	Metres Climbed	Stages
1	Souillac	Gramat	28	45	613	16
2	Gramat	Figeac	28	45	201	17
3	Figeac	Entraygues-sur-Truyère	36	58	433	18
4	Entraygues-sur-Truyère	St-Geniez d'Olt	33	53	554	19
5	St-Geniez d'Olt	Mende	41	66	960	20

Depart ⌂ Mende ✈ Nîmes

Cévennes Ardèche and Rhône

Arrive ⌂ Mende ✈ Nîmes

Day	From	To	Miles	Km	Metres Climbed	Stages
1	Mende	Villefort	35	57	532	21
2	Villefort	Pont d'Arc	40	64	476	22
3	Pont d'Arc	Aiguèze	22	35	483	23
4	Aiguèze	Châteauneuf-du-Pape	29	46	114	24

Depart ⌂ Orange 8miles/13km from Châteauneuf-du-Pape ✈ Avignon or Marseille

Provence

Arrive ⌂ Orange 8miles/13km from Châteauneuf-du-Pape ✈ Avignon or Marseille

Day	From	To	Miles	Km	Metres Climbed	Stages
1	Châteauneuf-du-Pape	Sault	42	68	947	25, 26
2	Sault	Forcalquier	33	53	310	27
3	Forcalquier	Moustiers-Ste-Marie	37	60	629	28
4	Moustiers-Ste-Marie	Castellane	50	81	1293	29, 30
5	Castellane	Nice	57	91	746	31, 32

Depart ⌂ ⛴ ✈ Nice

France en Vélo

BEST STAGES FOR...

We've handpicked our favourite places along the route and we hope you find them to be special, too. As you ride you'll discover many others that will form part of your unique memories of the trip, and become the story of your journey.

Tracks of Le Tour

St-Malo to Pontorson *p40* The start of your journey is almost exactly on the finish-line of the St-Malo stage of the 2013 race.

Fontevraud l'Abbaye to Parthenay *p88* Loudun is where the peloton rolled in, the day after the young Scot David Millar triumphed at the Futuroscope time trial in 2000.

Mende to Villefort *p170* Mende is multiple-stage start and finish town as well as hosting another pro bike race, Le Tour du Gauvedan.

Villes-sur-Auzon to Sault *p204* Le Tour has finished on the summit of Ventoux nine times.

Gréolierès to Nice *p242* Le Promenade des Anglais in Nice featured in the team time-trial in the 2013 edition of the race.

Wild Swimming

Chalonnes-sur-Loire to Brissac-Quincé *p72* Quiet river swim with a small beach.

Lusignan to L'isle Jourdain *p100* Secluded and tranquil, a tree-lined stretch of the Vienne river.

Souillac to Gramat *p138* Invigorating swim in the Ouysse.

Villefort to Pont d'Arc *p176* Swim under the iconic arch and dive from nearby rocks.

Gréolières to Nice *p242* Stand under a thundering waterfall a short step from the route.

Getting off the Beaten Track

Pontorson to Fougères *p46* Quiet back lanes of Brittany barely touched by traffic.

Parthenay to Lusignan *p96* Wander between the high hedgerows and fields typical of the *bocage* landscape.

Brantôme to Hautefort *p120* From *Périgord Blanc* to *Périgord Noir* enjoy exploring the distinctive differences in the scenery.

Figeac to Entraygues-sur-Truyére *p150* Tranquil, easy riverside riding in one of the least-visited areas of France.

Sault to Forcalquier *p212* Experience a quieter side of Provence.

Fortresses and Châteaux

Fougères to Vitré *p52*
Fairytale castles mark the start and
the end of this route.

Craon to Chalonnes-sur-Loire *p66*
Visit some of the most spectacular
châteaux on the Loire.

**Brissac-Quincé to Fontevraud
l'Abbaye** *p78*
Along the river and through Saumur
you will see many classic buildings.

Rochechouart to Brantôme *p114*
A grand château at Rochechouart
starts this stage of riding.

Brantôme to Hautefort *p120*
Touristy but elegant Brantome leads
to the impressive but little-known
château in Hautefort.

Exhilirating Descents

Souillac to Gramat *p138*
Enjoy the helter-skelter descent
from Rocamadour.

Villefort to Pont d'Arc *p176*
Wooded descent from the Col du
Mas de l'Ayre to Les Vans.

Villes-sur-Auzon to Sault *p204*
Gorge de la Nesque finishes with a
beautiful descent through limestone
formations.

Balcons to Castellane *p230*
A gradual descent allows you to take
in the view almost without pedalling.

Gréolières to Nice *p242*
1,000m of continuous descent all
the way to the Mediterranean. A
fantastic way to finish the journey.

Challenging Climbing

Souillac to Gramat *p138*
The undulating upward roads around Rocamadour rewards
you with fantastic views.

St-Geniez d'Olt to Mende *p162*
Through Marvejols you will be treated to a quiet climb via
shady woodlands.

Mende to Villefort *p170*
Col des Tribes is a long climb but with easy gradients.

Ventoux *p208*
Not strictly part of the route but a must for any racing fan.

Moustiers-Ste-Marie to Balcons *p226*
Climbing through Europe's largest canyon, you look down
on emerald-green waters.

Stunning Views

**Chalonnes-sur-Loire to
Brissac-Quincé** *p72*
Corniche Angevin is one of
the most spectacular roads
of the region.

**Brissac-Quincé to
Fontevraud l'Abbaye** *p78*
Admire the languid river
and the elegant château on
its banks.

Villefort to Pont d'Arc *p176*
From the top of Col du
Mas de l'Ayre you will be
able to see Ventoux.

Pont d'Arc to Aiguèze
p182
The Gorge de l'Ardèche
road looks down on the
many meanders and twists
of the Ardèche river.

**Moustiers- Ste-Marie to
Balcons** *p226*
Vertiginous views down
into the steep-sided Gorge
du Verdon.

Dégustation

Vitré to Craon *p58*
Sip a cider on the farm where it is made and walk in the apple orchards.

Brissac-Quincé to Fontevraud l'Abbaye *p78*
Treat yourself to a sparkling glass of *crémant* in Saumur .

Figeac to Entraygues-sur-Truyère *p150*
If you have finished riding for the day fill your bike bottle with wine in Entraygues-sur-Truyère.

Aiguèze to Châteauneuf-du-Pape *p190*
Riding through the most famous wine-producing village in the world calls for a glass to be raised.

Châteauneuf-du-Pape to Villes-sur-Auzon *p196*
At Terra Ventoux enjoy wine with a view of the iconic mountain.

Foodie Heaven

St-Malo to Pontorson *p40*
Oyster lovers are in for a treat in Cancale. Sit on the wall and enjoy the freshest oysters of your life.

Brissac-Quincé to Fontevraud l'Abbaye *p78*
Mushrooms may seem a familiar food, but there is more to learn at the Musée du Champignon.

Brantôme to Hautefort *p120*
The woods around Sorges are home to the truffle; don't pass through without a taste of this magic ingredient.

Hautfort to Les Eyzies *p126*
On the *foie gras* trail. If you put your ethical considerations aside, this is the best place to enjoy it.

Villefort to Pont d'Arc *p176*
Arriving in the plateau at Les Vans, you will be greeted by stalls of fresh fruit and vegetables.

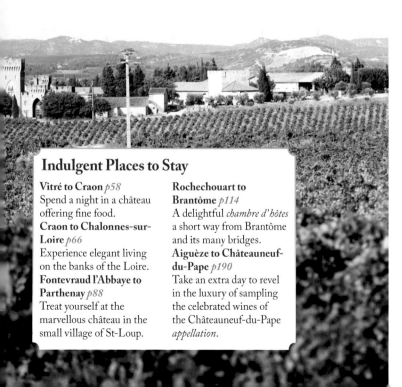

Indulgent Places to Stay

Vitré to Craon *p58*
Spend a night in a château offering fine food.

Craon to Chalonnes-sur-Loire *p66*
Experience elegant living on the banks of the Loire.

Fontevraud l'Abbaye to Parthenay *p88*
Treat yourself at the marvellous château in the small village of St-Loup.

Rochechouart to Brantôme *p114*
A delightful *chambre d'hôtes* a short way from Brantôme and its many bridges.

Aiguèze to Châteauneuf-du-Pape *p190*
Take an extra day to revel in the luxury of sampling the celebrated wines of the Châteauneuf-du-Pape *appellation*.

High Points

St-Geniez d'Olt to Mende *p162*
Goudard - 1,020m

Mende to Villefort *p170*
Col des Tribes – 1,130m

Villefort to Pont d'Arc *p176*
Col du Mas de l'Ayre - 846m

Moustiers-Ste-Marie to Balcons *p226*
Source de Vaumale – 1,180m

Castellane to Gréolières *p236*
Col de Luens – 1,054m

FRENCH HOSPITALITY

Travelling by bike is the ultimate ice-breaker. During the early days of the Tour de France, riders would raid bars with proud owners offering them liquid refreshment. Today's tourist rider gets an equally warm response with cafés always happy to top up your water.

In a cycling-mad country such as France, travelling by bike is an easy way to meet people and cyclists are treated with great respect.

Many people travelling to France seem to have absorbed the misconception that the French are rude and inhospitable hosts; this is rarely the case. However, the warmth of your welcome is very much dependent on your behaviour as a guest. This is the critical difference between French hospitality and the service culture seen in other countries where 'the customer is always right'. The exchange in France is more equal; both host and guest have roles and etiquettes to observe.

As a visiting guest there is an expectation for you to greet your hosts warmly and show respect to their establishment. A café in Nice, to make the point clearly, introduced a graded price list for their coffees. '*Un café*' was charged at €7 whereas '*Bonjour, un café, s'il vous plait*' just €1.40, and missing out the '*Bonjour*' raised the price to €4.25. A few pleasantries and an attempt at speaking French goes a long way towards breaking through any perceived frostiness.

Eating

Enjoyment of food is an integral part of French culture, meal times are observed rigidly and lunchtime is sacred. The ceremony surrounding food even extends to the humble picnic. In most villages you will find a small picnic area (*aire de pique-nique*) or *plan d'eau*, a quiet spot by a pond or lake. Passers-by will often offer a cheery '*Bon appétit!*' if they see you tucking into your sandwich.

You don't need to carry vast amounts of food supplies. Many villages have a *boulangerie* so you will never be far from a warm, fresh baguette, although you should be wary of lunch time and Sunday closing. In rural communities you may find a *place de multi-services* – a concentration of all essential village services including a *dépôt de pain*. In France cafes and bars are essentially the same thing, both provide a welcome caffeine fix for cyclists, however you are just as likely to see a farmer drinking a *petit blanc* (small white wine) at 8am as a coffee. In Provence there will be old men with glasses of cloudy yellow pastis vying for space at the bar with those chatting over coffee.

When eating out don't be shy about ordering the *menu du jour*. It is often the cheapest option and, most importantly, it is also the freshest because it is prepared each day with what is on offer from the local market or suppliers. It will give you a good taste for regional specialties and which produce is in season. To go with your food, try ordering wine by the *pichet* (jug) occasionally. It will be the basic *vin de table* but is usually a good locally produced wine. *Pichets* often come in 250cl or 500cl, perfect for when a whole bottle isn't required!

A preoccupation with provenance of food and 'buying local' is currently in vogue in many countries, but in France it is engrained in the culture. Fierce parochialism is authentic, not a marketing tool. As you cycle through you will notice that a type of cheese that was prolific in one stage can't be found anywhere just 30 miles further along the route.

France is unequalled in its flavours. The incredible diversity of terrain, soil type and climate influences the wide variety of food you will find on your plate or the drink in your glass. From the hefty beef steaks found in the north to the *foie gras* and truffles of the Périgord and the abundance of fresh vegetables in Provence, your meals will be a reflection of the landscape you have ridden through.

Accommodation

There is a wide range of accommodation available and there are suggestions for each stage, focusing on three main types: a good quality hotel, *chambre d'hôtes* or a campsite.

Chambres d'hôtes are essentially Bed & Breakfasts, although some may also offer an evening meal on request. The welcome is more intimate and personal than in a large hotel, your hosts will be happy to share their knowledge of the area and the rooms themselves are often interesting and character-filled.

The trend for boutique sites or glamping isn't as widespread in France as other countries, and many campsites resemble small holiday villages. Most *communes* have a municipal campsite run by the *mairie*; they are very good value and often smaller and quieter than commercial sites. Such campsites tend to be elaborate affairs with pools, bars, restaurants and launderettes – the kind of places that a family would go to for a week.

Camping à la ferme provides a more rustic experience but such sites are rare, as this type of camping is not so popular with French tourists, who make up the greatest proportion of the holiday market.

Consider the type of accommodation you need in respect of the riding you plan to do. After a full day in the saddle it will be good food and a comfortable place to rest that your body craves most. If your end-point is somewhere you wish to explore thoroughly, or you have booked beautiful accommodation with visions of time to relax, plan a shorter day. No matter how fit you are, a long ride, especially in the heat, isn't conducive to doing much more in the evening than enjoying a satisfying meal and relaxing with a drink. Nothing beats the feeling of contented tiredness after a long ride.

Terroir

Terroir is often applied solely to wines, but for the French it is a far deeper and complex emotional connection, not just to wine but to food.

Food is taken seriously, not in a self-conscious way but out of respect for the land that produced it and the skill of those who made or prepared it.

Good produce is treated with respect at the market, in the kitchen, and by the diner. Mushrooms are honoured and truffles worshipped.

The provenance of food is important, not just as a guarantee of quality, but because of the connections with the land. *Terroir* includes all five senses.

As you ride through the landscape you will observe the changing colours of the hills and soil, the variety of animals grazing, of trees and crops growing. You will smell the herbs and flowers that line the roadside and hear the insects working in amongst them.

In the evening, those same flavours, sights and aromas will be served to you on a plate to touch, taste and savour. As you eat and drink your way through France you will learn as much about a region in the restaurant as you do on the road.

Timings

Despite being perfectly comfortable with breaking the rules when it suits, some things in France are done with clock-work regularity. One of the key things to know is lunch times. Outside the hours of noon to 2pm, you will struggle to get a meal and any request for the lunch menu will be greeted with, 'not possible, not possible,' as the chef sharpens his knives in the kitchen. Yet a starving cycle tourist can often be surprised by offers of help. By some miracle, bread and cheese may materialise if you look particularly pathetic, but it's not a technique to be relied on!

You may also find it hard to get a coffee in a restaurant after 11.30am, as the staff will be focused on keeping tables clear for lunch. Nearly everyone stops for a proper sit-down meal; manual workers will strip out of dirty overalls to go to the café or restaurant and a two-hour lunch break is still the norm.

The majority of France does not subscribe to the 24-hour culture that pervades many other countries. An example of this can be seen in the *Route Barrée* signs you will undoubtedly encounter on your trip. For example, road works in the UK often happen overnight or at weekends to cause users as little inconvenience as possible. In France, the work takes place during the working week and the road may be closed between 9am and 5pm.

Leisure time is still held in high regard: on Sundays everything is closed except for three key shops which are usually open in the morning: the *boulangerie* for your bread, *boucherie* for your meat to prepare Sunday lunch and you may find a *fleuriste* so you can take flowers for your hostess or decorate your table. You will often be wished '*Bon dimanche!*' ('Have a good Sunday!'). Sunday is still a day of rest.

ST-MALO: LE GRAND DEPART

Exploring St-Malo

The granite-walled town of St-Malo was originally a fortified island at the mouth of the Rance river. Now joined to the mainland, it is the most visited place in Brittany.

In summer, the *intra-muros*, the old city 'within the walls', can feel a little hectic but head up one of the many flights of steps to access the walled ramparts that embrace the old town. Take in a lungful of fresh sea air and the views out to sea and over St-Malo's extensive beaches, which are revealed at low tide.

Looking out to sea from the walls you will find the foreboding Fort National, a former prison, to the east and the small rocky tidal islet of the Grand Bé to the west.

The islet, which you can walk to at low tide, is the resting place of celebrated writer and local hero, François-René de Chateaubriand. His autobiography, *Memoirs From Beyond the Grave*, was widely acclaimed and he is considered the founder of the French Romantic movement in literature.

Looking inwards to the town, the rows of houses in the *intra-muros* exude the confidence and wealth of the 17th and 18th centuries. The majority, however, had to be painstakingly restored after being destroyed during World War II. St-Malo takes great pride in its maritime history. Sailors from the port were the first Frenchmen to reach Canada and were also renowned pirates – local merchants at one stage held 25 per cent of all the gold in France!

If you are staying the night in St-Malo, take a stroll past the official start point of the trip along the promenade, which extends eastwards. The promenade begins 200m outside the *intra-muros'* most prominent entrance, the Porte St-Vincent. Along the promenade, too, you can often enjoy wonderful vistas and great sunsets from the sea wall. In the morning, however, the landscape changes when the arrival of mists from the Channel create an ethereal, even eerie atmosphere.

After watching the sun set, head into the *intra-muros* to explore the labyrinth of lanes in the old town. Keep walking beyond the restaurants and shops, as the lanes often lead to small friendly Breton taverns, where you can raise a glass of local cider to your journey ahead.

Far more than just a ferry port, St-Malo boasts the most impressive walled citadel on France's northern coast as well as large stretches of sandy beach. The wide, sweeping bay to the east of the town makes a great starting point for your journey, and the train station and nearby Dinard airport complete the range of options to help you get here relatively stress free.

Getting to the Start

The most apt way to arrive at this historic port from the UK is by ferry. If arriving from continental Europe, you will find St-Malo has good train links with the rest of France and beyond. If you are coming from further afield, flights from around the globe land at Paris Charles de Gaulle from where you can catch a train direct to St-Malo from the airport without the hassle of the Paris *metro*.

Boat

The Ferry Port is right in the heart of St-Malo, next to the *intra-muros*, and the approach from the sea is spectacular. Start your French experience early by sailing with Brittany Ferries (www.brittany-ferries.co.uk) from Portsmouth. Their overnight crossing is perfect, if you're pushed for time. It arrives around 8am so you could start pedalling after your morning *pain au chocolat* should you wish. Condor Ferries (www.condorferries.co.uk) will also take you across the Channel from Poole and Weymouth via Guernsey/Jersey. Remember to book your bike in advance if travelling as a foot passenger.

Plane

Dinard airport is just a short 20-minute taxi ride across the Rance Estuary from St-Malo. The airport is served by Ryanair (www.ryanair.co.uk) from the UK airports of London Stanstead, East Midlands and Leeds Bradford. If arriving from outside Europe, your best bet is to fly to Paris and catch one of the frequent trains to St-Malo. Rennes is a 50-minute train ride south of St-Malo, has an airport served by Flybe (www.flybe.co.uk) from Southampton, Exeter and Manchester in the UK, as well as Dublin. Aer Arann also fly from Ireland (www.aerarann.com) during the summer from Cork. Air France (www.airfrance.fr) link Rennes to Paris. From Rennes airport it's a 15-minute taxi ride to the station.

Train

St-Malo is served by frequent direct trains from Paris, Gare de Montparnasse (3 hours 30 minutes). Alternatively if arriving at Paris Charles de Gaulle, take the TGV direct from the airport to Rennes before changing to a local train for St-Malo (4 hours 30 minutes). Check out www.voyages-sncf.com for tickets and timetables. For useful information on how to get you and your *vélo* on the train to St-Malo look at www.bikes.sncf.com or call Voyages SNCF on 0844 848 5 848. Most trains accept bikes but it's advisable to check, and you nearly always need to book in advance. St-Malo train station is just 1km from the official start on the promenade.

Car

Hop (www.hop.fr) fly from Nice to Rennes, so you could always leave your car in St-Malo and return for it via the short train ride from Rennes. If you are lucky enough to be dropped off at the start, there is plenty of street parking one block back from the Promenade in St-Malo. The further away from the *intra-muros*, the easier parking becomes.

Sleep

Hotel

Malouinière le Valmarin
Built in the early 18th-century by a wealthy
ship-owner. Near the ferry terminal but with a
peaceful, large rose garden, perfect for pre-trip
planning. With just 12 rooms, the welcome is
refreshingly personal and warm.
7 Rue Jean XXIII, 35400 St-Malo
00 33 (0)2 99 81 94 76
www.levalmarin.com

Chambre d'Hôtes

Le Gai Courtil
The 2-minute stroll to the beach more than
compensates for the 25-minute walk to the
intra-muros. Small and homely – a refreshing
change from the larger hotels in town.
16 Avenue du General Lanrezac, 35400
St-Malo
00 33 (0)2 99 56 92 46
www.chambresdhotessaintmalo.fr

Campsite

La Cité d'Aleth
A great location on a headland to the south-
west of the town, overlooking the ferries as
they come and go against the backdrop of the
intra-muros.
Allée Gaston Buy, St-Servan, 35400
St-Malo
00 33 (0)2 99 81 60 91
www.ville-saint-malo.fr/campings

Eat

Table d'Henri
On the promenade with a large glass
frontage affording great views back to
the Fort National at the start of the route.
The emphasis is on fish, including fresh
Cancale oysters. There is also a wide array of
restaurants in the *intra-muros*.
4 Chaussée du Sillon, 35409 St-Malo
00 33 (0)2 99 40 50 93
www.latabledhenri.com

Drink

Le café du coin d'en bas de la rue du bout de la
ville d'en face du port....**La Java**
A cider and coffee bar packed full of personality
from its owners to the décor, which includes
old dolls on the wall and swings at the bar.
There are lots of small hidden drinking dens
waiting to be discovered in the *intra-muros* with
invariably warm welcomes.
3 Rue Ste-Barbe, 35400 St-Malo
00 33 (0)2 99 56 41 90
www.lajavacafe.com

Supplies

Food:

Crêpes are inescapable in St-Malo with plenty
of opportunitites to munch on a sweet crêpe
or its savoury counterpart, the *galette*. There
are plenty of *boulangeries* and a couple of small
supermarkets within the *intra-muros*.

Bike:

Concept Vélo
Near the train station for any final spares.
12 Rue Théodore Monod, 35400 St-Malo
00 33 (0)6 23 36 50 40

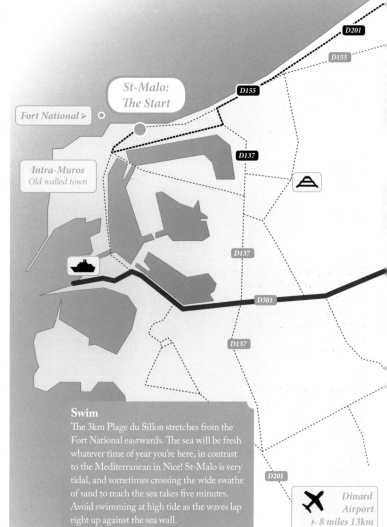

Swim

The 3km Plage du Sillon stretches from the
Fort National eastwards. The sea will be fresh
whatever time of year you're here, in contrast
to the Mediterranean in Nice! St-Malo is very
tidal, and sometimes crossing the wide swathe
of sand to reach the sea takes five minutes.
Avoid swimming at high tide as the waves lap
right up against the sea wall.

BRITTANY

SLURP the freshest oysters of your life while sitting on the sea wall in Cancale.

WALK the perimeter walls of St-Malo to get a true feel for this fortified town, surrounded on three sides by sea.

SIP cider in the hay at harvest time and wander through the orchards.

JOIN the locals in a bar to enjoy some banter and betting in this keen horse-racing region.

IMAGINE the scenes of siege and war that once surrounded the picture-book castles of Fougères and Vitré.

ASCEND the many steps up to Mont St-Michel for a closer look at this iconic Benedictine abbey.

ST-MALO TO PONTORSON

Stage 1: *38miles 61km*

Hugging the coastline, this first stage gives a true taste of Brittany. Enjoy fresh oysters in Cancale before searching for the misty outline of Mont St-Michel across the marshes and vivid colours of the Côte d'Émeraude.

The official start of the route is located at the viewpoint, a wider section at the start of the promenade that overlooks the distinctive outline of the Fort National. From the *office de tourisme* just outside the walls of the old town, cross the road towards the promenade. The starting point is immediately to the right of the slipway as you look out to sea.

The viewpoint is a great spot for photographs to mark the start of the journey. In a short while you will be leaving the sea behind you, and it won't be seen again until arriving at the Mediterranean in Nice.

Don't be dismayed if the fort is shrouded in St-Malo's infamous sea mist. Although very atmospheric, mornings often dawn dull here but the mist soon burns off, leaving clear views of the golden sands and the Channel with its shifting shades of blue and grey. The fort is on the l'Ilette rock and, depending on the tide, it is either an island or a short walk across the sand.

When the French flag is flying you can visit the fort, which has a long and often grisly history. Originally a place to light beacons and to hang criminals, the fort was built in the late 1600s. During the Second World War, citizens of St-Malo were imprisoned there by the German occupiers in order to prevent an uprising.

St-Malo to Rothéneuf

St-Malo has a large sweeping bay. Standing on the promontory opposite the fort you can appreciate its wide curve as it disappears out of view. This is the direction you will soon be riding in, heading east along the coast away from the walled town. Once you have collected all the souvenir snaps you need, it's time to begin your ride. You can walk with your bike along the seafront promenade away from the walled town until the road becomes two-way after about 200m. Alternatively start with the flow of traffic, almost immediately you will reach a roundabout by the *office de tourisme;* turn left here signed Paramé. There is a cycle lane that takes you alongside some car parking and docked boats. At the end, 800m from the start point, turn left, then immediately after turning you will see the sea directly in front of you. Turn right at the lights to re-join the seafront road.

OYSTERS

For a truly authentic oyster-eating experience, Cancale really is the only place to go. Cancale's oyster beds produce 15,000 tonnes a year and have long been considered amongst the best in France. The Romans ate them and Louis XIV had them brought to Versailles for the court to enjoy. There are many stalls selling oysters and they are as fresh as can be, straight from the beds within sight of the stalls. You can choose your size and choose your quality. If you have only ever eaten oysters in restaurants you will be amazed by how big some of the larger ones can be! The stallholders will hand you a plate with your chosen oysters and a couple of lemon quarters. The tradition is to sit on the sea wall to eat them, throwing the shells into the ever-growing pile on the beach beneath. If you prefer a bar experience, Le Tangon, also to the left at the roundabout, will serve you a glass of something very delicious and cold with some bread and butter to pad out your oysters and fill your stomach. But for a truly authentic experience, sit and eat on the sea wall.

Keep following this road for 1.5km until you reach a left-hand fork for Rothéneuf. The road becomes significantly quieter here and there is a cycle path. This area is known as the Paramé hotel district which sprang up once there was no more room for tourist accommodation within the city walls. The houses along here are more imposing and the road becomes significantly quieter. Stay on this road following signs for Cancale par la Côte. You reach Rothéneuf 8km after leaving St-Malo and here the cycle path ends.

Rothéneuf to Cancale

In Rothéneuf there is a sharp right then left bend but simply continue to follow signs for Cancale. 3km after leaving the town you'll see a very pretty bay on the left-hand side, the first of several along this section of the route. From here on, the route becomes much quieter and more rural with fields lining the roadside, but frequent glimpses of the sea remind you of where you are.

A further 5km after the first pretty bay you spot, you'll see Anse du Guesclin. This particular bay is worth a short stop, or you could even linger a while for a picnic and a swim as it is stunningly picturesque. There is a wide view of the Channel with an isolated house perched atop a rock island. Marram grass and fennel give way to a wide sandy bay with dunes to recline and sunbathe in. A truly peaceful and secluded spot.

Just 5km from here you'll see a sign for Pointe du Grouin, a small 1.5km detour from the route. The road takes you round a U-shaped one-way system to allow stunning views of the headland. If you venture down here you may be treated to a view of Mont St-Michel, its distant spires rising in the east through the sea mist that often covers this area.

Rejoining the route, continue to follow signs to Cancale for another 3km where you will enter the town. Turn left at the lights here, it will be signposted Centre Ville. At the crossroads go straight over towards the church. In front of the church you will see a statue of three ladies dressed in classic Breton costume, collecting oysters in the traditional manner, sea water draining through their loosely woven baskets. Turn right in front of this fountain. When you arrive at the roundabout on the seafront turn left for the oyster stalls or right to continue with the route. If you are a fan of fresh oysters we highly recommend you take the left turn!

Cancale to St-Broladre

Leave Cancale along the seafront, keeping the sea on your left. The road climbs up away from the sea and at the junction at the top, turn right signposted Mont St-Michel. At the main road, the D76, turn right again. Continue along this road until 8km after Cancale where you will see a right turn to Mont St-Michel and Dol-de-Bretagne on the D155. Follow this road and you will loop around to ride underneath the road that you just crossed. The D155 hugs the coastline, offering superb views across the marshes. A green line, from which the Côte

d'Émeraude gets its name, separates the grey of the land and the grey of the horizon. The road passes through several small villages with an abundance of café-bars and oyster sellers. After 4.5km you will reach Vildé La Marine. Go straight over the small roundabout here.

A further 4km takes you into Le Vivier-sur-Mer. Here the route stays to the left on the D797 and you will continue along by the sea for a further 5km before the route begins to turn inland towards Pontorson. This is a significant moment: you will be turning your back on the sea and will not be seeing it again until the Mediterranean in Nice.

The road now takes you between fields where garlic is a popular crop. When the garlic is being pulled from the soil you can smell it all around you, and the air is impregnated with its pungent scent. Roadside stalls sell fresh garlic if you want to buy some. Continue in the direction of Pontorson on the D797 to the small village of St-Broladre.

MONT ST-MICHEL

Mont St-Michel makes a striking silhouette against the skyline as it rises out of the bay, linked to the mainland by the thinnest thread of causeway. One of the first sites to obtain a UNESCO World Heritage listing, Mont St-Michel has long been a significant religious centre. The first church was built on the site in 709.

Dramatic seen from a distance, its construction and architecture is breathtaking when explored more closely. Its three levels built on to the granite rock have undergone many additions and alterations over the centuries, including fortifications in the 14th-century that allowed it to withstand a 30-year siege.

Mont St-Michel provided a dream backdrop for photographers when the route of the first time trial of the Tour de France 2013, curved round in front of the iconic abbey. Sadly, cyclists are no longer able to ride along the causeway so you have to leave your bike at the free bike parking near to the Place du Barrage.

From here you can continue on foot or on one of the shuttle buses. The walk takes approximately 30 minutes, so it's not ideal if you are wearing stiff-soled cycling shoes; the cobbled streets are not cleat-friendly either, so taking a change of shoes is a good idea.

Many feel Mont St-Michel is best viewed from a distance to avoid the descending hordes of day trippers, though an early morning or evening stroll can be highly rewarding.

St-Broladre to Pontorson

10km after St Broladre as you approach Pontorson, you will cross two roundabouts in quick succession. Head straight over following signs to Pontorson on the D797. At this point you enter Normandy for a very brief sojourn – you will be leaving again near the start of the next stage. At a traffic-light controlled T-junction, turn left in the direction of Centre Ville, then carry straight on at the roundabout still signposted Centre Ville. The stage ends at the next mini-roundabout. Turn left at the mini-roundabout for a detour to Mont St-Michel. Continue straight up the Rue de Mont St-Michel, where you'll find the *office de tourisme,* for 9 km past plenty of tourist paraphernalia until you reach the sacred mount at the road's end. If you are pressing on to the next stage, simply carry on straight over the mini-roundabout continuing along Pontorson's main street.

Pontorson takes its name from the French for bridge, *pont,* and from Orson, a Norman leader who was commissioned to build the bridge by the father of William the Conqueror. Pontorson, although near to Mont St-Michel, is not as touristy as you might expect. Although it caters for the tourist traffic, with several hotels and numerous *chambres d'hôtes*, its hotels are basic in character.

Sleep

Hotel
Le Grillon

A small, basic hotel with only 5 rooms on the main street of Pontorson, but warm and welcoming. It also has a popular *crêperie* and restaurant.

37 Rue Cousenon, 50170 Pontorson
00 33 (0)2 33 60 17 80
www.le-grillon-pontorson.com

Chambre d'Hôtes
Le Grenier du Jardin

A beautiful but simple attic bedroom complements the equally beautiful tucked-away small garden. With many artistic but discreet decorative flourishes, this is a lovely place to stay within walking distance of the main street.

31 Rue de la Libération, 50170 Pontorson
00 33 (0)2 99 97 48 41
www.legrenierdujardin.com

Campsite
Camping Haliotis

On the banks of the Cousenon river, this busy family site is perfectly situated for walking into Pontorson. A wide range of facilities including pool, bar and wifi.

Boulevard Patton, 50170 Pontorson
00 33 (0)2 33 68 11 59
www.camping-haliotis-mont-saint-michel.com

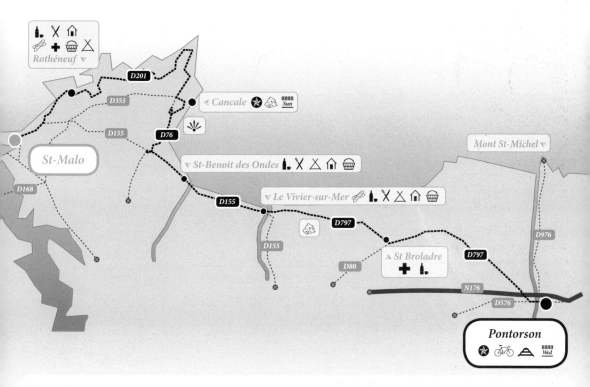

Supplies

Food

Pontorson has several *boulangeries* and the main street contains a typical range of small shops including a *pharmacie*. There is a supermarket on the Rue de Mont St-Michel if you need to stock up.

Bike
Cousenon Motoculture

There is no bike shop in Pontorson but in an emergency a tractor and scooter shop sells bicycle tyres and tubes. Located on the edge of Pontorson on the D975 in the direction of Ducey.

Parc d'Activités, 50170 Pontorson
0033 (0)2 33 30 11 40

Eat

Le Grillon

The busiest restaurant in Pontorson, popular with visitors and locals alike. The atmosphere is lively and the food good value, particularly if you opt for a three- course menu.

37 Rue Cousenon, 50170 Pontorson
00 33 (0)2 33 60 17 80
www.le-grillon-pontorson.com

PONTORSON ⊕ FOUGÈRES

Stage 2: *23miles 37km*

Taking you south-east away from the sea, the route winds through the tranquil back lanes of rural Normandy and Brittany. Cycling through small farming communities with golden fields of hay and deep green pastures, this stage ends near the famous Château de Fougères.

Leaving Pontorson

Starting at the mini-roundabout on the main street, begin where the first stage ended and continue heading east out of Pontorson in the direction of Avranches. There are two right-hand turns on leaving Pontorson, which are the key to unlocking the hidden lanes of this idyllic south-west corner of Normandy.

The first turn is 800m after pedalling away from the mini-roundabout; immediately after the Total garage turn right onto the D30. The second turn comes less than 200m after crossing the railway line where there are a series of small roads off to the right. Take the third possible right, which is signed D112, Vessey.

This region is littered with lots of lovely, enticing country lanes and you have the opportunity to unintentionally explore some of these, as the myriad farm tracks and lanes constantly criss-cross each other. This is one of the trickiest sections of navigation on the whole trip – the majority of the route has nowhere near as many junctions as the lanes provided for Normandy farms. However, if you stick to the principle that you always follow the D112 for 17km all the way to Coglès (except for a couple of short, dog-leg interruptions which are outlined), you'll enjoy a smooth almost traffic-free passage.

Pontorson to Argouges

4km after leaving Pontorson follow the D112 round to the right at a bend signed Vessey, then immediately after it, turn left on the D112 at a small mini-roundabout that looks decidedly out of place in this land of tractors and trailers. After a further 2km (6km in total from the outskirts of Pontorson) you will reach Vessey, a modest village you may hardly notice as you cruise through it, the eagerness of getting underway transferring its energy to your pedals. After following the road straight through Vessey, the route undulates gently through farmland with mistletoe-clad trees dotted sporadically amongst the fields.

2km after Vessey the D112 is punctuated by the D40, and the road ends at a T-junction. Turn right on the D40 for 200m before turning immediately left as the D112 continues, signed Argouges. After 1.5km the route reaches Argouges, bending

PARIS—BREST—PARIS

Fougères has a great cycling history. In 2013 it was the *ville de départ* for Stage 12 of the 100th edition of the Tour de France. Tour aficionados will remember this as the year Chris Froome stormed into the Yellow Jersey. Stage 12 was a flat section from Fougères to Tours and was all about the sprinters, and more importantly, who could stay on their bike. After a series of big crashes Marcel Kittel from Germany pipped Britain's Mark Cavendish to the line in Tours.

Every four years Fougères welcomes one the world's most famous long-distance cycling events, when Paris–Brest–Paris riders pass through the town. The Audux Club Parisien organises the 600km ride from the capital to Brest on the Atlantic coast and, in the ultimate test of mental and physical endurance, the same 600km route back again! The ride is continuous and unsupported and it's not uncommon to see a rider grabbing a few hours' sleep on the roadside.

Legend has it that during the first race in 1891, a Breton baker struck by the heroics of the cyclists passing his *boulangerie* at 4am as he prepared the next day's produce, vowed to create something in their honour. The resulting *gâteau Paris-Brest* is a wheel-shaped choux pastry filled with a rich praline cream. Packed with calories, it is now sold in many *boulangeries* all over France and at restaurant tables worldwide, making at least some aspects of the Paris–Brest accessible to all.

round to the right in front of the church. There is a *boulangarie,* which keeps sporadic opening hours, tucked on the inside of the bend.

Moments after the bend our friend the D112 is interrupted by its larger cousin the D12. Take a right here at the T-junction as the road ends, then take care to take the second left (after around 200m) onto the D112 as it begins again, signed Coglès 6km.

Argouges to Coglès

On leaving Argouges, shortly after passing newly-built houses, stay on the main road, which forks left at a crucifix. The road rolls gently upwards. In summer the hedgerows are thick with a cocktail of foxgloves, daisies, dandelions, ferns and the odd nettle providing a heady scent and the gentle buzz of working bees.

You could be forgiven for thinking you were in rural southern England. Through the gaps in the hedges, you see a land dominated by corn and healthy-looking cows. 4.5km after leaving Argouges, turn right at a crossroads marked by a tall crucifix on your left-hand side, signed Le Petit Pas. Here there is less focus on signs as locals like to keep these gorgeous lanes a mystery.

Immediately after your right turn by the crucifix you should see a sweet-chestnut wood running along the right-hand side of the road. The route descends slightly to a junction approximately 1km after the crucifix. Simply follow the main route as it bends round to the right and after a further 0.5km, as it bends sharp left, ignoring the driveways to local homesteads. You will cross a small modest stream by a lone house.

It may be easy to miss, but this stream represents the point where the route is re-united with Brittany as we leave Normandy behind on our journey south. This humble border has not always been peaceful as Bretons have fought fiercely to defend their cultural traditions and independence throughout the ages. Though few people now speak the Breton language, Brittany retains the strongest sense of identity of any region of mainland France. Bretons are the first to mount fierce protest at any Parisian policy that may hit the local agricultural economy.

After crossing the stream and its invisible frontier, you arrive in Coglès. Turn left at the T-junction in Coglès on the D15. To reach the true centre of the village turn left at the church and a *boulangerie* and café can be found on the adjacent Place de l'Église.

Coglès to St Germain-en-Coglès

Continue on the D15 out of the village, a slightly wider road with markings in the middle which passes over the *autoroute,* connecting the two principal cities of this part of France: the administrative capital of Brittany, Rennes and the Normandy port of Caen. 4km after Coglés turn right at a crossroads onto the D103, signed Montours 2km. Our route continues on peaceful roads to this mid-sized village.

After 1.5km, on the outskirts of the village, turn left at a crossroads signed Montours, D17. The road rises uphill slightly for 500m before winding through the narrow centre of the village. In the centre you will find a *boulangerie* on the right and a sporadically open restaurant on the left. By the church follow the D17 signs to Fougères as the route bends right, then immediately left by the unusually modern-looking *mairie* and small cultural centre.

The route winds its way through a mixture of grazing land and wheat fields for 5km to the next slightly larger settlement of St-Germain-en-Coglès. On the way to St-Germain-en-Coglès, 3.5km after Montours, keen botanists or those cyclists who like to 'watch the flowers grow', during more leisurely rides, should take a left at the Parc Floral sign to reach the Parc Botanique de Haute Bretagne, indisputably the best botanic gardens in Brittany.

St-Germain-en-Coglès to Lecousse

In St-Germain-en-Conglès follow the D17 through the village taking the left exit at the roundabout at the village end, signed Fougères. Immediately after the roundabout, on the left, a small car park provides access to a short local walk through a water garden, the Jardin de l'Eau. Each of the 11 small village *communes* of the Coglès area has its own board, indicating each community's sense of pride as well as displaying tourist information in these rarely visited villages.

The route bisects a cycle greenway, 2.5km south of St-Germain-en-Coglès. Such greenways or *voies vertes* are part of a large network of over 1000km cycle ways that criss-cross Brittany. They are mainly gravel but are accessible to all and offer a great family cycling holiday in the region.

The remainder of this stage from St-Germain-en-Coglès to Fougères is lined by small hedgerows with plentiful ferns. In French, *fougère* means fern. 6km after St-Germain-en-Coglès the road reaches the village of Lecousse, its modern-looking housing a testament to the expansion of Fougères.

Lecousse to Fougères

At the traffic lights in Lecousse, turn left onto the D155 to Fougères. After 300m at a roundabout next to the Intermarché supermarket take the first exit signed Centre Ville. Then descend a short hill to a roundabout at the bottom. The stage officially ends here, but if you are carrying on towards Vitré, take the second exit signed Centre Ville.

Whatever time of day you finish this stage or pass through on your ride, we recommend you take the first exit signed Rennes and continue 300m until you reach the Château de Fougères on your left (keep a lookout as it is slightly set back from the main road). It is worth taking a few minutes to stroll around the Place Raoul II, a medieval square, with plentiful seats and cafés on a sunny day and a great view of the imposing château, which is in turn set against the backdrop of the fortified old town.

The fortifications are very impressive – the château is built on a natural rocky outcrop of solid granite, the site of an old wooden fort destroyed by Henry II in 1166. And when it comes to medieval defences, the Château de Fougères breaks the mould, owing to its unusual location beneath the old town which overlooks the structure from the top of an imposing rock face.

An overgrown but impressive moat, home to wildflowers and trickling waterfalls, encircles the château. The structure, like that of Vitré, was part of the ultimately unsuccessful defences of the Duchy of Brittany, which finally merged into the Kingdom of France in 1532. Some well-preserved medieval streets link the château with the old town, but are best explored on foot owing to the combination of ramps and stairways. These climb towards the Place aux Arbres through the *jardin public* and afford great views over the ramparts.

Sleep

Hotel

Hôtel des Voyageurs

A central 3-star option situated uphill from the château on a small roundabout offering comfortable rooms.

10 Place Gambetta, 35300 Fougères
00 33 (0)2 99 99 08 20
www.hotel-fougeres.fr

Chambre d'Hôtes

La Lanterne

Situated a stone's throw from the château drawbridge in the heart of Fougères' medieval streets. Smallish but quirky rooms offer a warm welcome away from traffic-filled roads.

110 Rue de la Pinterie, 35300 Fougères
00 33 (0)2 99 99 58 80

Campsite

Camping Municipal de Fougères

A basic but well-run campsite just outside the ring road on the east of town. From the centre of town follow the D17 towards La Chapelle Janson.

Route de la Chapelle Janson, 35300 Fougères
00 33 (0)2 99 99 40 81

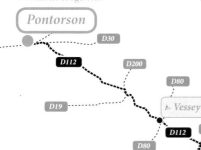

Eat

Eating out

Head for Place Raoul II, a medieval square adjacent to the moat that surrounds the château. There are plenty of outside tables where you can devour a Breton crêpe or savour a more formal meal.

Supplies

Food

Saturday is market day, or for the basics head to the supermarket you passed at the top of the hill before the descent into town. There are many *boulangeries* and a smaller supermarket in the *centre ville*.

Bike

Ulteam Sport

Well-stocked bike shop with a great central location, just 200m from the Hôtel des Voyageurs, in the opposite direction along the one-way street.

41 Rue de la Forêt, 35300 Fougères
00 33 (0)2 56 47 12 15
www.planetecycle.com

Drink

Place Raoul II is also a good place for a post-ride drink and perfect for supping an evening Breton cider. During the day the square also boast a *salon de thé*, great for a moment's pause if you are passing through, on towards Vitré.

FOUGERES TO VITRE

Stage 3: *19miles 30km*

The flattest stage of the route takes you on predominantly rural roads from one castle to the next, starting from the medieval Château de Fougères on its granite rock, and finishing at the well-preserved Château de Vitré, perched high above the town.

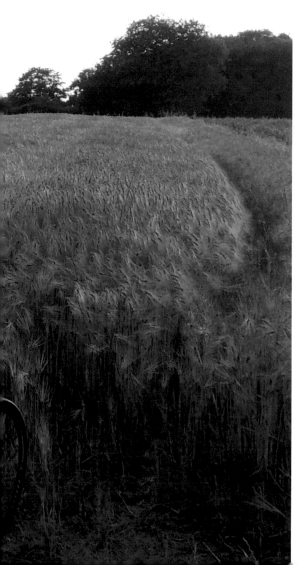

Leaving Fougères

Starting at the roundabout near the château below the main part of town, take the Rue de Rennes signposted Centre Ville which leads you slightly uphill and crosses over the river.

At the first roundabout take the first exit, effectively straight on, and from the second mini-roundabout with the Hôtel des Voyageurs Best Western on your left, turn right for the Rue de Tribunal over a short cobbled section between shops, signposted Vitré. At the next roundabout take the third exit, then immediately turn right signposted Vitré, then at a further roundabout take the second exit signed Vitré.

At the traffic lights get into the right-hand lane to continue straight on toward Billé and Javené, ignoring the left-hand turn to Vitré. From here the route is much quieter and avoids the main road. After 2.5km you will reach a roundabout where you will be crossing straight over the ring road around Fougères. Care is needed here but the road is relatively quiet with large breaks between traffic to cross. The route now follows this road all the way to Vitré

Javené to St-Christophe-des-Bois

In a further 1km you will pass the sign to Javené off to your left. Continue straight on, the first village you cycle through will be Billé in another 4km. The countryside here is mainly open fields. Occasionally you will pass sullen-looking cows watching the road, and the occasional isolated house. Billé is a little livelier with the very much out-of-context Ibérique Tapas Bar on the right as you enter the village, along with the usual all-purpose cafe/bar that can be found in most small villages.

After Billé the landscape is mainly wheat and maize fields in the summer season, with occasional pockets of woodland. 2km after Billé you will enter Combourtillé – look out for the red telephone box on the left-hand side, an iconic British symbol.

At the exit to the village there is another equally striking symbol, a very red and imposing crucifix. The route is predominantly flat and it is easy to bowl along between the fields and patches of trees and maintain a good pace with very little effort required. In a further 6km from Combourtillé you will reach St-Christophe-des-Bois, another quiet little hamlet with a *boulangerie* and café.

St-Christophe-des-Bois to Vitré

4km after leaving St-Christophe-des-Bois you will enter Taillis, a slightly bigger village than those you previously passed through. As you exit the village look out for the very small Chapelle du Sacré-Coeur on your left. Unlike many of the ornate and imposing churches and chapels we pass in this region, it is striking in its simplicity. From here the riding becomes much more interesting as you start to descend between patches of chestnut woodland on wide, open, sweeping bends. Not particularly fast or technical it continues to add to the sensation of a very tranquil section of riding.

6.5km after leaving Taillis you arrive at the by-pass for Vitré. Follow signs for Vitré Nord crossing straight over the roundabout. At the next junction turn left signposted Centre Ville. At the roundabout head straight over. The road drops down through some of the old town buildings, giving you a flavour of the medieval town you are entering.

If you look up you will catch occasional views of the castle high above you. At the traffic lights turn left, signposted Centre Ville. Shortly after to your left are some lovely cafés housed in half-timbered medieval houses. If these whet your appetite then it is definitely worth spending some time exploring the narrow streets and castle itself, as this is just the perimeter of the old town.

The stage finishes on the right outside the *office de tourisme* and the station. From here you can continue with the next stage or take a break and absorb the atmosphere in this medieval town or, if staying overnight, you can experience the almost film-set perfection of its well- preserved buildings.

Vitré
Vitré describes itself as the *Porte de Bretagne*, the gateway to Brittany and its position on the borders of Normandy, Maine and Anjou meant that it held an important role in defending

THE DUCHY OF BRITTANY

Brittany has one of the strongest cultural identities of any part of France and is known for its strongly independent nature. If you speak to a resident they will be careful to tell you that they are Breton not French.

Brittany resisted the rule of Charlemagne, unlike the rest of France, and successfully defended itself against Norman invasion. It remained autonomous and largely prosperous until various wars and political marriages brought it under French rule, the final large region to be amalgamated.

There is a perception that Brittany is a particularly poor region, however, in the middle-ages it had a thriving economy with a merchant fleet trading in Spain, Portugal and Northern Europe. Those who support Breton independence point to this as a reason for the region to be given more autonomy. Currently it is dependent on central government for subsidies and funding.

Brittany still has its own language, which is taught in a very small minority of schools and although spoken by only a few people , it is still in use. The connection to both Welsh and Cornish languages are strong, since they come from similar Celtic roots, and the Breton flag resembles the Cornish flag.

Breton music and traditions are a source of pride and a way of maintaining the region's distinct cultural identity.

the Duchy of Brittany. A fortress has been on the site for over a thousand years with parts of the present castle dating back as far as the first part of the 13th-century. During its long history the castle has seen many periods of turmoil, experienced fire and provided a refuge from both war and plague. Although many modifications and changes have been made, particularly during the medieval period, the castle appears largely unaltered, as do the narrow streets and stone houses tucked below the walls, making it easy to step back in time.

Despite its appearance Vitré is no Disney set. It is a very active and busy town despite its fairy-tale castle backdrop. In amongst the twisted buildings of the old quarter you will find lively bars and places to eat. Market day is Monday, with stalls in front of Notre-Dame church and is worth a visit, even if you are just passing through. The narrowness of the streets and occasional cobbled sections means the old town is best explored on foot. The slower pace gives you the chance to observe and notice the different style of houses, with their overhanging gables and varying heights and layouts.

Sleep

Hotel
Le Petit Billot
A 2-star hotel just a few minutes walk from the castle, fairly basic but friendly and welcoming. There is a garage for bikes.

5 Place du General
Leclerc, 35500 Vitré
00 33 (0)2 99 75 02 10
www.hotel-vitre.com

Chambre d'Hôtes
Madame Faucher
A traditional house full of character, with shared bathroom between the two rooms. Very peaceful location with a easy short walk to the old *centre ville*.

2 Chemin des Tertres Noirs, 35500 Vitré
00 33 (0)2 99 75 08 69
www.bnb.faucher.info

Campsite
Municipal St-Étienne
A pleasant municipal campsite on the ring road with a free bus service in season. Well-maintained with a swimming pool and good basic facilities.

Rue d'Argentré, 35500 Vitré
00 33 (0)2 99 75 25 28
www.mairie-vitre.fr

Supplies

Food
Vitré has plenty of shops for all your needs within walking distance from the centre of the old town – everything from traditional *épiceries*, to the essentials such as a *pharmacie* and small supermarket.

Bike
Vélo Naturel
Situated in an out-of-town shopping complex near the Hyper-U supermarket. It is very well stocked with knowledgeable staff and a good workshop.

9 Rue du Fougeray, 35500 Vitré
00 33 (0)2 99 74 57 12
www.velonaturel.com

Eat

Auberge Le Saint Louis
In one of Vitré's many half-timbered buildings traditional French cuisine is served in a dark-panelled room creating an ambience of elegant and lavish old style dining .

31 Rue Notre Dame, 35500 Vitré
00 33 (0)2 99 75 28 28
www.aubergesaintlouis.fr

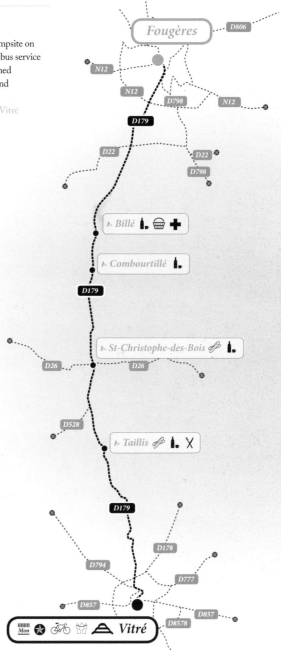

VITRE TO CRAON

Stage 4: *25miles 41km*

A deeply rural stage which leaves behind the
Breton flags and crosses into the *département*
of Mayenne, a ride through small farming
communities and past their fertile fields on
tranquil back lanes, before arriving in the town of
Craon famous for its château and chariot racers.

Leaving Vitré

From the square in front of the station by the *office de tourisme* start the stage by taking the Rue de la Liberté, signed Rennes. Immediately after leaving the square at the first roundabout take the second exit straight across signed Ernée. At the next roundabout in front of the church take the first exit marked Toutes Directions.

The route goes over a bridge above the railway line before meeting a third roundabout where you take the last exit signed Laval and Ernée. After following the railway line on your left for 300m you arrive at your fourth and final roundabout in quick succession. Take the second exit signed Laval and Erbrée (not Ernée), D857. Continue straight on the D857 ignoring turn-offs. The road can sometimes be busy, depending on the time of day, but a cycle lane soon emerges at the edge of the road, which is well respected by French drivers. The route heads out of town past a plethora of garages and agricultural suppliers but your efforts on this short busy section will soon be rewarded with great, quiet country roads.

The edge of Vitré to Mondevert

3.5km after leaving the square in Vitré, at a large roundabout with a campervan area on the left, take the first exit signed Erbrée, D29. The departure from the main D857 road onto the D29 marks a significant change to a much narrower road with modest markings in the middle, as the urban fringe immediately gives way to rural quiet.

The route arrives in Erbrée 3.5km after leaving the large roundabout. Continue straight over the mini-roundabout then straight on at the *boulangerie* (though note you have to give way). The bar/café in Erbrée is called 'Ty Gwen' or white house, a name just as commonly found in the Welsh valleys as rural Brittany, and a reminder of the close links these two languages share.

Continue through Erbrée, following signs to Mondevert, passing the *pharmacie* on the left as you leave the village on the D29. 2km after Erbrée as the route passes over the Paris to Rennes *autoroute,* take the second possible exit at the two roundabouts either side of the highway bridge, which in both instances are signed Mondevert.

Immediately after the *autoroute* junction you cycle into Mondevert, literally translated as 'green world'. Mondevert has a small *alimentation* if you forgot any supplies before leaving Vitré. At the crossroads in Mondevert continue straight across on the D29, Rue de la Forêt, signed Le Pertre 7km.

Mondevert to Le Pertre

The Rue de la Forêt is apt as you are about to enter a lovely, narrow section through the Forêt du Pertre, with stacks of logs at the end of tracks disappearing into the woods. Consisting primarily of beech trees the area looks spectacular in the throes of autumn, while in spring and summer this certainly is a green world. The road continues straight through the forest for 5km undulating gently. After emerging from the cool of the forest the land either side is frequently occupied by horse stables. Horse racing is a religion in these parts.

Take care on the violent speed bump which greets you on entering the village, then at the end of the road at a T-junction with the *bibliothèque* in front of you, turn right. Like many small villages in this region, Le Pertre is well-served with an array of facilities you are unlikely to find in any British village of a similar size - though whether they are open or not is the perennial question! If you are looking for a good place to munch your picnic follow the sign to Plan d'Eau between the buildings in the village centre to a small lake.

Le Pertre to Beaulieu-sur-Oudon

Continue past the Place de l'Église in Le Pertre following the road round to the left past Le Sulky, a bar that takes its name from a type of chariot racing. Under 100m after passing the bar, turn right immediately after the restaurant Les Deux Provinces, signed D33 Beaulieu-sur-Oudon. The restaurant name gives you a clue to the fact you are about to cross the border from Brittany into the *département* of Mayenne. Cycle along the border for 2km keeping on the principal route, the D33, ignoring the opportunity to fork right. 2km after leaving Le Pertre at the unmarked *département* border, the road crosses over a new bridge and becomes the D142.

The Mayenne is one of the most rural French *départements* making it great cycling country. It is often looked upon as unsophisticated and the *Mayennais* are sometime the butt of jokes for French city dwellers. Many tourists fly past Mayenne on the *autoroute*, heading to better-known areas such as the Loire or the Dordogne. Though many French also look fondly on Mayenne as a place that empitomises the part mythical *La France Profonde*, a rural idyll linked strongly to the sense of *terroir*. In Mayenne you'll find places that embody what many consider the real essence of France. The self-sufficiency of local farmers means they are deeply connected to their land. They have their feet planted literally and metaphorically on the ground and are immersed in their landscape.

HORSE RACING AND HIPPODROMES

If you come here in July you will find little interest in the Tour de France peloton; this is horse racing country. Craon's hippodrome hosts 9 meets of national and international races, attracting over 70,000 race goers during the season. Traditional horseracing is often eclipsed by the *sulky*, a type of racing synonymous with this corner of France, where the jockey sits on a light two-wheeled cart pulled by a briskly trotting horse.

Locals love a flutter, which they indulge in while buying cigarettes and sipping a drink. Just look for the PMU green sign with a picture of two horses. Inside, you are guaranteed to find a gaggle of locals nursing coffee, cider or beer and clinging to their slips at any time of the day. A key part of culture in this region, such betting stations can be found in even the smallest of cafés and bars.

Beaulieu-sur-Oudon to Craon

4.5km after leaving Le Pertre the route arrives at a stop sign in Beaulieu-sur-Oudon. Turn left, with a local bar on the inside of the junction, then shortly after, follow a short one- way system round to the right at the village church, turning right immediately after the church, signposted Méral.

As you leave the village the route passes the now dried-up, old village washing area, then continues past farmsteads. It is a further 5.5km to Méral, crossing straight over a larger road 2km after leaving Beaulieu-sur-Oudon. At the crossroads by the bar in the centre of Méral continue straight across on the D142. To find the village facilities, turn left at the crossroads leaving the route for 50m to the Place de l'Eglise where you'll find a restaurant and information board showing religious *randonnées* (walks) connecting local churches.

If you're feeling peckish or need fuel for a long day of bagging multiple stages, you could do worse than sample a *menu du jour* at a local restaurant tucked away in one of these modest Mayenne villages, which are usually superb value.

The choice will be very limited but cooked fresh on the day, it's sure to be delicious; not *haute cuisine* but hearty local food. Despite being a small village Méral is famous for its harvest festival and *pommes d'amour* (toffee apples, literally 'apples of love') indicating the importance of the orchards to this market farming region.

Even small rural villages are not escaping the modern signs of expansion: you'll pass new-build houses on the outskirts of Méral that lie opposite the local horse-racing track. Continue 9km straight along the D142 to Livré-la-Touche, interrupted after 4.5 km by a crossroads where you simply continue straight across the main route. Birdsong and the odd squirrel darting around will accompany you along these fairly flat, winding countryside lanes.

At the mini-roundabout on entering Livré-la-Touche take the second exit (forking left), but take care as the locals have not yet put up a road sign to mark the entrance to their village. At the crossroads in the centre of the village by the church and bar, continue straight as the Rue de Bretagne becomes the Rue d'Anjou. The name Anjou will be familiar to wine aficionados especially those fond of a rosé, and although you have to turn your two wheels a significant number of kilometres still to see your first vines, the street name is testament to your progress south as the Loire draws ever closer.

Arriving in Craon
4.5km after Livré-la-Touche you pedal into Craon on the D142. With a No Entry sign ahead follow the road round to the right, before turning left at the crossroads signed Centre Ville.

After about 300m, at a break in the terraced housing and locally owned shops, the road crosses a small bridge, the Pont Neuf, over the Oudon river. Look to your right as you cross to see the older, picturesque river bridge, the *petit pont*. 100m further on the left, the stage's end is marked by the church of St Nicolas, with one of the most powerful organs in western France. If the organ is silent you will be able to identify the church by its imposing size, looming on an embankment high to your left.

Craon is a small town of 5,000 inhabitants which is worth a look around. It is famous for its château, its *hippodrome* and its famous cheese, *La Chaussée aux Moines*, which was originally produced in a nearby monastery. Now very popular, the cheese is sold in supermarkets throughout the country.

Craon has a mixture of housing, both wealthy merchants' properties and working-class homes. Many of the grander houses on the older streets of Craon were built as the town grew on the back of salt trading, and in the days of *gabelle*, a compulsory tax collected from the sale of salt. The Cour de la Geôle was used as a prison for those caught trying to avoid the royal tax and selling salt illegally.

INDULGE

Château de Craon
This refined stately home was built in the late 18th-century with white limestone from the banks of the Loire, giving it a distinctive luminous aspect.

The château prides itself on locally sourced, wholesome cooking – the vegetables come from the potager, an impressive vegetable garden and small soft-fruit orchard, which back on to the adjoining town wall. The château boasts 40 hectares of grounds to explore, an English-style park and a French-style garden. You can follow the meandering banks of the Oudon for a 6km-stroll past grazing cattle, ducks and geese.

Loik & Hélène de Guébriant
Le Château, 53400 Craon
00 33 (0)2 43 06 11 02
www.craoncastle.com

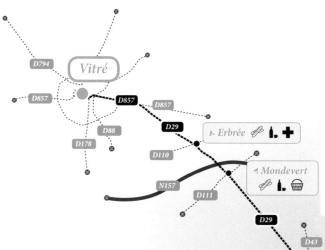

Supplies

Food

Craon's market day is every Monday on the Promenade Charles de Gaulle. There is a small, handy and well-stocked supermarket next to Bar La Station in the *centre ville*.

Bike

Cycles Fouillet Daniel
A mixed tractor, car and bike-spares store on a street named after Craon's twin town in Devon, UK. Useful in an emergency.
6 Boulevard Okehampton, 53400 Craon
0033 (0)2 43 06 19 14

Sleep

Hotel

Hôtel-Restaurant La Crêperie du Château
Simple but excellently located rooms opposite the château. The restaurant offers much more than crêpes and is one of the most popular in town.
14 Avenue de Champagné, 53400 Craon
00 33 (0)2 43 06 10 33
www.hotel-restaurant-craon.com

Chambre d'Hôtes

Le Demeure de l'Ile
Set in the heart of town by the *petit pont* on the Oudon, the 18th-century home has been magnificently restored with access to a tiny fairytale-like, sheltered, wooded seating area on a small island in the middle of the river.
Chantal Bretaudeau, 16 rue du Vieux Pont, Craon
00 33 (0)2 43 06 37 07
www.demeuredelile.com

Campsite

Camping du Mûrier
Next to a small lake on the edge of town, but thanks to the compact nature of Craon just half a km to the *centre ville*. Located next to a small *plan d'eau* (lake), it can be a popular site so you may not be at one with nature but it does have a wide range of facilities
Rue Alain Gerbault, 53400 Craon
00 33 (0)2 43 07 35 60
www.ville-craon53.fr/camping-du-murier

Eat

Le Quatre-Épices

Here, a modern twist is given to fresh local products from Mayenne, which vary with the seasons. For simpler fare you will also find a couple of pizzerias in the centre near the covered market.
Espace Touristique du Mûrier, Rue Alain Gerbault, 53400 Craon
00 33 (0)2 43 06 05 25
www.lequatreepices.fr

Drink

Le Pressoir

At *cave à pommeau* (cider farm), just half a km from the town centre you can discover the different stages of production and sample some apple or pear cider. For authentic local mingling, in particular on market day, try a beer in Bar la Station on Place 11 Novembre.
Route de Château-Gontier, 53400 Craon
00 33 (0)2 43 06 17 90
www.fermedupressoir.com

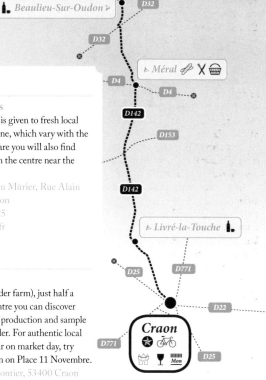

PAYS DE LA LOIRE

IDLE on one of the many islands dotted along the Loire river.

SPOT the first vineyards of the journey whilst cycling the beautiful Corniche Angevine.

LINGER by the Loire, with a chilled glass of rosé and a delicious picnic.

SPLURGE on a night in a château to experience the extravagance of aristocratic living.

TOAST your trip with a glass of sparkling Saumur *crémant* in one of the many *caves*.

FEEL the peace and solemnity of Fontevraud-l'Abbaye.

CRAON ⊙ TO CHALONNES-SUR-LOIRE

Stage 5: *39miles 62km*

Winding rural lanes give way to
straight but undulating roads with
each crest crowned by a church, a
clear visual target to lure you on.
In the closing kilometres of this
stage you reach a key landmark on
your journey when you cross the
Loire river and finish on its banks.

Craon to Châtelais

tarting with the church on your left, ride towards the roundabout and turn right. The space on your right holds a vibrant market on Mondays and is a great place to pick up food for the rest of your day. Go straight over at the next roundabout, which features an elaborate contemporary statue of a horse.

Follow the D771 in the direction of St-Nazaire along a tree-lined avenue. At the next roundabout turn left following Segré, D25. The next roundabout will come in quick succession; continue straight on signposted Châtelais. Within a few hundred metres you will pass the sign showing you are leaving Craon. Surrounded by open fields, you will see many grazing horses as you are close to the *hippodrome*.

Shortly after leaving the edge of Craon, take the left-hand fork signposted Chérance 3.6km. Between the broad expanses of open fields you will be able to look across to rolling hills in the distance, a subtle change in landscape from the flatter earlier stages. Occasionally an isolated oak or chestnut can be seen in amongst the fields.

When you arrive in Chérance, go straight on through the village turning left when you reach a T-junction, and then almost immediately right, signed Châtelais 5km. Continue on this road until you reach Châtelais. A gentle descent takes you to the Oudon river that you crossed in Craon. A short climb follows and, as you reach the crest, a fantastic view of the roof tops of Châtelais and its church greets you.

Châtelais to Segré

When you enter Châtelais turn right at a T-junction. With the imposing church on your left, take the left turn for the D193 in the direction of L'Hôtellerie-de-Flée and Nyoiseau. Châtelais is a good little town to explore with a small musuem dedicated to archaeological finds in the region. It is open by arrangement only but there are three phone numbers on the door and almost certainly one of the keyholders will be available to let you in and show you around.

Follow the D193 through Châtelais, and at the end of the village cross a small bridge and then take the right fork, toward Nyoiseau (it looks more like a straight on) on the

D193. Along here you will see yet more horse paddocks and a small *hippodrome*, the road undulating gently between them. In 4.5km at a T-junction with the D71, turn left towards Nyoiseau and Segré. You will shortly pass the *Ecomusée du Domaine de la Petite Couère*. A mixture of animals, wildlife and a recreated 18th-century village, it is one of the most highly rated attractions in the area, but with so much delightful countryside to view and so many authentic small villages to pedal through, little will be lost if you by-pass it.

After 1km you enter Nyoiseau, which has a *tabac* and *boulangerie* but little else. Nyoiseau merges directly into the next village Brèges, so stay on the D71 and at the end of Brèges continue straight over the roundabout. In 3km you reach a much bigger roundabout on the outskirts of Segré. At the first roundabout take the second exit and at the second roundabout take the third available exit signed Segré-Centre.

You are now following the Rue Ernest Renan, a back-way into town with the river on your right. Follow Centre Ville at a mini-roundabout with a spider sculpture. Cross over the river by the *mairie* and follow Rue Victor Hugo to the crossroads with Rue Gambetta, then turn right here signposted D280 direction Cholet. Go straight on at the next roundabout continuing to follow signs for Château de la Lorie and Cholet. As the road starts to bend round to the right and climb, take the left turn in the direction of Marans, D961.

INDULGE

Château de l'Epinay

This 16th-century château is now a luxurious *chambre d'hôtes*, carefully decorated to display the charm of the building. Many original features remain and the collections of 18th-century furniture and art give a real sense of the grandeur of château life in days gone by, but now with all the modern luxuries you could wish for.
Hosts Patrice and Valerie Montuoro will give you a very warm welcome, as will their three dogs! Breakfast is a sumptuous affair with lots of delicious options to choose from – perfect fuel for the day in the saddle ahead of you. A billiards room, natural swimming pool and canoes to use on the river provide plenty of ways to relax when not on your bike.

49170 Saint-Georges-sur-Loire
00 33 (0)2 41 39 87 05
www.chateauepinay.com

Segré is a fairly busy working town and, although it is well cared for and pretty, unless you need supplies or to visit the bike shop, it is not a place to while away too much time when there are other more picturesque places still to visit and more riding to be done.

Segré to La Pouëze
Shortly after leaving Segré you will pass a turning for Château de la Lorie, one of the most graceful châteaux of this region, off to the left. Unlike many grand houses, which feature a mish-mash of different styles as each generation rushes to put its stamp on the building, subsequent owners have instead made sympathetic additions that retain its symmetry. The ornate marble ballroom crowned with a musicians' gallery is very evocative of a time of courtly elegance.

Continue to follow the D961 straight on at the next two roundabouts, following signs for Marans and Vern d'Anjou. 3.5km after the last roundabout, you will pass through Marans, then follow the signs toward Vern d'Anjou, D961. Marans has a small shop, a *tabac* and a bar. Like so many villages around here the most impressive building is the church, which you can see on your left as you pass through.

The road from here is straight as a die, and you will be able to see as far as the next village even as you depart the current one. Each crest is crowned by a church with the road a roller-coaster in between the spires. 4.5km after Marans you will reach Vern d'Anjou, a small village with a *plan d'eau* off to the right that makes a nice picnic spot. At the crossroads in the centre, go straight over in the direction of La Pouëze D961.

A further 6km brings you into La Pouëze where an ivy-covered house stands next to a dramatic gold-covered crucifix at the entrance into the village. One of the key local industries here was slate mining until the mine closed in 1997. Its head-frame above the mine shaft is now a *monument historique* and the local community is working towards its restoration. You can find out more about the stone of this region at the *Musée du Granit* in the next village, Bécon-les-Granits.

La Pouëze to St-Georges-sur-Loire
After 5km the route pases through Bécon-les-Granits before the long, straight road continues in undulating waves to the next village, St-Augustin-des-Bois. The spire of the church appears on the horizon before St-Augustin-des-Bois, but you have to plunge down one hill and climb the other side before arriving in town. Keep your speed up on the descent and you'll make it some of the way up the next rise on momentum alone.

4km after St-Augustin-des-Bois you will reach a high spot with a view towards the Loire river, although you cannot see the river itself, the shapes of spires and towers emerging in

the misty distance is worth slowing down for. A further 3km brings you into St-Georges-sur-Loire.

Both the *mairie* and *bibliothèque* are housed in an incredibly elegant building with a spacious park laid out in front. Although the park is not maintained to the standards of the grounds of a wealthy château, the elements of symmetry and order can still be seen in the square lawns and avenues of trees. The Château de Serrant in St-Georges-sur-Loire is open to the public but only for guided tours.

St-Georges-sur-Loire to Chalonnes-sur-Loire

From St-Georges-sur-Loire the road becomes significantly busier as the route approaches one of the main crossing-points of the Loire. It helps that the road is slightly downhill, so you are able to maintain a good speed easily, and it is also wide, so you do not feel squeezed.

4km after leaving St-Georges-sur-Loire you cross the first channel of the Loire. The Loire has many small islands, and at this crossing-point you move from one island to the next to cross the full width of the river. There are two more crossings before you reach Chalonnes-sur-Loire: the second has a cycle path with a barrier between you and the traffic; and the third, the biggest of the bridges, also has a separated area for cyclists, although the sign here suggests that you walk across. At the end of the final bridge, turn immediately left to end the stage on a pretty tree-lined road alongside a cobbled quay. There are bankside benches offering river views for a well-earned rest.

THE LOIRE

The Loire is France's longest and laziest river and drains a fifth of the country's land area. It starts its 1,020km journey in the Massif Central flowing north toward Orléans before turning south-west towards Saumur, and then west to where it empties into the Atlantic at St-Nazaire.

Its progress becomes significantly slowed by silt in its lower course, resulting in sand bars and small islands that dot the channels. Numerous bridges mean that, on occasion, you can cycle between islands as well as alongside the banks.

While it is very tranquil today, the Loire has seen its fair share of strife: it formed the boundary between the French and English during the Hundred Year War and the Wars of Religion – both sides drowned their enemies in its waters.

The most lasting influence, and one of the greatest tourist attractions today, is the trail of elegant châteaux built by the royalty of France and their courts. They were attracted by the beauty of the Loire valley and found the leisurely pace of the river suited their own languid way of life.

Sleep

Chambres d'Hôtes

There is no hotel in Chalonnes-sur-Loire but there are two *chambres d'hôtes* next door to each other on the cobbled quay where the stage ends. Both cater for cyclists and are perfectly situated for walking into the small town or enjoying an evening stroll by the river.

Maison Beausoleil
64 Rue St Maurille, 49290 Chalonnes-sur-Loire
00 33 (0)2 41 77 95 67
www.chambres-beausoleil-chalonnes.com

Logis des Mariniers Maison d'Hôtes
35 Quai Victor Hugo, 49290 Chalonnes-sur-Loire
00 33 (0)2 41 68 02 64
www.logisdesmariniers.com

Camping

Camping le Candais
With good facilities and near to the Loire, this campsite is close to areas where river swimming is permitted – perfect for a post-ride dip.
Route de Rochefort,
49290 Chalonnes-sur-Loire
00 33 (0)2 41 78 02 27
www.campingterreoceane.com

Supplies

Food
You are unlikely to find specialist food shops or produce aimed at tourists but you will find the everyday items you may require within the few streets near the bridge in Chalonnes. There is a supermarket on the Route de Chemille, the D961.

Bike
100% Vélo – Segré
On the way into Segré the route almost takes you past the door. It is reasonably well stocked with up-to-date products.
22 Bis David d'Angers 49500 Segré
00 33 (0)2 41 26 02 14

Cycle Lefrançois
Look out for the front half of a bike sticking out of the shop wall above you. A good workshop for any mechanical problems.
18 Rue du Vieux Pont, 49290 Chalonnes-sur-Loire
00 33 (0)2 41 47 00 90
cycleslefrancois.canalblog.com

Swim
If you fancy a dip after a hot day in the saddle you will be able to find easy and safe access to the river near to the campsite Le Candais on the Louet branch of the Loire river, off the D751 in the direction of Rochefort-sur-Loire.

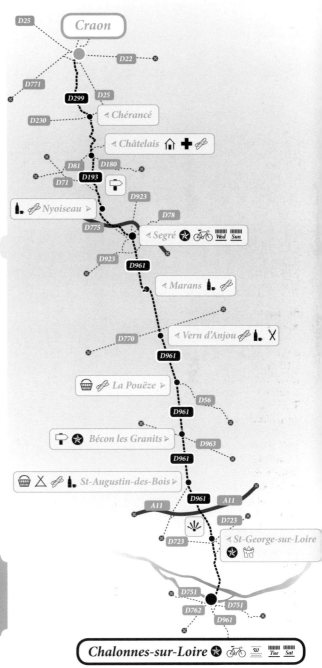

CHALONNES-SUR-LOIRE ⊤⊙
BRISSAC-QUINCE

Stage 6: *22miles 36km*

Chalonnes-sur-Loire to Corniche Angevine

With the river on your left and your back to the bridge, follow the road round until you meet a T-junction. Turn left here and keep an eye out for the distinctive half-bike sticking out of the wall on the bike shop. At the roundabout go straight over, taking the second exit signposted Rochefort-sur-Loire on the D751 to start the Corniche Angevine.

1km from the start you will pass Le Layon on your right, a lake with a picnic area and a pleasant spot to sunbathe, however, there is another good opportunity for a sunbathe and a swim in Rochefort-sur-Loire in 9km time if you prefer to keep pedalling.

Within a couple of kilometres of leaving Chalonnes-sur-Loire you will pass the Chapelle Ste-Barbe-des-Mines, commissioned in 1858 by the widow of the director of mines in Chalonnes-sur-Loire in his memory. It was used by those who worked in the mines nearby. The building suffered badly during both wars and in 1945 a French soldier shot at the head of Sainte-Barbe's statue above the door. Marked for demolition in the 1980s, it is now owned by the local community and has been restored as a venue for events.

A couple more kilometres after the *chapelle* you will pass the first vineyards of the route – a significant moment. The Loire acts as a natural line drawn across France, dividing the cooler north from the warmer south. Before crossing the Loire you will have been sipping cider and passing through orchards, below the Loire you will start to see many more vineyards and *un verre du vin* is more likely to be the drink of choice. There is also a distinct change in climate. If St-Malo was cool and grey when you set off, then the Loire is often where the temperature starts to warm up and the sun to become a more predictable companion.

Corniche Angevine to Rochefort-sur-Loire

The Corniche Angevine winds its way along the cliffs of the rocky outcrop on the south side of the Loire. From the saddle you will be able to admire views across to some of the islands that dot the river. Later in the stage the route takes you across one of the largest of them.

Starting with the beautiful curves of the Corniche Angevine, the route winds its way past the first vineyards of the trip before becoming reunited with the Loire. The ride takes you along an island surrounded by France's longest river before turning south to Brissac-Quincé, which is dominated by its château.

The road climbs slightly, but with sufficient curves and a gentle enough gradient so that it never feels too challenging.

A further 3km of riding will see you winding up the *corniche* with occasional viewpoints to the left and the first of many wine *dégustations* that you will see along the route. You can call in for a small sample and find out more about the local vintages. When you arrive in Rochefort-sur-Loire you will be able to find some wild swimming and picnic opportunities if

you take the D106, signed Béhuard left over the bridge and follow signs for the piscine turning first right into Chemin du Port signed Le Parking. The river swimming is 200 metres after the swimming pool.

Rochefort-sur-Loire to St-Jean-de-la-Croix

Leaving Rochefort the road follows a meandering path between the vines. A glance to the left shows small rounded hills with the ubiquitous church spire or steeple rising up from many of them. In 4km you reach the small village of Denée, described as *une petite cité de caractère*. There is an interactive info point on the wall of the art gallery behind the small Proxi supermarket. It is simple to use and offers a wealth of information on the local area. Despite its proximity to the Loire and popular tourist routes, this particular village feels very much lived-in, friendly, open and chatty. The residents seem happy going about their daily life with the flow of visitors neither a help nor a hindrance to it.

1km outside of town, on a slight downhill, there is an obscured left turn to St-Jean-de-la-Croix on the D132. It is soon after the Proxi supermarket, so begin to slow down as you pass. Initially a narrow lane, it widens slightly and you will be treated to some beautiful easy pedalling. Soon after the turn you will cross a bridge over a small lake and not long after

LADY ANGEVIN

Lady Angevin was the nickname given to Renée Bordereau, a Frenchwoman born in nearby Soulaines-sur-Aubance in 1770, who disguised herself as a man and fought in the Royalist Cavalry during the Vendée wars. The unit she led threw six hundred republican soldiers into the river Louet from Roche-de-Mûrs, in the commune of Mûrs Erigné. She was reputed to be a brave soldier and skilled tactician. Her memoirs are still in print today.

that you will see a purpose-made picnic spot on your right – a raised up plinth with good views.

Just over 1km from the end of the lake you will cross a bridge. Though you may not realise it, you are now riding on an island, situated mid-stream in the Loire. Surrounded by lush green fields and trees you are only a hundred metres or so from the river but seldom see it. 2.5km after crossing the river onto the island you will arrive at a row of pretty cottages and a church in the very small hamlet of St-Jean-de-la-Croix.

St-Jean-de-la-Croix to Mûrs Erigné

All of the small villages along this stretch have traffic-calming measures in place to help keep the speed down to match the tranquil nature of the area, but traffic is never particularly busy and you are likely to see more cyclists than cars. The cottages you pass are mainly small, simple affairs. There is none of the grandeur of riverside châteaux along this stretch, but this makes it all the more homely and pleasant.

1 km after leaving St-Jean-de-la-Croix you will enter Vieux Port Thibault, the neighbours in newer Port Thibault are just across the water. 2km from here the road comes closer to the river edge, again allowing a clear view of the water, and there is a beach area slightly set back from the road and partially concealed by a bank. Another 3km of flat riverside cruising brings you to a view of Les Ponts-de-Cé which is split across both sides of the river. The bridge with its eleven arches can be seen from the route, however, you will be heading around to the right so will not be crossing over it.

At the roundabout take the second exit, straight on, staying on the D132. Follow this between some fairly modern-looking houses with an elaborately large traffic island splitting the two carriageways. At the end of this road you will arrive at a traffic- light controlled T-junction. Turn right here for Brissac-Quincé.

After a few hundred metres you will pass over the Pont du Louet, and say *au revoir* to the island. Another small bridge takes you into Mûrs Erigné, where you will spot a rather lovely old Michelin sign on a wall on your left showing Poitiers one way and Cholet the other. Shortly after this turn left signed Brissac-Quincé, D748.

Mûrs Erigné to Brissac Quincé.

Immediately after taking the left to Brissac-Quincé take the first right, signposted St-Melaine-sur-Aubance, ignoring the sign that says Brissac-Quincé 9km as this will take you to the dual carriageway. Continue for 200 metres to a crossroads

with a stop sign, then head straight over. At the first mini-roundabout turn right, first exit. The road continues another 200m to another mini-roundabout where you need to continue straight over, taking the second exit. You will then cross over the A87 *autoroute* to Paris. Turn immediately left on the D127 signposted St-Melaine-sur-Aubance.

1km after the *autoroute* turn right at the roundabout signposted St-Melaine-sur-Aubance on the D127. Follow the road between the vines that line each side of the road. After 2 km you reach a bridge over the Aubance itself. There is a picnic area off to the right which would make a very pleasant place to stop and eat, or even dangle your feet in the water. At the T-junction turn left, signposted Brissac-Quincé D123 and remain on the same road for the final 4 km.

After St-Melaine-sur-Aubance the road is slightly more wooded for a short while with a pleasingly easy slightly downhill gradient. After 2km you cross over a small bridge. The next 1km is through more vineyards and as you turn toward Brissac-Quincé for the final kilometre you can see the town and its château on the hill above you. The stage ends 500 metres after the roundabout at the gates to the château.

Brissac-Quincé

The town of Brissac-Quincé is built on a small hill facing the château. To get from the castle there is a series of winding bends that spiral you up to the *centre ville* or, on foot, a more direct set of steps takes you from one level to the next.

Although relatively small, Brissac-Quincé has a real sense of grandeur and timelessness, mainly owing to its pleasing

buildings. The cobbles of the narrow streets gleam and the white walls and clean lines of the buildings are simple and elegant, even where there is a mix of architectural styles and time periods.

Several of the restaurants have been situated so that their terraces have panoramic views of the castle. There are far worse ways to spend an evening than sipping a chilled glass of Loire rosé and watching the sun set over the domed roof and turrets. Brissac-Quincé has twice hosted the Championships of France for hot-air balloonists or rather *Le Championnat de France de Montgolfières*, named after the brothers who invented the first hot-air balloon. The brightly coloured balloons rising above the silhouette of the castle can be an amazing sight.

CHATEAU DE BRISSAC

High on its hill, Château de Brissac is an impressive sight, made even more so by its status as the tallest castle along the Loire.

Begun by Charles de Cossé, governor of Paris and marshal of France, it was established on top of an older fortress.

As with most châteaux, various periods of building and alteration continued through the centuries. The front features a 17th-century domed pavilion sandwiched between 15th-century towers.

Fifteen rooms are open to the public including the bedroom of Louis XIII and the opera theatre built in 1883 and still used for concerts today. The gardens can be explored and the wine cellar offers occasional tastings.

One of the best views of the château is from above. If you take a walk into the town and stand outside the *office de tourisme* looking down on the castle, you will be able to see the glory of all its towers and facades as well as the expanse of gardens.

Sleep

Hotel
Le Castel
Whilst being the only hotel in town, it is also worthy of a recommendation thanks to its helpful staff, terrace area for post-ride drinks and its position with a view of the castle. It is also within walking distance of the town.

1 Rue Louis Moron, 49320 Brissac-Quincé
00 33 (0)2 41 91 24 74
www.hotel-lecastel.com

Chambre d'Hôtes
Moulin de Clabeau
2km before you reach Brissac-Quincé this secluded and peaceful *chambre d'hôtes* has bedrooms full of character with lovely old beams in an old watermill.
Just off the route, signed from the D123, 2km before Brissac-Quincé.

00 33 (0)2 41 91 22 09
www.gite-brissac.com

Campsite
Camping de l'Etang
At the vineyard of Domaine de l'Etang this 4-star campsite has a wealth of facilities and provides the opportunity to taste the wines on-site. The family leisure park may not be to everyone's taste but within the 8 hectares of the site you will be able to find a quiet corner.

Route de St-Mathurin, 49320 Brissac-Quincé.
00 33 (0)2 41 91 70 67
www.domaine-etang.fr

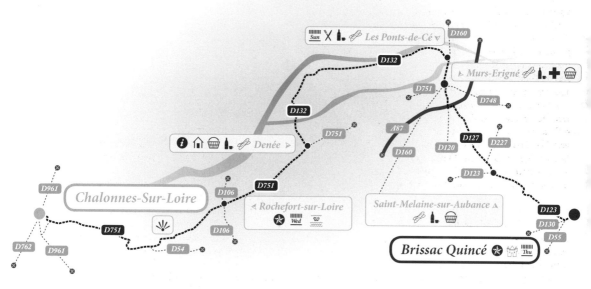

Swim
10km into your ride you reach the village of Rochefort-sur-Loire. Take the D106 to your left, head over the bridge then turn right into Le Port. You will find a river swimming spot located 200 metres past the swimming pool.

Supplies

Food
There is a limited number of small shops in Brissac-Quincé but you should be able to get your basic daily supplies from the three *boulangeries* and one *épicerie*. If you need more extensive shopping head to the Parc des Activités, an-out-of-town shopping area.

Eat

Le Haut Tertre
Primarily a *crêperie* but also offering salads, *galettes* and more substantial meals. Simple modern décor inside and an outside terrace for warmer days. Food is simple, tasty and good value. All you need after a day in the saddle.

1 Tertre, 49320 Brissac-Quincé
00 33 (0)2 41 91 79 95

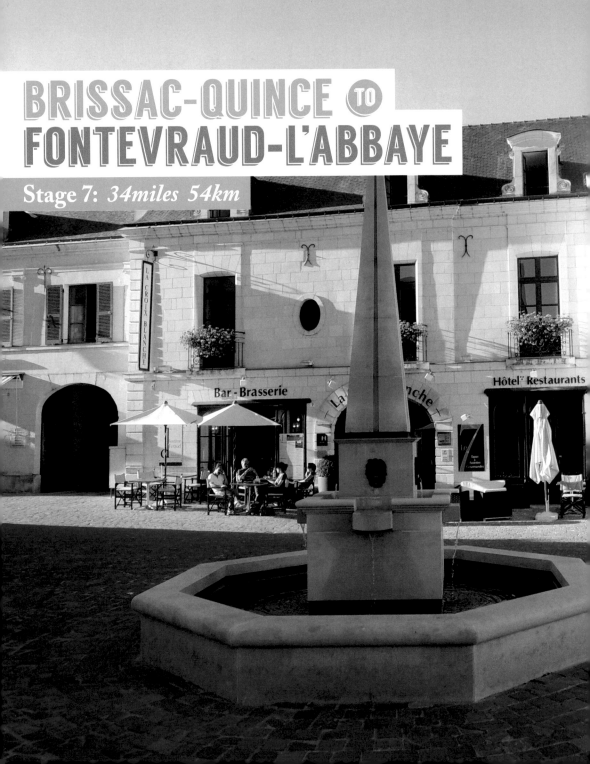

BRISSAC-QUINCE ⓣⓞ FONTEVRAUD-L'ABBAYE

Stage 7: *34miles 54km*

TABAC · VINS · CADEAUX

A ride through the heart of the ancient province of Anjou, an area ever popular with cycle tourists. Pedal along the banks of the Loire, past *caves* of the famous Saumur sparkling wine, and through a small forest *en route* to the atmospheric old streets of Fontevraud l'Abbaye and its impressive monastic complex, the largest in France.

Brissac-Quincé to St-Rémy-la-Varenne

The stage starts in front of the château with a very short climb up to the *centre ville*. After surging up the switchbacks you arrive at the main square. With *Le Clemenceau* restaurant in front of you, turn right down the narrow, one-way Rue du 14 Juilliet.

Most towns have a street of the same name in honour of Bastille Day, which marked the start of the French Revolution. 200m down the street, turn right again signed St-Mathurin on the D55, pedal over a bridge over a dual carriageway, and shortly after you'll find yourself reunited with familiar vineyards that line the route.

4km after leaving Brissac-Quincé, the route passes through the adjacent farming hamlets of La Croix Viau and Bouhière. After a further 2km the route crosses straight over the D751 at Château de Bois-Brinçon, with views across the vineyard to the castle. The route continues on the D55 with a sweeping right-hand bend in front of the château.

After the château, carry straight on passing an old windmill in the hamlet of Le Bourg Dion. 6km on from the château turn right and then immediately right again, by a picnic area under a cluster of trees on your left, signed Gennes 10km, D132. If you cross the Loire river you've just missed the turn. The route now flirts with the southern banks of the Loire all the way to Saumur, the regional capital of Anjou.

You are now on the *Loire à vélo* route so you may meet other cyclists journeying from its source to the Atlantic. Depending on the time of year, water levels in the Loire vary wildly; it can look like a silt-choked stream in the late summer months and a roaring river in early spring, when the snow melts near its source high in the Massif Central.

Less than 1km after you've made your two right turns, you'll find a short cobbled section in St-Rémy-la-Varenne, the first of a string of small villages adjacent to the Loire. The *office de tourisme* is through a small archway, and the old priory with its peaceful garden is round the back if you need a break.

St-Rémy-la-Varenne to Le Thoureil

2km after St-Rémy, at the Vins d'Anjou cave at St-Maur is
your first significant sighting of the wide expanse of the Loire.
After a further 2km you arrive in Le Thoureil, where the road
runs right against the Loire with the wall on the left forming
the river's bank.

There is an impressive and clear view of both banks of the
river, which is unusual because the Loire has many islands and
channels throughout its lower course.

In the days when the Loire was a working river, Le
Thoureil's position allowed it to develop as a busy river port.
Although the mariners' cottages and merchants' townhouses
are the only survivors of this era, it is still possible to imagine
life here in the golden age of boatmanship.

Through the *office de tourisme* you can arrange a trip on a
toue, also known as a *gabare*, a small, 18th-century wooden
boat with a cabin, which was the traditional means of
transport and commerce on the river.

The boats have unusually flat bottoms to help them navigate
the river's shallower channels. When not shipping goods,
mariners found time to play *tilleuls*, a form of bowling using
the flat hulls of their boats. The game's origins may also
lie with Spanish prisoners, who dug out trenches to build
embankments along the Loire in the 18th-century.

They played using ball-bearings from the region's
windmills. Today the Saumur region alone has over 140
tilleuls and *boules* clubs, which form an important part of
village life.

Le Thoureil to Gennes

After Le Thoureil the route is set back further from the river,
rejoining it after a couple of kilometres. 4km after leaving Le
Thoureil the route arrives in the small town of Gennes.
Turn right at main road signed Saumur, shortly after take the
second exit left off a mini-roundabout, again signed Saumur,
D751 at the Café de la Paix.

Gennes was an important religious and commercial centre
in the Gallo-Roman period. In the 1980s excavation of an
amphitheatre on a hill above the town revealed it to have the
capacity for up to 5000 spectators at gladiatorial contests – the
largest Roman amphitheatre in western France.

Should you have time, you can visit the family-run Moulin
de Sarre, one of the last working watermills in France that still
produces flour from wheat crushed by a traditional grindstone.
Gennes also boasts a megaliths' mountain-bike trail, which
tours the region's many neolithic landmarks.

Gennes to Saumur

300m after the mini-roundabout, on your way out of town to Saumur, you will notice the prominent pink colours of the bike shop Cycle Obsession. Continue on this road for 15km until Saumur. 2km after leaving Gennes you arrive in Cunault, with its château built on a rocky outcrop.

However it is Notre-Dame that takes centre stage in Cunault, the longest Romanesque church without a transept in France. If you peer inside you may notice that religious motifs have been placed up high so they don't interfere with the elegance of the pure architectural lines. If you prefer cafés to churches, try Le Cale at the edge of the village, which has some well-positioned tables for a coffee by the river.

After just 1km you reach the small twin villages of Trèves and Préban. Restaurant, La Cave aux Moines, proudly advertises snails, mushrooms and wine.

SAUMUR'S SPARKLING SUBURBS

Every building in the suburb of St-Hilaire-St-Florent seems to be used for wine-making and the most celebrated product is sparkling Saumur *crémant*. You can visit any of the rock-carved cellars where the wine matures and enjoy a complimentary *dégustation*, remembering of course too much *vin* won't mix well with your *vélo*!

Although the Loire is most famous for its rosé, the vineyards of Anjou that surround Saumur are the largest in the Loire with 20,000 acres and 32 *appellations d'origine contrôlée*, producing not just rosé but respectable reds and whites.

The beautiful vine-laden land lying between Saumur, Montsoreau and Le Puy-Notre-Dame through which you cycle before Fontevraud is often referred to locally as the green-and-golden triangle.

The most prestigious wines of the region are the sparkling *Saumur Brut* and *Crémant de Loire*, which many argue are as good as champagne but without the price tag.

Shortly after the route passes through the hamlet of St-Jean. At this point the Loire can just be made out through clusters of trees off to your left, as you ride through the small villages of Chênehutte and La Mimerolle.

3.5km after La Mimerolle, just before the outskirts of Saumur, there is an interesting Musée de Champignon on your right, easily missed on this quick flat section but worth a peek for the wide variety of fungi. The humidity and temperature of the caves that dot the river valley are perfect breeding-grounds for mushrooms.

Arriving in Saumur

From the Musée de Champignon it is a further 4km to Saumur *centre ville* but first you pass a line of *caves* of renowned sparkling wine producers on your right as you enter the town. After passing the *caves*, carry on straight over a roundabout signed Bagneux, then straight over a smaller roundabout passing under a road bridge carrying the Saumur by-pass.

After just under 2km of riding through a residential part of Saumur, take the third exit left at a roundabout which takes you across the Pont Fouchard over the Thouet river. Saumur *centre ville* is sandwiched between the Thouet and Loire, with the confluence at the northern edge of town.

Immediately after crossing the river take the exit right at the roundabout signed Varrains, D93. If you wish to visit the *centre ville* simply carry straight on taking the second exit at this point.

Saumur

Aside from sparkling wines, Saumur is home to the French cavalry academy and the Cadre Noir riding school. As with many Loire towns, if you explore Saumur's *centre ville*, you will find a prominent château high up above the other buildings.

The château has not always been so stable and has only recently re-opened after the collapse of a slope. This led to the toppling of the north-west bastion towards the river in 2001, requiring over a decade of painstaking restoration work.

Saumur also boasts Europe's largest dolmen lying in the garden of a bar in the suburb of Bagneux. Although many mark burial sites, the purpose of this dolmen is unknown and remains a mystery as no bones have been found.

You can sip a drink marvelling at how and why neolithic man might have hauled 500 tonnes of stone to create this large chamber. To reach the site, which is on private land, at the roundabout before crossing the Thouet take the first exit, signed Cholet, and follow the signs.

Saumur to Fontevraud-l'Abbaye

Following the D93 out of town towards Varrains, keep in the right-hand lane to avoid looping back to town. Shortly after, continue straight across taking the second exit signed D93, Varrains. The road linking Saumur with Varrains can be busy because the settlements have expanded into each other, a cycle lane runs along the side of the road for 5km after the bridge.

With the new-build housing of Varrains on the right and vineyards on the left, take the fourth and final exit at the roundabout signed D205 Souzay-Champigny.

The road curves its way gradually upwards through rows of vines. You are rewarded with peaceful riding all the way to Fontevraud through a mix of oak woods, wheat fields and grapevines. Sandwiched between touristy Saumur and the honeypot of Fontevraud, this face of the Loire is not often seen unless on on two wheels.

After just under 3km, in Champigny turn left at the T-junction signed Souzay D205, following the road round a one-way system before turning right onto the D145 signed Fontevraud l'Abbaye. From Champigny it is 7km to Fontevraud climbing a little through woodland before descending gently to a roundabout just outside Fontevraud.

Arriving in Fontevraud-l'Abbaye

At the roundabout take the third exit sign-posted Centre Ville, Abbaye Royale. To reach the village centre, pass the war memorial and car park on your right before turning right shortly after at an old well, with a small sign marked Hôtel Abbaye Royale. After 200m you reach a fountain in front of the entrance to the grand abbey and Europe's largest monastic complex, which makes this village so popular.

Founded in the early 12th-century 38 different abbesses, often of royal blood, presided over a mixed order of monks, nuns, lepers and reformed prostitutes until 1792.

The abbey is the resting place of 15 of the Plantagenet family, including the mysterious Eleanor of Aquitaine who is buried alongside her husband Henry II, their son Richard the Lionheart and daughter-in-law, Isabelle of Angoulême. Napoleon decided to turn the complex into a prison in 1804 and it remained in use until 1963.

Even if you are not an ardent abbey enthusiast, the sheer scale of the complex is impressive. If you can't be enticed though the door, the village itself is worth an exploratory stroll. You could follow *les circuits de patrimoine* through the streets – walks that offer a refreshingly human side to history with perspectives on village life through the eyes of many different historical characters.

The weight of history and calmness pervade this entire village, even the path linking the large car park near the war memorial to the church of St-Michel is a beautifully kept, tree lined avenue.

LOIRE A VELO

The Loire is one of the best regions for cycle tourists anywhere in the world, with its mix of friendly terrain, interesting sights and excellent cycling infrastructure. Many rental locations along the Loire will allow you to drop your bike off further along the valley, enabling you to undertake a place-to-place trip.

Loire à Vélo is also the name of an official 800km route that follows the upper reaches of the river from Cuffy, in the department of Cher, to St-Brevin-les-Pins in Loire-Atlantique. At least 50% of the route is traffic-free. Look out for the green-and-blue Loire à Vélo indicators.

Anjou Vélo Vintage

In homage to the history of cycling, for one June weekend each year Saumur hosts the Anjou Vélo Vintage. The town is overrun by traditional vintage bikes, their riders dressed in retro vélo outfits. The event involves a range of activities from a *musée du vélo* to music, but the highlight is a vintage *sportif*, with riders pedalling round the countryside on three different loop rides.

Sleep

Hotel

Hostellerie La Croix Blanche
By the fountain on the main square with classic beamed ceilings. The bells of the abbey wake you in time for an ample breakfast.
7 Place Des Plantagenêts, 49590 Fontevraud-l'Abbaye
00 33 (0)2 41 51 71 11
www.hotel-croixblanche.com

Chambre d'Hôtes

Alienor
Welcoming limestone house in the heart of Fontevraud, just 600m from the abbey.
Régine et Jean-François Biette,
43 Avenue des Roches, 49590 Fontevraud- l'Abbaye
00 33 (0)2 41 40 12 69
www.fontevraud-alienor.com

Campsite

Le Camping de l'Isle Verte
This is in Montsoreau on the banks of the river, 5km north of Fontevraud. It is equally picturesque and enjoys its status amongst the elite as one of *les plus beaux villages* of France.
Avenue de la Loire, 49730 Montsoreau
00 33 (0)2 41 51 76 60
www.campingisleverte.com

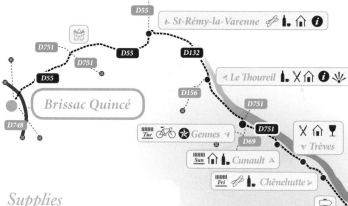

Eat

La Licorne
Pass underneath the unicorn (*licorne*) above the door for traditional gourmet cuisine in an 18th-century mansion close to the abbey.
Allée Ste-Catherine, 49590 Fontevraud-l'Abbaye
00 33 (0)2 41 51 72 49
www.la-licorne-restaurant.com

Supplies

Bike

Unusually, you have a choice of bike shops en route from Gennes to Saumur, reflecting the popularity of cycling along the Loire.

Cycle-Obsession

Very helpful store, well-stocked with spares. You could even try a tandem if you have time, and you'll be flying along the flat roads of the Loire.
14 Route de Saumur, 49350 Gennes
00 33 (0)2 41 40 74 41
www. cycle-obsession.com

Véloland City, Cesbron Cycles

A new store for Saumur, unfortunately 4km from the town centre in Distre, but well -stocked and run by a respected nationally affiliated chain.
Rue de l'Avenir (à côté de Jouet Club), 49400 Distre
www.veloland.com

Supplies

Food

Fontevraud market is on a Wednesday morning. The village has some local artisan chocolates and biscuits, but Fontevraud isn't the best place for basics. The *boulangerie* has plenty of options and has an interesting *salon de thé*, Le Trois Lys, at the side.

Drink

If you are pining for a cup of tea, head to Chez Teresa. Fontevraud is not known for its nightlife but the outside courtyard terrace and bar at La Croix Blanche makes an atmospheric spot for a sundowner, so there's no need to be completely monastic.

POITOU - CHARENTES

FOLLOW in the footsteps of pilgrims up the medieval lane of Vaux St-Jacques to the gates of Parthenay.

CRUISE past the cornfields of northern Poitou, enjoying the friendliest gradients of the journey.

STUMBLE across some of most well-preserved Roman ruins in France at Sanxay and Cassiomagus.

PEDAL through the pastoral *bocage* watched only by fields of docile-looking cows and sheep.

REVEL in the rural quiet along the banks of the Vienne river south of Confolens.

FROLIC in the cool, deep waters of the Vienne – perfect for a post-ride swim.

FONTEVRAUD-L'ABBAYE ⓣⓞ PARTHENAY

Stage 8: *48miles 77km*

After lingering in the Loire, this is a stage of real pedalling progress due south, in two distinct sections. Loudun church spire teases you from 15km away on the straightest section of road on your whole journey. After this, the route winds through the wheat fields and grazing land of the Thouet valley to the unassuming but history -steeped town of Parthenay.

Fontevraud-l'Abbaye to Loudun

rom the fountain in front of the abbey entrance follow the sign to Couziers, to your right as you look at the building. You ride alongside the abbey wall on your left for 0.5km, giving you an idea of its sheer scale. As the road forks, take the right-hand road down a small lane away from the wall. After 1.5km along the lane, which is lined by small embankments on either side, you reach the main road. Turn left here and follow this road for 22 km all the way to Loudun.

This Roman road is ruler-straight, although it undulates up and down in places, all the way until Loudun, which was established as a gateway to Poitou and originally home to a large fortress.

The road's straightness is interrupted in only one instance, 3km after joining the main road, where the terrain is too steep for it to go straight up. Here, the road bends right then left to a heady 110m – a very modest elevation but one of the highest points in this relatively flat stage.

Just after you begin to descend, depending on your speed, you may notice a mushroom-growing farm on your right. Mushrooms are big business in this area and much sought after, not only for Parisian restaurant tables but also internationally.

The road then forms a beautifully sweeping, and seemingly never-ending, right-hand bend that makes a gradual descent.

The distant spire of Loudun church can be seen from 15km away, beckoning you on. The view is framed by woodland running along either side of the road. Your progress along this stretch of road will depend upon your relationship with the wind gods.

A southerly breeze is nice and warm, but it can seem like you are hallucinating, chasing the church as it runs away from you. A cool northerly, on the other hand, makes it look as if the spire is growing closer, and appearing faster than your legs can turn.

When a roundabout interrupts your direct path, continue straight across travelling due south, signed Loudun 8km. As Loudun draws closer the woods give way to corn fields, then at a second roundabout carry straight on to Loudun over the railway line.

Loudun

Arriving in Loudun *centre ville*, with the remnants of the old town walls ahead of you, turn right signposted Thouars. Keep in the left lane and go straight on, following the town walls on your left down a tree-lined avenue. The road descends slightly. When you arrive at a T-junction, turn left signed Autres Directions. Continue straight on at a set of traffic lights, turning right 400m after the lights, signed Chalais D63. This is a difficult turn to spot but well worth looking out for as it avoids a busy section of *route nationale*, which trucks trundle along at speed, heading south to the regional capital of Poitiers. If you get to an Esso garage you have gone too far. This route takes you on a pleasant, semi-circle around the *centre ville* anti-clockwise. It can also be done clockwise by aiming for Chalais D63, although riding round the eastern side of town is busier.

Loudun is a working town that has seen more prosperous days as a major transport centre, indicated by the ring road, which acts as a hub. From it, the straight-as-a-die roads act like spokes, departing from every angle into the countryside. With the arrival of the *autoroute* Loudun lost a lot of its significance as a strategic crossroads for trade. However, it does boast a small *vélodrome* and had its moment at the centre of cycling. On July 2nd 2000, Loudun hosted the end of the second stage of the Tour de France, which started 194km away at the Futuroscope theme park. The previous day in the opening stage at Futuroscope, a young scot name David Millar opened the tour by claiming victory in the prologue.

Situated inside the inner ring road is the old town, which is worth an amble if you have 15 minutes to spare. It is set up a slight hill, with winding lanes of limestone buildings interspersed with the odd square with a fountain. Even unimpressive looking French towns are rich in history. With a 10th-century square tower on the high part of town and the 13th-century Porte du Martray marking the western entrance to the town, Loudun has many hidden layers. You will find plenty of *boulangeries*, and possibly some will be open, if your energy levels need boosting after the long, straight journey from the Loire.

Loudun to Moncontour

Leaving town on the D63 signed Chalais, in quick succession you continue straight across at a stop sign, straight on at mini-roundabout and then straight across the heavily trafficked bypass. The D63 is a narrow country lane which, 2km after crossing the bypass, reaches the small farming hamlet of Mazault. In Mazault, the road passes through a narrow channel of stone farm buildings, which have been built into the limestone rock in places.

Here, look out for and take the left signed Chalais D63. After 1km in Chalais by the church, continue straight following the D63 signed St-Cassien 3km. The road narrows through a small woodland before opening back up to fields.

In St-Cassien turn left, signed Martaize D63, and keep straight on, ignoring side turnings. As you head out of the village the route opens and flattens out. 1km after St-Cassien

turn right at a T-junction onto a wider road, signed Martaize 2.5km. This is open country with big skies and barley. On your left as you enter Martaize you will find a wooded picnic area, perfect for shade or shelter, depending on the weather.

In the village, follow the road straight on signed Moncontour 8km, D52. At this point bend round to the left, and if you need any facilities the centre of the village is just 100m away. There is a small supermarket and a bar, which looks more like someone's front room, as is often the case in smaller villages. As you round the corner on leaving the village, you may notice you have completed the quickest kilometre of your life (that is, if you haven't diverted to the bar) as the sign at a mini- roundabout where you continue straight on announces Moncontour 7km!

The ride to Moncontour, past an array of cornfields, is quick and flat, as indeed is the remainder of the stage to Parthenay. But if time permits there is a multitude of medieval and more ancient sites of interest in smaller towns and larger villages, either on or adjacent to your route. After flying through the corn for 7km, turn right into the large village of Moncontour on the D52 then, shortly after, turn left at a T-junction entering the village along a tree-lined avenue.

The elongated, agricultural village of Moncontour is famous for its nearby water-ski lake, out of view from the road, and the impressive donjon (look up to your right as you ride along the main street). If your legs are yearning for some climbing to interrupt this pancake-flat second half of this stage, you could always ride the 40m up to the donjon (a defensive and lookout tower), built in 1020 and still remarkably intact. From the base alone there are commanding views over the fertile plains, which have been farmed and feuded over for over a thousand years, as well as of the route south to the abbey church spire in the next village of St-Jouin-de-Marnes. In July and August the tower is open so you can go up to the top.

Moncontour to Airvault

At the end of the long main street in Moncontour, turn right signposted Airvault, D52. After 2km through flat farmland, turn right at the T-junction onto the D37 to St-Jouin-de-Marnes. Shortly after, the route enters St-Jouin-de-Marnes dominated by its 11th to 12th-century abbey on the right as you enter the village. It is one of the most beautifully positioned abbeys in the region, looking north over the hayfields of the very gently sloping Dive valley. This is some accolade in an area of stiff competition on the pilgrimage route to Santiago de Compostela. However, even monastic life was not quiet enough for everyone and Généroux, a monk, fled the old monastery in St-Jouin-des-Marnes to live as a hermit. His home was a cave, 6km to the west on the banks of the river Thouet, and the village of St-Généroux is named after him.

Shortly after passing the abbey, turn left at a large, triangular village green, signed Airvault, D46, across the hypotenuse side of the green by a small bar. Persist with the unusually patchwork surface for the first 3km as the straight road soon reverts to the silky smooth surface you have become accustomed to in France.

MAGIC MUSHROOMS

Northern Poitou might not be home to the hallucinogenic variety, but the mushroom business in this region is booming and employs more than 2,000 people. Just south of Fontevraud, you cycle past large-scale mushroom farms, where rotting hay bales combine with other organic waste inside dark growing sheds to create the moist conditions for growth.

Anjou, which we have just left, is responsible for supplying 75% of France's cultivated mushrooms. There, dark caves in limestone cliffs along the Loire, not growing sheds, provide the perfect conditions.

Production started in the 19th-century with *champignons de Paris* – the name reflecting the old cultivation methods in disused quarries around Paris. The market is becoming increasingly lucrative as foodies and restaurants worldwide seek exotic varieties such as shitake.

After a 9km flat section without a single bend, you arrive in Airvault. Continue straight on at the crossroads signed Parthenay D46, paying attention to the stop sign, or alternatively turn right following Centre Ville to look at the centre of town.

Airvault has a small but pretty *centre ville*, its main street located atmospherically in its own mini-valley below the more modern parts of town. It has a grand, ornate, old market hall that springs to life on a Saturday morning. There is also a museum of folk arts, focusing on traditional daily life, which is housed in the former Augustine abbey, as well as an elevated château with crumbling walls overlooking the church. Abbeys and churches seem to be ubiquitous in this region, which is dominated by corn and Catholicism.

Airvault today displays much of its medieval past, with its underground spring, quaint streets and half-timbered houses. It is also renowned for its world music and dance festival in the second week of July, but perhaps less well-known for a didgeridoo festival, when the haunting music echoes around, amplified by the natural acoustics in this small valley.

Airvault to St-Loup-sur-Thouet

Leaving Airvault on the D46 to Parthenay, you pedal past a pretty, well-tended traffic island of flowers and a small water-wheel on the right with a *boulangerie* and café-bar. On the left there is a good picnic spot under a dual line of trees, where you can sometimes watch locals playing *boules* on the walkway. When leaving, first cross over the level crossing and then head straight across the roundabout, taking the second exit signed Parthenay D46, before going over the second level crossing at Fief Barreau. Barley rustles in the breeze on your left as the road by-passes a sprinkling of new houses on your right.

Just under 4km after leaving Airvault, the route descends for a few hundred metres, quickly twisting to the right under a railway bridge by the banks of the slow-flowing, lily-choked Thouet. Momentum may carry you around the next bend to the left over the river but, just before riding over the river bridge, you could turn right to look further into the village of St-Loup-Sur-Thouet, signed Centre Ville.

The village has a rich past and is a pretty place to stop for lunch or morning coffee. In the 16th-century, St-Loup had a burgeoning middle class, thanks to its booming tanning industry, taking cattle hides from the grazing country to the upper reaches of the valley to the south. A canal was excavated to make use of the water from the Thouet, which now envelops the whole village. The principal street, Rue Théophane

Bernard, is made up of 16th-century, half-timbered houses with intricate stonework and beams. It leads to an elegant château where you can stay the night.

St-Loup-sur-Thouet to Parthenay

After crossing over the Thouet, turn left signposted Gourgé 7km, D138. In a contrast to the arable open land of the early part of this stage, high hedgerows now divide up lush green pastureland.

This landscape of irregular shaped fields and meadows bounded by hedges choked with brambles, gorse, oak and chestnut trees is known as *paysage bocager* and is the legacy of farming in the middle ages.

The hedges offered protection against the weather and facilitated the production of fruit and firewood. This quiet upper reach of the Thouet valley seems a world away from the large agri-industries around Loudun.

3.5km after St-Loup-sur-Thouet the road forks. Keep left on the principle route to Gourgé crossing the railway line shortly after. A further 2km on turn left on the D137 to Gourgé, you pass a crucifix with Gourgé church in view on the hill. Once in the village continue past a small Vival supermarket, avoiding the right-hand fork signed Parthenay. The route bends left, with the 10th-century church of St-Hilaire on the inside of the bend.

Turn right immediately after the church. It's now 11km to Parthenay on the D134 as indicated by a classic Michelin touring sign nailed to a house wall. You will know if you've gone too far as you will end up descending to the Roman bridge over the Thouet. Pass a *boulangerie* on your way out of Gourgé and continue riding through the *paysage bocager* landscape until you reach the outskirts of Parthenay at Chatillon-sur-Thouet.

Arriving in Parthenay

There are a series of roundabouts to negotiate for a pleasant ride into this town with a medieval heart, but modern levels of traffic on, its outskirts. At the first roundabout you come to, continue straight across; you can see the church on a hill ahead of you indicating the centre of town. At the second roundabout take the first exit signed Parthenay and continue straight on at the third and fourth roundabouts, taking the second exits in both instances. The road then passes under a railway bridge arriving at the fifth and final roundabout in quick succession. Take the second exit which is to the left, signed Parthenay-Centre. You may notice a painting on a house which gives some insight into the history of the town before crossing a bridge over the Thouet.

Parthenay is nestled into the inside of a meander of the river, with the old town based on a rocky promontory. Many of the city's fortifications and its stone castle are still visible. To your right you can see the impressively preserved 13th-century Porte Mediévale below, guarding the entrance to the *quartier historique*. Half a kilometre after crossing the river, the stage finishes at a roundabout with the large, urban space of the Place Robert Bigot and its bandstand on your right.

Despite all this history, on first glance, Parthenay can look like a modern town with little character, especially if you're feeling weary from a long stage in the saddle or a day of multiple stage-bagging, but it's definitely worth exploring. Follow the labyrinth of streets down towards the river and you will come across the Rue de la Vaux St-Jacques, which was the main thoroughfare in the medieval town, containing

INDULGE

Château du Saint-Loup

Fit for a film set 20km before the end of the stage in Saint-Loup-sur-Thoet. Complete with moat and drawbridge, this 17th-century *monument historique* was built on the site of an old feudal castle.

Rooms are decorated with handcrafted furnishings, and you could even opt for one of the restored 15th-century dungeons.

79600 Saint-Loup-sur-Thouet
00 33 (0)5 49 64 81 73
www.chateaudesaint-loup.com

the majority of Parthenay's many, late 15th-century, half-timbered houses. These were built by wealthy merchants as places of business as well as residences. The street is still very much a residential area and is lined with people's homes. Refreshingly, the buildings have not been taken over by souvenir-shops and cafés, which is the often case in popular and better-known regions of France.

At the bottom of the street, just before the 13th-century Porte de St-Jacques which guards the gateway to the centre, you will find the *office de tourisme* next to an excellent free and informative museum revealing Parthenay's history. You can also walk up the gate tower attached to the bridge for a great view over the river, but it is equally impressive looking back up the Rue de la Vaux St-Jacques. You can probably imagine what this street would have been like in medieval times, when weary pilgrims from Normandy, Brittany and England would trudge through the town gates at all hours, looking for lodgings and sustenance on their long, religious journey to Santiago de Compostela. With one fifth of your own trip complete, it is a great opportunity to look southwards and reflect on your own journey so far.

Sleep

Hotel

Les Jardins St-Laurent

A short walk east of the *centre ville* with a pool and attractive terrace area for post-ride drinks. The hotel also has a restaurant if your legs are too tired to explore the town.

6 Rue Michelet, 79200 Parthenay
00 33 (0)5 49 64 70 30
www.jardins-saint-laurent.com

Chambre d'Hôtes

Monsieur et Madame Giboury

At the higher end of the Rue de la Vaux St-Jacques with character filled rooms, next to the site of the old medieval market.

10 Place du Vauvert, 79200 Parthenay
00 33 (0)5 49 64 12 33

Campsite

Le Bois Vert.

Not everyone's idea of tranquillity, but you can't fault the range of services at this quality 4-star campsite. Part of the large *base de loisirs* riverbank recreation area 2km south-west of the centre.

14 Rue de Boisseay, 79200 Parthenay
00 33 (0)5 49 64 78 43
www.camping-boisvert.com

Supplies

Food

Parthenay has a general market on a Wednesday but is most famous for its cattle market, held on the same day. This is one of the largest in France and much of the local economy is based on animal husbandary and the supply of quality beef.

There are plenty of *boulangeries* around the centre and a supermarket at the southern end of the town, which is busy and feels like the whole town is shopping there.

Bikes

Vélo Gatine

Named after the traditional name for Parthenay and its surrounding local farming area, this well-stocked shop is located on the ring road south of town. Follow the directions out of town on the next stage, but then turn left onto the ring road at the roundabout should your *vélo* need some fine-tuning or some stronger medicine.

3 Rue Verdun, Pompaire, 79200 Parthenay
00 33 (0)5 49 71 11 92
velogatine.wix.com/magasin-velo-gatine

Fontevraud-l'Abbaye

D147
D39
D39
D147
D347
D759

Tue | Loudun ▶
D61
D759
D63
D14
D59
D59
Chalais ◀
D52
St Cassen ▶
D52
D347

▽ Martaize

▽ St-Jouin-des-Marnes ▽
D37
D52
D147
D37
▽ Moncontour
Sun
D46

D725
D725
St-Loup-sur-Thouet ▶
D46
▽ Airvault *Sat*

D46 | D138

D137

△ Gourge
N149
D134
D938
D19
N149
D949
Parthenay
D743
Wed

Eat

La Citadelle

There are lots of brasserie options in Parthenay but this restaurant is ever-popular with a warm ambience and a range of traditional French food, particularly *grillades*.

9 Place Picard, 79200 Parthenay
00 33 (0)5 49 64 12 25
www.restolacitadelle.com

Drink

For evening re-hydration there is usually a gaggle of locals on the terrace outside Pub Le Skipper in the Place du Donjon.

PARTHENAY ⒯⒪ LUSIGNAN

Stage 9: *27miles 43km*

Secluded back lanes banked with flower-studded hedgerows take you through the pastoral landscape surrounding Parthenay to the more open countryside of the Vienne region, ending at a surprising power-house of medieval France.

Parthenay to Vausseroux

tarting at the roundabout with the bandstand and Place Robert Bigot on your right, head uphill to the top of the square, also signposted Centre Ville. At two mini-roundabouts in quick succession continue straight on.

At the third roundabout turn left, third exit, toward St-Maixent l'Ecole remaining on the D938. You will go over a level crossing and then at the next roundabout go straight over again, still following St-Maixent l'Ecole, D938. In 1.5km you will enter La Maladerie, where there are some large out-of-town supermarkets and a pharmacy.

2.5km after entering La Maladerie you pass through Pompaire, but once past this point the hedgerows take over from houses and the scenery becomes much more rural. Views of grazing land fill the early part of this stage – much of the land around Parthenay is pastoral, and the area has a long tradition of producing excellent meat.

6.5km after leaving Pompaire, take the left turn signposted Vausseroux 5km on the D21. The roadsides typify this area's *bocage* landscape with small fields and high hedgerows. The lush green verges are studded with daisies and purple flowers, bobbing in the shade cast by the hedgerows and occasional tall chestnut or oak. Sadly much of the *bocage* is being lost owing to the advent of industrial- style agriculture dramatically changing the appearance of the landscape and limiting its diversity. Keep an eye out for a distinctive style of gate know as *gâtine*, which is unique to this area. After 4.5km you will reach Vausseroux. At the T-junction turn left signposted St. Martin du Fouilloux and Ménigoute, D738. Take the next right signposted La Pagerie 5km and Ménigoute 9km, D21.

Vausseroux to Sanxay

Another 5km brings you into La Pagerie, where in summer, nasturtiums and geraniums colour the walls and gardens. Stay on the D21 signposted Ménigoute 4km. Look out for a perfect example of a *gâtine* on the left, 1km after you leave La Pagerie.

When you arrive in Ménigoute, at the T-junction turn left in front of the Auberge des Voyageurs signposted Sanxay, D21. The small town of Ménigoute is to your right. If you

wish to explore, turn right at the T-junction and then take the first left. This will bring you to a large *terrain de boules* which acts as a traffic island for a one-way system. Here you will find the two churches, one 11th-century and one 15th-century, a small museum and an *auberge* perfect for a quiet coffee stop. On leaving Ménigoute, turn right signposted Sanxay and Lusignan, D21.

3 km after leaving Ménigoute you will see a sign to your left – Site Gallo-Roman de Sanxay. This is one of the most important and best-preserved historic sites in France.

Sanxay to Jazeneuil

1km after passing the site you will enter the outskirts of Sanxay itself. Go straight at the mini-roundabout and then over a bridge crossing the Vonne river. At the T-junction turn right, signposted Jazeneuil and Lusignan.

Riding through Sanxay, keep an eye out for some interesting gothic-looking wall decorations and the old water pump at the end of the village before you cross back over the Vonne.

2km after leaving Sanxay take the left turn signposted Jazeneuil and Lusignan, D26. The landscape here begins to change, the hedgerows are lower and the fields broader and more open. 3.5km after the turn you will cross the *autoroute*. Surrounded by pastoral scenes, you do not expect to have the rush of Paris-Bordeaux traffic flowing underneath you. The road is now named the D94.

Jazeneuil to Lusignan

In 2.5km you arrive at Jazeneuil. Follow the road round to the right, signposted Lusignan 6km. You will pass a petrol station with antique-looking pumps that is also a coffee shop, bar and general stores. It is clearly the heart of the small village, with people coming and going to pick up some gossip or perch at the bar with a beer.

Continue on the D94. The fields here are significantly bigger than those nearer Parthenay – large fields of wheat and sweet corn border the road, with the occasional field of sunflowers.

The road is predominantly flat and makes for easy pedalling, so the final 4.5km into Lusignan will pass very pleasurably. Fields start to give way to houses and the first sign you are entering a town will be the school on your right. At the junction turn left into Lusignan, signposted Centre Ville and cross over the railway.

Follow the one way system round to your left to finish this stage of the ride in front of the *hôtel de ville*.

Lusignan

On arrival, Lusignan seems an unprepossessing town, but it was once home to some of the most powerful men in France. The Lords of Lusignan in the 12th-century held such grandiose titles as King of Jerusalem and King of Cyprus. Their fortress, the Château de Lusignan, was one of the greatest in France and although it was completely destroyed, some remains are visible in the 18th-century gardens near the *office de tourisme*. An exhibition tracing the epic history of the Lusignan family can be found on the Rue de Chypre.

The streets of Lusignan are a history lesson in themselves: restoration work is currently being undertaken to revive the western walls of the town, the medieval bridge, two towers and moat. The 20th-century buildings have been removed and the original wall has been excavated.

SITE GALLO-ROMAIN DE SANXAY

Built in the meander of the river Vonne, Sanxay was an important place between the 1st and 4th centuries. With its temple, theatre and baths, it functioned as a sanctuary offering thermal cures. The first excavations were carried out by Father Camille de la Croix in the 19th-century.

Free to wander the site, you are able to immerse yourself in imagining how life would have been and to appreciate the sheer scale of the construction, often a more peaceful and pleasurable experience than being hurried round in a guided group.

The amphitheatre is once again being used for its original function – staging performances. Attending one would certainly be the best way to appreciate this amazing construction.

Sleep

Hotel

Le Chapeau Rouge
A hotel since 1643, its central location is ideal for wandering the quiet streets of Lusignan or a walk in the 18th-century pleasure garden.
1 rue de Chypre, 86600 Lusignan
00 33 (0)5 49 54 09 08
www.le-chapeau-rouge.com

Le Saint Georges – Hotel and Restaurant
More hotels can be found in Vivonne 11km into the next stage. Vivonne is a growing town on the edge of a motorway just south of Poitiers. It lacks the historical ambience of Lusignan but does have this 3-star hotel and restaurant. Take the left off the first roundabout as you approach Vivonne; the hotel is well signed from here.
12 Grand Rue, 86370 Vivonne
00 33 (0)5 49 89 01 89
www.hotel-st-georges.com

Campsite

Camping de Vauchiron
A relaxed municipal campsite, well-positioned close to the river where you can swim and sunbathe. There is a snack bar on site and fresh bread delivered daily.
Chemin de la Plage, 86600 Lusignan
00 33 (0)5 49 43 30 08

Supplies

Food

All the basics can be covered in Lusignan itself, which has a variety of small shops near the finish of the stage in the place in front of the *hôtel de ville*. There is a market selling fresh produce on Wednesday mornings and a larger supermarket on the outskirts of the town.

Eat

Le Bistroquet

A varied menu including both traditional and less-sophisticated options if you just want something simple and filling after your ride. Also offers accommodation.
34 Avenue de Poitiers, 86600 Lusignan
00 33 (0)5 49 53 45 83

LUSIGNAN ⓣ L'ISLE-JOURDAIN

Stage 10: *35miles 56km*

A stage of connections that show how Roman roads and crossing points of rivers can shape a landscape. From Vivonne at the confluence of three rivers, to the minor fording points of the Clouère river and the vast viaduct at L'Isle Jourdain, this stage is shaped by rivers – not so much riding along them as crossing over them.

Lusignan to Vivonne

Starting in the Place du 8 Mai and facing the *hôtel de ville*, turn right down Rue Raymondin on the corner by the pharmacy. The road is slightly downhill until at a T-junction with a Stop sign, you turn right signposted Niort. Pass the Ste-Catherine pizza restaurant on your left and take the second turning on the left, Route de Vivonne, signed Forêt de Saint Sauvant.

Just over 1.5km after leaving Lusignan you will come to a roundabout; go straight over signposted Vivonne 13km, D742. After 5km you will reach a crossroads, 1km to your left is the village of Celle-l'Evescault and its 13th-century church. The road along here can be fairly busy but it is wide and straight, so you never feel squeezed by traffic. The open expanses of arable land have far reaching views and are only occasionally broken up by small copses.

In a further 5km you reach the first roundabout on the outskirts of Vivonne; go straight over following D742. The road makes a 90-degree right turn and crosses over the N10. At the roundabout, go straight over again signposted Château Larcher. If you wish to turn into Vivonne take the third exit to your left, where you will find a large variety of shops, accommodation and an *office de tourisme*.

Vivonne is at the confluence of the Palais and Vonne rivers, where they join the Clain. It was a fording place on the Roman road to Poitiers and grew in size as a resting place for travellers. Proximity to Poitiers and ease of access now make Vivonne a popular tourist spot. Its rivers are a focal point of tourism with good fishing, a man-made beach and kayaking, all within walking distance of the *centre ville*.

It boasts layers of history from Roman times onwards, with its 11th-century castle on a rock spur and the orignal settlement, now a large town, established at the foot. It's not a particularly beautiful town but on the banks of the rivers you can find peace and tranquillity.

Vivonne to Château Larcher

From the roundabout on the route to Château Larcher there is a short descent before crossing the Clain. You then have a short hairpin climb to bring you up above the town. The

gradient is very gradual and the sweeping corners aid your progress. From here you have 4km of predominantly straight but undulating road to reach Château Larcher. Turn right if you wish to explore the interesting small village of Château Larcher itself.

Built on the banks of the Clouère river, Château Larcher is a very well-preserved and peaceful old village. At the heart is a 12th-century Romanesque church and castle, with moat and towers still intact. The artefact of which the village is most proud is its rare *lanterne des morts* (death lantern), which can be found in the cemetery and is still used for religious festivals. It is a narrow, 8.5m high tower, more like a finger pointing upwards from around the memorial stones. A small plinth inside houses a lantern that throws light out of the tower through its many windows. There are only around 30 in existence, the majority of which are in the Limousin region.

Château Larcher isn't a village stultified by its weight of history. Every year the residents bring it to life with a grand medieval fair that lasts for 3 days. On summer evenings they have candle-lit explorations of the town, with theatre and dance taking place near to the walls of the castle. Whilst this is obviously a huge tourist attraction, as is the *Féerie de Noël*, when the town is specially decorated for Christmas, there is a strong sense of community amongst the inhabitants. This is no well-maintained museum but a living village. L' Auberge de la

Clouère is a place at the heart of regular entertainment. If you stop by of an evening you could be treated to anything from an Elvis-themed night with Alsace food, to live piano music or a gourmet feast. Even on a quiet night you are likely to find a few locals shooting pool – a rare sight in rural France.

Château Larcher to Gençay

Leave Château Larcher on the D742 toward Gençay. The first section is back to the now familiar *bocage* scenery, lightly wooded with fields and hedgerows, before coming to a wide, open expanse which is strangely reminiscent of the American mid-West. Giant pylons straddle fields of wheat with the looping wires running parallel with the road and a vast open sky above. A snapshot taken here would be enough to convince someone you had been to a different continent altogether. 8.5km after leaving Château Larcher you will arrive at the outskirts of Gençay; turn right at the roundabout signposted Gençay on the D741. As you head slightly downhill towards the *centre ville* you will pass the entrance to the Château de Galmoisin.

As you arrive at the entrance to the town and cross the stone bridge you will be able to see the Château Gençay above to your right. To your left there is a small park with a picnic area, a pleasant place to sit and eat while admiring the castle walls.

102

Keep following the D741 through the town. The *office de tourisme* is off to your right next door to the *mairie* on the Place du Marché. You will be able to find everything you need in this busy little town.

Château de Gençay, the buiding you saw as you arrived in the town, is the remains of a ruined medieval castle. Its high fortifications stand clear above the town and its thick walls and wide moat are still clearly visible. The castle played a significant role in the battle between English and French forces. It was besieged by the French commander, Bertrand du Guesclin, for three years before he finally entered the castle. The other significant building in Gençay is the elegantly restored 14th-century Château La Roche.

Gençay to Usson du Poitou
Follow the D741 through Gençay and turn left towards Confolens, (the sign reads D1 because the '7' and '4' have dropped off!). Go straight on at the roundabout and then after 3km turn left, signposted Brion. As you cross over the bridge there is a shelter and picnic table to the left, a good spot on a sunny day to relax and a dry spot to munch a sandwich if the weather is inclement.

VIADUCTS AND BRIDGES

L'Isle-Jourdain is dominated by its viaduct. It was built in 1881, opened to rail traffic in 1891 and closed in 1969. Its height and width, with graciously curving 20m-wide arches, make it a tourist attraction for the area. Bungee jumpers benefit from the viaduct's 50m- high arches, leaping into the air then barely breaking the surface of the water before the elastic pulls them back up. You can also cycle on the viaduct, which forms part of a cycle network.

The bridge that links the two sides of the town today is known as Pont St-Sylvain, and a bridge has existed at this point since the 11th-century. The bridge is named after St-Sylvain, a Christian martyr who, according to local legend, was put in a bag and thrown into the Vienne. He was later found in the village of Loubressac, meaning literally 'the bag opens'.

After 1km you will enter Brion, where the road heads round to the left by the church. There is another shelter and also a WC but little else in this very small hamlet. At the end of Brion, turn right signposted St-Secondin, D102. These narrow lanes are used by little more than farm traffic and for access by the few people who live in these small villages.

After another 4km you will reach St-Secondin. This is a slightly bigger villge and offers a *boulangerie*, bar and café if you need a snack or to fill your water bottles. At the crossroads go straight over then turn right on the D102, signposted Usson-du-Poitou. After a further 5km you will reach another crossroads where you turn right toward Usson 0.6km.

Usson-du-Poitou is in on the banks of the small Clouère river. Its first name was Roman and the town may well have developed as a crossing point of the river. In the middle ages it was very wealthy and there are numerous châteaux nearby that reflect its status.

The village itself has an 11th-century Romanesque church but among its most interesting features are the *Jardins de la Clouère* at the heart of the village. There is a picnic area, a wild garden with many varieties of local trees and a raised boardwalk over the marshy river edge. The gardens make a pleasant diversion if you need to stretch your legs after hours in the saddle.

To leave Usson-du-Potitou, turn left signposted L'Isle-Jourdain 14km, D102 (mysteriously the sign one side of the road says 14km and the sign on the other 15km). Take the next left as well, continuing to follow D102.

The next 10 km are shadowed by trees and broken up by occasional fields and the well-tended vegetable plots of the few houses you pass. At the T-junction, turn right on the D8 signposted L'Isle-Jourdain 2km. As you arrive in L'Isle-Jourdain you will first see the huge viaduct on your left. There is a small car park just beneath it which is the end of this stage and the start of the next. To reach the centre ville head straight on across the bridge over the river.

L'Isle-Jourdain

Dominated by the barrage and river, L'Isle-Jourdain is a haven for water sports, with water ski-ing and boating available on the Lac du Chardes, formed by the dam. Its relaxed atmosphere make it a popular but low-key holiday spot. The town itself is small but provides everything you might need. There are bars to quench your post-ride thirst and a couple of restaurants for evening meals.

A little spin around the town will reveal its church and, along its sometimes steep streets, an assortment of different styles of houses that reflect the town's growth over centuries.

Sleep

Hotel
Hôtel Val de Vienne
Slightly outside L'Isle-Jourdain, this hotel has a tranquil spot on the side of the river and is perfect for a post-ride swim. Extensive grounds that roll down to the river bank, outside pool and large comfortable rooms make this definitely worth a few extra kms of riding. To reach it, follow the directions of the next stage to leave L'Isle-Jourdain.
Port de Salles, 86150 Le Vigeant
00 33 (0)5 49 48 27 27
www.hotel-valdevienne.com

Chambre d'Hôtes
Le Lion d'Or
This character-filled, 12th-century house in the centre of town is within walking distance of bars and restaurants.
15 Place d'Armes, 86150 L'Isle-Jourdain
00 33 (0)5 49 48 59 94

Campsite
Le Lac de Chardes
An excellent municipal campsite at the site of the old railway station. It has a pool with slides so is popular with families, but it is also possible to find a quiet corner. Within walking distance of the town centre and also of the viaduct.
86150 L'Isle-Jourdain
00 33 (0)5 49 48 72 46

Drink

Café de la Paix
In the centre of town, it offers basic meals such as pizza but has an attractive outside terrace where you will find local workers enjoying drinks at virtually every hour of the day, from mid-morning to nightfall.
9 Place d'Armes, 86150 L'Isle-Jourdain
00 33 (0)5 49 48 23 86

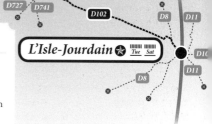

Supplies

Food
Although a relatively small town, in L'Isle-Jourdain you will find a good quality *boulangerie*, a *tabac* and small supermarket which will have sufficient to keep a hungry cyclist on the road.

Eat

Esprit Restaurant et Bar,
A friendly, family-run restaurant offering a slightly more sophisticated menu than other places in town, and in a relaxed warm environment. Their food showcases dishes typical of the region and there are also very reasonably priced *menus du jour*.
1 Place du Poitou, 86150 L'Isle-Jourdain
00 33 (0)5 16 80 03 11

L' ISLE JOURDAIN ⓉⓄ ROCHECHOUART

Stage 11: *37miles 60km*

A gentle ride heading south through the little-visited and peaceful Vienne river valley on some of the quietest back lanes of the whole journey. After the pretty village of Exideuil, the route undulates away from the river past Gallo-Roman ruins to star-struck Rochechouart, which is dominated by its château.

L'Isle-Jourdain to Availles-Limouzine

The stage starts at the junction under the old railway viaduct that dominates the skyline of L'Isle-Jourdain. If you stayed in the town, retrace your steps across the bridge, taking your first left before the viaduct. If continuing from the last stage, turn immediately right after the viaduct signed Le Vigeant, D8, and also signed for the Circuit Automobile du Val de Vienne racetrack. If you are planning to stay at Hôtel Val de Vienne, follow the green-and-white signs.

Keep following the road as it rises slightly away from the river, ignoring a right-hand fork to Le Vigeant. 4km after leaving town at a crossroads there is another green-and-white sign for Hôtel Val de Vienne pointing to the left. If you wish to stay, follow this turn for 1.5km down to the river to reach this wonderfully secluded spot. Shortly after the turning to the hotel you will pass a motor-racing circuit on your right.

Continue straight along the D8 to Availles-Limouzine, riding high above the banks of the Vienne. You get occasional glimpses of the river on your left and it is relatively flat, so you can make good progress southwards. 11km after leaving L'Isle-Jourdain, there is a great view northwards of the Vienne. 14km after leaving L'Isle-Jourdain the route drops gradually before entering the village of Availles-Limouzine.

At a T-junction in front of the hotel, turn left signed Autres Directions, D8. In quick succession the route passes a small market square and the *office de tourisme* on your left before you fork right towards Confolens on the D8. Availles-Limouzine used to be an enclave of the traditional *langue d'Oc* speakers in a region where the *langue d'Oïl* dominated.

Availles-Limouzine to Confolens

As you leave the village on the D8 to tackle the 13km to Confolens, keep an eye out for an array of old ploughs in amongst hay bales on your left-hand side. It is 6 gently undulating kilometres to the next village of Lessac. The Vienne is out of sight but you can see land sloping slightly away to your left. Before you reach Lessac, via a short descent, you cross the border from the *département* named after its largest river into the Charente. In Lessac keep left at the

mini-roundabout signed Confolens, then follow the main road through the village. Keep left on the main road, leaving the village signed Ste-Radegonde, 2km distant.

Keep left at the mini-roundabout on entering- Ste-Radegonde, squeezing between classic houses with antique shutters. Just before a bridge turn right to Confolens; however, it is worth riding onto the bridge to see a crumbling château perched above the Vienne on the opposite bank. Ste-Radegonde's sister-village of St-Germain-de-Confolens on the eastern banks of the Vienne has a restaurant, water-fountain and a picnic area with a nice view of the château. The road to Confolens climbs away from the river then drops down into the town.

3km after Ste-Radegonde, take the exit on the left signed Limoges at the first mini-roundabout. At the second mini-roundabout by the Hôtel Mère Michelet keep right again, signed Limoges. Here you will find the slightly non-traditional French café named 'Le Twickenham' on your right. Rugby fans might be disappointed, though, as it seems to bear little connection to the game despite the name.

Confolens

The Vienne river splits Confolens in half and your 500m on its main road may seem a little traffic-choked as it is a key crossing point of the river. As you cross you get a view of the Pont Vieux, the medieval bridge to the left which connects the modern, western side of town you have just left with the older, eastern part. For a time this was the only bridge between Chabanais and St Germain. To look around the small *centre ville* turn left up the main street immediately after the bridge.

Confolens takes its name from the French for confluence, owing to its location at the point where the river Goire meets the Vienne – this is fitting as it was an ancient meeting-point for *Oc* and *Oïl* language speakers. The Vienne acted not only as a linguistic barrier between speakers of the *langue d'Oc* to the east and *langue d'Oïl* to the west but also as a frontier between the rival dioceses of Limoges and Poitiers on opposite sides of the river. Paradoxically the town's Pont Vieux functioned as a key trading point uniting the populations on each side.

Confolens' half-timbered medieval houses in Rue Pinaguet, as well as its Renaissance houses, may not be as plentiful or as well-preserved as Parthenay's but they are still worth a look. The Chemin du Moulin à Huile leads to a small watermill which has being lovingly preserved and could almost belong in a Constable painting. It was originally used in the booming tanning industry; later locals brought walnuts and rapeseed so the oils could be extracted, right up until the 1960s.

Confolens to Exideuil

This part of the stage is one of the quietest sections of riding on the whole 1,000-mile journey, but it takes attentiveness to access the bounty of lost lanes on leaving Confolens. After crossing the bridge with the *centre ville* to your left, follow the main road as it bends to the left, signed Limoges. Immediately after the bend, fork to your right on a small lane marked only by a small 'Cycleway 43' and a blue 'P' parking sign.

Take care not to miss this turn. It is the first possible, right after the river. If you start to climb and pass a Renault garage you have gone too far.

This route takes you on quiet, single-track, back lanes alongside the eastern banks of the Vienne, where fields of corn and hay slope down to the Vienne river on your right, and the only sounds you can hear are the calls of cuckoos. It is often hard to tell if the river is actually flowing, but the water is heading north to join the Loire.

4km after Confolens keep left and pass through the small farming hamlet of La Brousse, after which the road bends away from the river. 2km beyond La Brousse at a stop sign, turn right to Chirac, which is 8km to the D59. You are now deep into cow country, and it may be difficult to avoid getting the evidence left by the animals underneath your front wheel.

PAYS DE LA METEORITE

200 million years ago, one of the biggest meteorites ever to hit the earth landed 4km west of Rochechouart. It was 1.5km in diameter, weighed 6 million tonnes, and travelled at a speed of 20km per second, hitting the ground with a magnitude that would have measured 11 on the Richter scale.

Although the 20km crater, or *astroblème*, the meteor created is almost completely eroded and indiscernible, it has left its mark on Rochechouart and its locale.

The meteor brought about unique geological changes as the speed of impact and heat generated transformed the underlying rocks. Known as *brèche* rocks, these look like they come from the moon's surface.

They have been used in the construction of, and integrated into, many local buildings, not least the château. Peruse the pavement outside the Espace Météorite Paul-Pellas on Rue Jean Parvy to see a selection of different *brèche* used throughout the town.

Many centuries before the development of Rochechouart, this metamorphic rock was used in the construction of the Roman baths at Cassinomagus, just a short detour off this stage.

The route sweeps back down towards the banks of the Vienne reaching a crossroads after 5km. Continue straight across towards Chirac, D59. This is a granite area, which stretches down from the rugged terrain of the Massif Central. However the landscape here is gentle with plenty of pasture for raising livestock, but you will also see cultivated fields.

In Chirac avoid following the main road as it bends left, unless you want to see the small village's 10 different apple trees on a mini *promenade des pommes*, each showcasing a different variety. This gives a sense of the pride locals take in their distinctive *terroir*, no matter how small the community.

As the main road bends left, carry straight on down a lane with the church on your right, pedalling through a narrow section between houses when leaving the village as indicated by the 2.2m width-restriction sign. A little under 2km after leaving Chirac at a stop sign, turn right for a quick 1km descent down to Exideuil. Take care as it's easy for your bike to gather momentum and propel you onto the single-track bridge across the river and into the village of Exideuil. After the bridge at a T-junction, turn left onto the D370. Exideuil is a pretty village with facilities including a *chambre d'hôtes*, and a beautiful shelter where you could tuck into your supplies.

Exideuil to Rochechouart

Pedalling out of Exideuil you cross the railway line and begin to climb away from the Vienne for the last time. After 1km at the large and sometimes busy roundabout, take the 4th exit signed Chabanais. Most of the traffic now heads round the town on a bypass, whereas the route takes you the 1.5km to the town's main square. Immediately you arrive at the square on your left, turn right signed Rochechouart, D29. Pass around the square before bending right over a level crossing.

The route climbs gradually through the outskirts of the town. Despite its power in medieval times, little evidence of it remains in modern Chabanais as most of the town was rebuilt after suffering heavily during the Second World War. The French Resistance destroyed the town's bridge in 1944 to cut key communication links and hamper Nazi efforts, but this did not stop parts of the town being torched.

Follow the D29 to Rochechouart, a total of 9km. After 4 km of overall gradual climbing away from the Vienne valley, as the river turns east and the route presses on south, you pass through the village of Chassenon.

There is a picnic area on your left, set against the backdrop of the beautiful 14th-century church of St-Jean-Baptiste. On a hot day, the tap, tucked away behind the phone box under the trees is very welcome. On leaving the village, the road becomes flatter and you will see the first of many signs marked Route Richard Coeur de Lion. Whilst King Richard the Lionheart is often thought of as an English King, he rarely set foot in England and as Duke of Aquitaine his connection with the land you are riding through is much stronger.

Half a kilometre after leaving Chassenon you have the opportunity to delve even further back in time as indicated by a sign to your right marked Cassinomagus. This Gallo-Roman *parc archéologique* includes an exceptionally well-preserved Roman baths with a web of multi-layered aqueducts, linking boiler rooms with brick ovens and swimming pools, all easily identifiable.

After the turning to Cassinomagus it is just under 5km to the stage end in Rochechouart. On your way you enter both the Parc Natural Régional Périgord and the *département* of the Haute Vienne.

Arriving in Rochechouart

The stage ends at a distinctly strange half-roundabout, where the road you are riding on meets the main D675. Take your first exit right for *centre ville* or second right signed St-Mathieu, D675, to continue onto the next section.

Rochechouart's handsome château at the southern tip of the *centre ville* mostly dates from the 15th-century. It houses a museum of contemporary art as well as the *hôtel de ville*. Much of the rock used to build the château originated from outer space when a meteorite landed on the site of the town. Rochechouart is a pleasant place to spend an evening and is rarely crowded, even in the height of summer. But if you require a higher standard of hotel, continue on the next stage to Brantôme in the Dordogne.

OC OR OIL?

The Vienne river, which you follow for a large part of this stage, once formed a frontier between two distinct linguistic zones with Occitane speakers to the east and *langue d'Oïl* speakers to the west. Both were older versions of French, which took their names from how the language expressed 'yes'. *Oïl* later became *oui* and was adopted more widely than *Oc*, which is now spoken only by a handful of people in the Languedoc region. The ancient pre-medieval province of Occitanie encompassed not only the South of France but Spanish Catalonia and Italian Piedmont.

Sleep

Hotel

La Météorite

A small 7-room, 2-star option right in the heart of town with a decent-sized summer terrace. If you are a large group, the Hôtel de France next door and of a similar standard, has slightly more rooms.

1 Place Octave Marquet, 87600 Rochechouart

00 33 (0)5 55 02 86 80

www.lameteorite.com

Chambre d'Hôtes

La Grenouille Joyeuse

This house, made from the rock of the meteor impact, offers 2 comfortable rooms and a warm welcome, a stone's throw from the town square.

1 Rue du Grippe, 87600 Rochechouart

00 33 (0)5 8719 47 23

www.la-grenouille-joyeuse.com

Campsite

Camping de la Météorite

Situated 1km south of town and accessed by the D10 next to the Plan d'eau, this 4-star campsite has plenty of facilities.

Lac de Boischenu, 87600 Rochechouart

00 33 (0)5 55 03 65 96

www.campingmeteorite.fr

Supplies

Food

There are numerous *boulangeries* and *pâtisseries* dotted around the *centre ville* and a supermarket in the direction of St-Junien.

Bike

Météore Moto

Bike shop is a generous term but this motorbike and mechanical dealer on the D675 toward St-Junien has a range of useful spares in an emergency from tyres to tubes – just ask the helpful staff behind the counter. The opening hours are longer than a traditional bike shop.

50 Avenue Jean Jaures, 87600 Rochechouart

00 33 (0)5 55 03 04 24

www.meteore-moto.fr

Eat

Auberge Le Roc de Boeuf

A homely inn complete with open fire, wooden beams and a range of inviting menus in different price brackets.

Le Moulin de La Côte, Route Babadus, 87600 Rochechouart

00 33 (0)5 55 03 61 75

www.lerocduboeuf.com

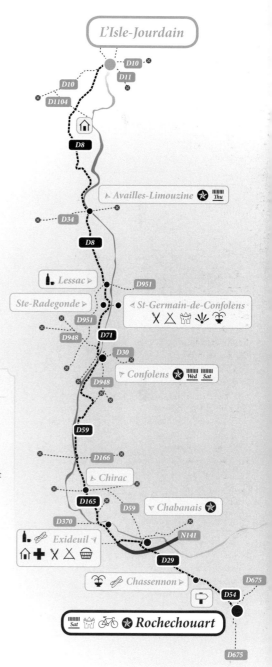

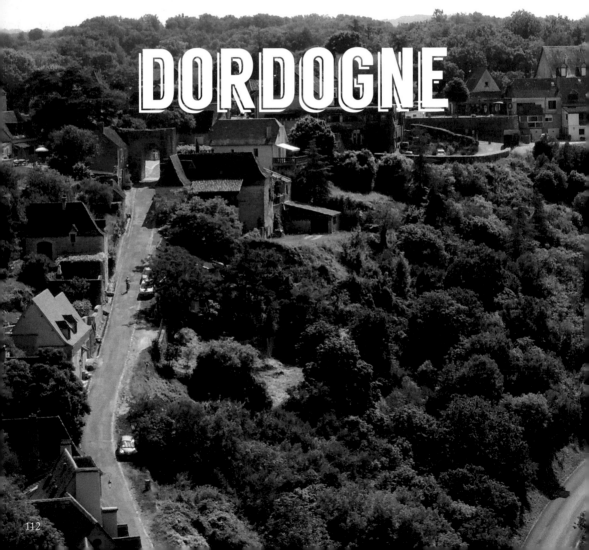

DORDOGNE

TWIST through the helter-skelter of roads offering dramatic views of Rocamadour.

ROLL along the quiet, wooded riverside lanes of the *Périgord Noir*.

INDULGE in sumptuous meals of *foie gras* and truffles as a reward for your day in the saddle.

STROLL the medieval streets and twisting alleyways of Sarlat-La-Canéda.

MEET Cro-Magnon man and your prehistoric ancestors in the caves of the troglodytes.

DELVE beneath the workaday exterior to discover the medieval heart of old Souillac.

ROCHECHOUART  TO
BRANTOME

Stage 12: *39miles 62km*

Effortless navigation allows you to roll along the hills of Haute Vienne into the Dordogne as the route follows the D675 due south. Almost the entire ride is spent in the sparsely populated Parc Naturel Régional Périgord–Limousin passing through a patchwork of green meadows, clusters of chestnut trees and lashings of wild flowers, before reaching picture-postcard Brantôme, entirely surrounded by the Dronne river.

Rochechouart to St-Mathieu

Starting the stage at the semi-roundabout junction near the entrance to the *centre ville* head out of town on the D675, signed St-Mathieu. After a short descent the stage starts with a treat. Look to your right after leaving town to see a view of Rochechouart on its hilltop.

This stage may be on the same road nearly all the way, but it is a welcome contrast to the ruler-straight roads and landscape dominated by churches and flat arable land north of the Loire River. The D675 winds its way through woodland and pastures bounded by fern-choked hedgerows.

The road is by definition a main route, but traffic is light in this sparsely populated area. After 6km of winding, mild undulations, followed by a gentle 2km climb, you pass through the small town of Vayres with a welcoming café on the left and a *boulangerie* on the right, should you require sustenance. This early part of your stage sees you pedalling through the *Bocage Limousin*, initially near a small forest just south of Rochechouart before passing fields which are dotted with the distinctive red of the Limousin cattle, known for the quality of their beef.

After Vayres the route climbs steadily for 1km before a 2km descent to a bridge over a small river. Subsequently it regains its height and the fields turn back into woodlands. The 8km from Vayres to St Mathieu become increasingly rolling and more wooded, interspersed with the occasional golden fields. If you happen to be riding on an autumnal weekend you may see locals with rifles peering between dense trees. No need to worry; they are looking for wild boar, which forage in the woods.

St-Mathieu to Piégut-Pluviers

In the small town of St-Mathieu turn right in front of the *mairie* to continue south on the D675, signed Nontron. Just south of St-Mathieu, after 2km, the stage crosses from the Haute Vienne and enters the Dordogne. You are now riding through the Massif des Feuillardières characterised by its clumps of chestnut trees and small rivers. Chestnut trees are abundant in this area, fuelling the large number of charcoal forges. The chestnut is a symbol of the region and an important part of the economy. Local craftsman, relying on traditional skills and techniques, use the versatile wood for fence posts and to make furniture.

Blink and you will miss the village of Champniers-et -Reilhac, 2km after entering the Dordogne, but turn off to the right into the *centre ville* and visit the inviting restaurant if you fancy spoiling yourself. You may also notice the first example of the distinctive Dordogne architecture on the village church. The towers in the region are squat with square bases, and feature a lip that overhangs like the brim of a top hat.

Continue on the D675 and 6km after Champniers-et-Reilhac, which include a welcome 2km descent, you reach the twin settlements of Piégut-Pluviers. The main road by-passes the *centre ville*, which is a pretty town 1km off the route reached by turning right on the D91 by the Elan garage. It has a 23-metre high donjon tower surrounded by a *motte naturelle* on a granite outcrop. If you are passing on a Wednesday, be sure to visit the market held there since 1642.

Piégut-Pluviers to Nontron
3.5km after passing Piégut-Pluviers the D675 takes you thorough the village of Augignac. There is not much to detain you other than a nice shady picnic area on the left just after the village. 8km further on, the route skirts the town of Nontron, a more workaday town than Brantôme. You can reach the *centre ville* by forking to the left amidst a trio of supermarkets or, if you are enjoying the downhill and miss this, turn left at the lights. If you have been into the *centre ville* retrace your steps to the traffic lights, turning left signed Périgueux. If you are riding past, simply continue straight on downhill at the lights on the D675. Nontron has the oldest working cutlery forge in France and a proud tradition in maintaining century-old knife-making techniques. Nontron is also home to the famous *Carnaval des Soufflets*.

Nontron to Brantôme
Take care on the fast-twisting descent on the road around Nontron *centre ville*, where some of the corners tighten. If you can squeeze a glimpse over your left shoulder you will see Nontron perched on its rocky outcrop. 1km after the traffic lights, as the route flattens out at Le Claud, you pass a rugby pitch on your left, the first signs you are entering the south-western stronghold of the sport.

Continue on the D675 for 20km to a roundabout just

INDULGE

Le Chatenet
This is the perfect place to unwind, yet just 10 minutes' amble from the town's restaurants. This *maison d'hôtes de charme* is a grand Périgord stone manor house built in the 17th-century by Lord de Giry, who also left his initials on the cobbled-stone veranda. Be sure to leave the large comfortable rooms for a spot of *billards* and to stroll past the walnut and fruit trees in the extensive, ever-changing garden.

Le Chatenet, 24310 Brantôme
00 33 (0)5 53 05 81 08
www.lechatenet.com

CARNAVAL DES SOUFFLETS

A tradition dating from the *carnaval* celebrations of the Middle Ages, this one is held in Nontron every other April. The townspeople dress up in nightshirts, cotton caps, clogs and masks and each carries a pair of bellows. With these, they attempt to blow air up each other's nightshirts, claiming they are chasing away evil spirits! Although the carnival is religious in origin, one theory held that it cleared the air in the town; another that the bellows targeted loose women!

before Brantôme. There are two descents and two climbs along the way, each 2km in length. On this stretch of the ride, just before Brantôme you enter the *Périgord Vert*.

Initially you may not notice much difference in the landscape, which is a patchwork of pasture, woodland, uncultivated meadows and intimate green valleys. The combination of lush valleys and relatively dry pastures, however, mcan the area is blessed with a wide range of flora, including 30 different varieties of orchids, many of which can be seen spiking the meadows in spring time.

In the final few kilometres before Brantôme, the route becomes flatter and passes tracts of cultivated land. At the roundabout, take the last exit for Brantôme and descend the final 1km to the town.

The descent will lead you straight onto a bridge, the Pont des Barris, one of Brantôme's six bridges across the tranquil River Dronne. To continue onto the next stage

simply follow the road through the *centre ville*. Brantôme is definitely worth a wander even if your usual approach to towns is to keep your head down and press on.

Brantôme

The 'Venice of Périgord' is Brantôme's tourist title, which is slightly ambitious given that it doesn't have any canals, though one thousand years ago monks cut the corner off a meander in the Dronne river to establish a mill-stream. As a result, Brantôme *centre ville* sits on an island in the Dronne, seemingly held in place by its six bridges, which anchor it to the mainland.

The 'Jewel of Périgord Vert' is a more apt title. Brantôme is achingly beautiful with parkland ringing the outer river banks. The Jardin des Moines is often lined with painters putting their own interpretation on the picture-postcard prettiness of the Pont Coude.

To visit the *office de tourisme*, in the old convent part of the *abbaye*, turn right just before crossing the Pont des Barris. As you ride into town, you will find a high street where all the shops are in a cave from restaurants to ice-cream sellers.

If you're around on a Friday in July or August make sure you catch the *Joutes Nautiques*, set against backdrop of the

abbaye. Although popular with tourists, this is very much a local event as the competitors' pride is at stake. Teams of ten take turns jousting each other on a platform at the front of a rowing boat, with the loser falling into the shallow waters of the Dronne.

PERIGORD

On this stage you will get your first taste of the Dordogne, one of the most visited regions in France, and so popular with the British that it is often referred to as 'Dordogne-shire'. But many French locals, as well as tourists, refer to roughly the same geographical region as Périgord – a term you will see frequently during the next few stages of riding. Périgord was the name of an ancient province, but perhaps more significantly, it refers to a rich variety of landscape

The far north of the *département*, entered on this stage of riding, is known as *Périgord Vert* for its verdant green pasture land, light woodland clusters and under-populated valleys. The next stage to Hautefort takes you briefly into the *Périgord Blanc* near Sorges, famous for truffle. The ride has a more open feel, and you'll notice the white of the area's limestone outcrops that occasionally stud the fields. Between Hautefort and Les Eyzies you enter the *Périgord Noir*, with its dense oak woodland.

To complete the colour scheme there is a fourth region, slightly to the south-west of the route. *Périgord*

Pourpre (purple) is a vine-covered landscape and the wines of Bergerac are famous. A bike is the perfect vehicle to travel through Périgord/Dordogne and get intimately acquainted with the landscape and its subtle changes in tone.

Throughout the Périgords the soil is noticeably rich and this is responsible for the region's distinctive *terroir* and *cuisine*. You will see duck and geese farmers selling high-quality meat and *foie gras*, as well as a range of market vegetables on offer, freshly picked from plots throughout the region.

Sleep

Hotel

Hôtel Charbonnel

On the island right in the heart of Brantôme on the banks of the Dronne river offering excellent views. This 3 star option has comfortable rooms complete with wood carved furnishings as well as a quality restaurant attached.

57 Rue Gambetta, 24310 Brantome
00 33 (0)5 53 05 70 15
www.lesfrerecharbonnel.com

Chambre d'Hôtes

Au Nid des Thés

Four individual styled rooms, also check out the adjoining a *salon de thé*, proprietor Sandrine also offers plenty of treats to indulge on from her days as a pastry chef in Paris. Not the cheapest rooms but a great location on the island.

13 Rue Victor Hugo, 24310 Brantôme
00 33 (0)5 53 02 75 49
www.au-nid-des-thes.fr

Campsite

Camping Puynadal

A smallish quiet site with more of a family feel than the big player Camping Peyrelevade but like most French campsites it still has plenty of facilities, including swimming pool and restaurant.

Route d'Agonac D69, 24310 Brantôme
00 33 (0)5 53 06 19 66
www.camping-puynadal.com

Supplies

Food

Market day is Friday when a maze of streets is taken over by local producers. Unfortunately the best cycling time is not the best truffle time, you would have to visit between December and February to sprinkle some magic on your baguette.

However all year round there's a wide range of fruit, fromage and charcuterie sellers. If it's not Friday visit the *boulangeries* that dot the streets of the island. There is a supermarket on your route out of town on the next stage of your journey.

Bike

Véloland

One of the widest ranges of spares and accessories you will find anywhere en route between St-Malo and Nice. It's up on your right just after the roundabout before your descent into the *centre ville*.

Route d'Anglouéme, 24310 Brantôme
00 33 (0)5 53 08 02 65
www.veloland.com

Eat

Les Jardins de Brantôme

You will be tripping over restaurants walking round Brantôme, but the menu and service at Les Jardins is inviting in the cosy dining terrace adorned with flowers. The emphasis is on using local producers from the *Périgord Vert*. They also have rooms. If you want something less gastronomique and simpler cycling fuel try 'Le Vieux Four' set in an ancient troglodyte cave on the same street for traditional *au feu des bois* pizza.

33 Rue Pierre de Mareuil , 24310 Brantome
00 33 (0)5 53 05 88 16
www.lesjardinsdebrantome.com

Drink

Brantôme is more renowned for its restaurants but the café/bar on the Place du Marché across from the abbaye make a good place for a drink.

BRANTOME ⓣⓞ HAUTEFORT

Stage 13: *32miles 52km*

Virtually empty roads lead you through three coloured regions of the Périgord – *Vert, Blanc* and *Noir* – in one of France's most sparsely populated areas. A stage of gourmet as well as scenic delights as you travel through the truffle capital of France and cross paths with the *Route du Foie Gras*.

Brantôme to Agonac

Starting from the bridge, Pont des Barris, where you finished the last stage, take a final look at the abbey on your right before setting off. Follow the road between the shops on the edge of town; the narrow streets Brantôme is famous for are off to your right. Within a few hundred metres you will cross the Dronne river for a second time. Again, pause here to look at the fabulous views, or at least pedal slowly across the bridge.

You will pass through an avenue of trees that leads you away from the town, then after 1.5km at the roundabout take the third exit left signposted Périgueux, D939, immediately after turn left signed, Agonac 12km, D69. The next 12km is classic *Périgord Vert* as you roll past fields edges with small patches of woodland. The road climbs sinuously up to small ridges along sweeping bends. It will feel like easy pedalling as the road draws you in with its teasing corners. Fields are undulating, with smooth mounded tops and deep hidden valleys.

There is a richness and sensuality to the landscape. As you ride past the varying greens, golds and deep-brown furrows of the fields, you almost want to reach out and caress them – the hills seem small enough to fit into the palm of your hand. It is a great road for a bike; you can relish the sensation of pushing into the many curves.

Agonac to Sorges

On reaching Agonac, go straight on at the Stop, turn left at the T-junction, then right over the bridge, signposted Sorges 10km. Cross the railway line then immediately turn left towards Sorges, D106. It is mysteriously now 11km, an additional 1km having been added since the bridge!

After Agonac the road climbs gently through chestnut woodland and open fields. Despite woods and rolling hills the sky still feels vast and the land spacious. The colours and shapes of the land beneath the wide open skies create the perfect composition.

With 4km to go you will see the church in Sorges on the horizon. In a further 3km you will reach a crossroads; head straight over toward Sorges 1km, D106. At the Stop sign turn right. Go straight past the *boulangerie* on your left and the church on your right.

One of the greatest treasures of the Périgord region, the truffle, is celebrated at the *Musée de la Truffe* in Sorges, on the main N21 running through the village in the direction of Périgueux. This little museum will tell you everything you want to know about truffles, from where they are found to how they are cooked and why, what is essentially a fungus, tastes so good and is held in such high esteem. Tastings are offered where you can try different types of truffle along with a glass of wine or champagne.

Sorges to Coulaures

At the crossroads, with the Auberge de la Truffe opposite, head straight over signposted Coulaures 9km D74. For the next 2.5km you will enjoy a great road surface and a gently downhill gradient. The open bends require little braking and allow mind and body to relax as you freewheel the descent. Unfortunately this doesn't last forever and a climb soon follows, then this pattern of lazy descents and gentle climbs continues as each curve in the road draws you on. In one of the most sparsely populated areas of France, this is a very quiet road and you won't see any houses until the next village.

7.5km from Sorges turn left for Coulaures D705, 2km. You will pass a sign for a *foie gras* farm offering *dégustation*. This isn't the prettiest road by any means and the earlier roads on this stage may have spoilt you with their beauty, but the section is short. In Coulaures, take the right turn signposted Tourtoirac 10km, D73, and cross the old bridge over the Loué river. Near the bridge you can see the 15th-century chapel Notre-Dame du Pont.

Coulaures to Tourtoirac

Following the D73, the road becomes more wooded as you enter the *Périgord Noir* and the road climbs from one valley to the next, the undulating woodland providing shade and respite from the heat when riding through the hot summer months. This is a country of *foie gras* and truffles; some of the best of France's larder can be found in this region and the woods are also a source of game. 1km outside of Tourtoirac you will pass a campsite and soon after, the abbey comes into view, its classic Dordogne towers appearing above the trees as you come down the hill toward a T-junction.

Turn right at the T-junction, cross over the bridge, and at the Stop sign turn left toward Hautefort 8km, D5. You will pass Tourtoirac's abbey, built in the 11th and 12th centuries, on your left as you leave. It has a very small but useful modern museum attached, if you are interested in the area. The abbey

is small but charming and peaceful, if you have time to poke your head around the door. Tourtoirac also has underground caves to explore featuring a subterranean river and a rich array of stalactites and stalagmites, only discovered in 1995. Unlike many other caves in the region these were never inhabited. Tourtoirac was home to Antoine Orélie de Tounens 1825–1878, a French lawyer and adventurer.

De Tounens was born into a family of farmers but managed to go to law school. He is an interesting character and there is much debate over what drove him along his life's path: whether it was a desire to rise above his humble background or whether he was simply spirited with a thirst for adventure, a dreamer with the determination to succeed.

After moving to Arucania , now part of Chile, De Tounens made his home among the Mapuche, growing his hair long, wearing traditional clothing and speaking the Mapuche language. The Mapuche lived in clans spread around the region and were at the time fighting Spanish invaders. With his knowledge of western diplomacy and tactics, De Tounens persuaded them they would have more success united under one leader, and so he became king of Araucania and then also of Patagonia. He wrote a national constitution, composed an anthem and designed a flag. The Mapuche saw him as a faithful and trustworthy ally but he was a challenge to the rulers of Chile, who eventually captured him and declared him insane, rather than reveal the extent of his influence. The French consulate intervened and he was deported to France.

Tourtoirac to Hautefort

After leaving Tourtoirac you will pass through the rich green farming land for which this part of the Dordogne is famous. Fertile fields are bordered with dense, dark woodland and occasional small farmsteads are dotted along the way. 7km after leaving Tourtoirac you will reach St-Agnan. At the crossroads head straight on toward Hautefort 2km, D62. From here the road continues slightly uphill, becoming steeper for the final 1km. The château itself is up to the right, although from this side you are almost too close to see it clearly; the views are better departing town on the next stage. The stage finishes in front of the ancient hospice, on a crossroads, where you will also find the *office de tourisme*.

Hautefort

Hautefort sits at the crossroads of three of the Périgords: black, white and green. Clearly, it takes its name from the château sitting grandly on the top of the hill. Although a small village

FOIE GRAS

80% of all *foie gras* is made in France and 90% of the French *foie gras* industry is based in the Périgord. Owing to concerns over animal welfare, the EU ruled that its production had to be limited to areas where it is already carried out.

In the Périgord a popular *Route du Foie Gras* takes aficionados of this controversial French delicacy around the many sites where it is made and sold.

If you are the kind of shopper who always reaches for the free-range eggs, then you are unlikely to be a fan, although you will be able to see the geese or ducks living happily outdoors in many fields along the route. The birds are kept outside to graze until the final phase of fattening, when they are brought into sheds.

The birds are fed *gavage*, a mix of grain and fat designed to fatten up the liver.

In the wild they would naturally consume more in preparation for migration, and their liver would swell to around 50g. For *foie gras*, however, it needs to weigh 300g.

Force-feeding is viewed by many as a cruel process, especially to produce a product whose high fat content is not exactly healthy for the end consumer.

However, *foie gras* is treated with great respect in French cuisine and is widely appreciated by diners all across France who eat it with a clear conscience.

the château, it's well-maintained stately gardens and Museé de la Médecine provide plenty of interest.

As with so many seemingly elegant châteaux, Hautefort started off as a fortress but by the 16th and 17th centuries it had become a place of leisure and its military purpose was subsumed beneath more graceful structures. It is unusually fine for this region, where many of the châteaux remained rough fortresses.

The château was almost destroyed several times, but remained intact during the Revolution because it was used as a prison. In the early 20th century when the incumbent died without an heir, it became severely dilapidated but was saved by Baron Henry de Bastard and his wife Simone, who fell in love with the place and meticulously restored it.

Simone's love and commitment to the château was severely tested when her husband died, and then just three years after restoration was completed, a fire raged through parts of building. Immediately she began the whole task

again, faithfully recreating the original. The restoration work extended to the formal gardens surrounding the château, including the spectacular creation of a geometric pattern of box hedges.

The Museé de la Médecine is housed in the former hospice for the poor, founded in 1669 by the same Marquis who gave the château its elegant makeover. There are similarities in the architecture of both, such as in the domed roof of the chapel.

The displays of horrific-looking medical instruments are enough to make your stomach churn and make you glad you are living in the 21st-century. The herb garden that surrounds the building is a more restful and pleasant experience.

Hautefort has limited options for accommodation and dining, though there is a second hotel in St-Agnan.

During the summer months there are evening events at the château, including candle-lit guided tours and live performances. If you wish to include these in your itinerary, it is definitely worth booking ahead.

Sleep

Hotel

Auberge du Parc

Located in the centre of town, just below the château walls, it provides good food and basic accommodation.

Place René Lavaud, 24390 Hautefort

00 33 (0)5 53 50 88 98

www.aubergeduparc-hautefort.fr

Chambre d'Hôtes

L'Auberge les Tilleuls

5km into the next stage in the village of Badefols d'Ans, this *auberge* offers traditional Périgord cuisine and simple accommodation.

Le Bourg, 24390 Badefols D'Ans

00 33 (0)5 53 51 52 97

Campsite

Camping du Coucou

Delightful lakeside camping 2km from Hautefort in Nailhac. Plenty of facilities including swimming pool, boules and a small supermarket.

Le Bois du Coucou, 24390 Hautefort

00 33 (0)5 53 50 86 97

www.campingducoucou.com

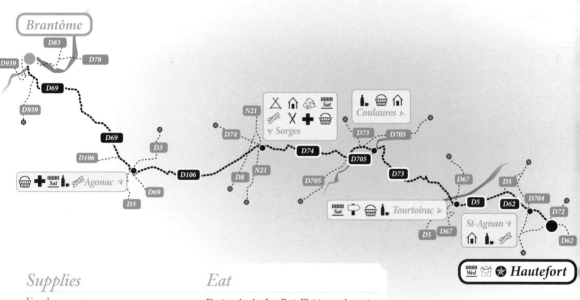

Supplies

Food

Hautefort has a range of small shops, selling enough to provide the basics for a picnic and to see you through the day, although choice is limited.

Eat

During the day Les Petit Plaisirs on the main square below the castle offers a lunchtime menu. For evening meals, the Auberge du Parc has a *menu terroir* and is on the *Route du Foie Gras*.

Place Eugène Leroy, 24390 Hautefort

00 33 (0)5 53 51 91 86

HAUTEFORT **TO** LES EYZIES-DE-TAYAC

Stage 14: *36miles 58km*

A journey through the 'cradle of mankind', this stage takes you past the famous cave paintings of Lascaux, the troglodyte caves of Roque Saint Christophe and finishes in Les Eyzies-du-Tayac where Cro-Magnon man, our earliest modern human ancestor, was discovered. Quiet riverside roads, wooded hill tops and small farm holdings give a real taste of the Dordogne.

Hautefort to Châtres

Starting on the crossroads with the Museé de la Médecine on your right, follow Badefols d'Ans 6km, D62. As you leave, look over your shoulder towards Hautefort for spectacular views of the château.

As soon as you pass the last of the village buildings, you will start to see small farms, fields of cows, and walnut trees. The cows you see are likely to be Limousin cattle raised for veal. Whilst agriculture is a key industry in this area it is operated on a small scale. The farmers, referred to as *paysans*, produce enough for themselves and for their local community rather than practise the industrial-scale farming found more often in the north.

Within 5km of leaving Hautefort, a view of the church tower and roof-tops of Badefols d'Ans opens up. The church, its roof along with that of the château showing clearly against the sky line as you approach the village, was built in the late-17th-century from the remains of a much older Protestant church destroyed by Louis XIV. The privately owned château was nearly destroyed by the Germans in the Second World War, as the resident family were known to be active within the Resistance.

Continue through Badefols until shortly after the end of the houses, then take the right, signposted Châtres 4km, D62. The softly moulded hills typical of the Dordogne create curves not corners, and for the cyclist this means no harsh braking or sudden turning to disrupt your ride. After 4km of this relaxing riding you will enter the hamlet of Châtres. The majority of the houses, church and *mairie* are up the hill to your right; the route, however, stays to the left of the memorial signposted Beauregard 5km, D62. That a hamlet, little more than a group of houses still has its own *mairie* and *poste* indicates the importance of community in France, and also how these services are critical to keeping rural communities alive.

Châtres to Condat sur Vézère

The quiet rural riding continues, as you roll between fields and small woodlands. After 4km, the route crosses over a motorway, known as *La Transeuropéenne*, a major road but you would barely know it is there, as at this point it is concealed in a tunnel.

2.5km after crossing the motorway you pass Beauregard village on your left. The road just skirts the edge, but should you feel the inclination to explore you will be rewarded with some interesting medieval streets tucked in amongst the modern housing.

Remain on the D62 signposted Le Lardin St-Lazare 2km. It is a long fast descent with good tarmac and sweeping bends, so you will quickly pick up speed. As you descend past the many orchards you cannot fail to notice the steam rising from the valley below. The source is the large papermill in the town. There has been a paper mill here since 1923, making use of local resources, plentiful wood and water from the Vézère river.

Take care through the town as you will have picked up some speed and there are many side roads. At the traffic lights, continue straight on towards Montignac 11km, D704. You may notice at this point that Les Eyzies and Sarlat are both signed in the same directions, and are the same distance. However, the route takes you to Les Eyzies first, past the many caves that were home to the earliest humans, before turning toward the romantic and picturesque medieval streets of Sarlat.

Half a kilometre after the crossroads, you will cross a railway track and then pass the mill. Shortly after you come to a Y-shaped junction, where you take the left fork signposted Condat, D62.

Condat-sur-Vézère to Montignac

Continue through the tree-lined avenue and cross the Vézère. Take the first right over the bridge signposted towards the Eglise and Commanderie.

It is a very narrow street, and you may doubt you have taken the correct turning, but when it pops you out opposite the river you will know you are in the right place. This is the confluence of the Colys and Vézère rivers and in the 15th-century they were a source of hydro-power for nearby mills.

In a further 3km you will pass the grand Château de la Fleunie hotel and restaurant, set amongst the trees. A luxurious 3-star hotel and spa, it may tempt you to consider cutting your ride short and relaxing for a while. The road climbs up a tree-covered hill behind the château, and a wooden platform built at the top as a viewpoint allows a spectacular view onto the river beneath.

Shortly after passing the château you will arrive at a

T-junction where you turn left to Montignac, D45. A strange one-way system sandwiches you between a wall and the river, but this only lasts for about a kilometre before you are reunited with the other carriageway.

Montignac

In 3km, after joining the D45, when you meet the D704, turn right signposted Centre Ville, then turn right again at the lights following the D704 over the bridge. At this point look left and you will see the next bridge that you will be crossing over – this elaborate one-way system loops you around the town. At the end of this first bridge turn left for Centre Ville Montignac, D704.

At the end of the road turn left again taking the D704 over the second bridge. Immediately after crossing the bridge, turn right on the D65 with the river close beside you on your right.

Montignac is a pleasant town for a coffee stop. It has many interesting niche shops tucked up its many alleyways. It is a town that has been inhabited since prehistoric times and you can trace its more recent history through the ramshackle tangle of 15th-, 16th- and 17th-century homes in the old town. Montignac is, however, most famous for the extensive prehistoric paintings in the Lascaux caves.

The caves, discovered by three teenage boys in 1940, were first opened to the public in 1948 but allowing in visitors damaged the fragile paintings and the caves were closed to the public in 1963. Lascaux II was developed, a replica of the caves and their paintings, just 200m away from the original site.

Montignac to Thonac

A pleasantly flat, easy section follows with the river on one side and fields backed with woodland to your left. After 4km you will see the Château de Losse on the opposite side of the river, constructed in 1570 by Jean II de Losse on medieval foundations. From this side it seems improbable that the château has defied the waters for so long, as it appears to be undermined by the river. 2km after spotting Château de Losse take the right turn across the river towards Thonac D65e.

Thonac to La Roque St-Christophe

At the mini-roundabout turn left signposted Les Eyzies D706. After 3km you will pass a sign to St-Léon-sur-Vézère, although the route by-passes the village it is a worthwhile detour as it is one of France's *plus beaux villages*.

The Romanesque church of St-Léon, on one of the pilgrims' routes to Santiago de Compostela, sits close to the river at the beginning of its meander. There are benches under the shady trees and this would be a good spot for a picnic. On a corner of the church, marks on the wall show where flood-water reached at different points in its history.

Aptly described as the 'artists village', four artists work and exhibit here – two painters, a jewellery maker and a wood carver. The wood sculpture by Olivier Legay is displayed in L'Atelier du Bois Dormant behind the information point. Strongly influenced by the environment of the *Périgord Noir*, his work uses local materials and captures a sense of prehistory and mythology.

The D706 traces its way around the outside of the meander that St-Léon-sur-Vézère sits within. 6km after the entrance to the village you arrive again at the river. Immediately after crossing, look to your left where you will suddenly notice a limestone rock-face that appears to have been lived in. This is the Cité Troglodytique de la Roque St-Christophe. This limestone wall, 1km long and 80m high, has been continuously occupied since Neanderthals first lived there 55,000 years ago, and the last inhabitants left just 300 years ago.

Even if you do not take the tour, it is worthwhile turning off to the left and riding as far as the car park underneath the base of the cliff. From the road you can clearly see the square-cut holes in the limestone which would have once supported beams and structures.

La Roque Saint Christophe to Les Eyzies-de-Tayac

Continue on the D706, this takes you all the way to Les Eyzies. Within this next section of riding you will see many signs for caves and museums. The area surrounding Les Eyzies as far as Montignac is referred to as the 'cradle of mankind' as there is much evidence that it was widely

CAVE PAINTINGS

The Vézère valley contains some of the finest examples of prehistoric cave art found anywhere in the world. Using basic flint tools for engraving and grinding pigments for colours, Cro-Magnon people were able to create incredibly skilful and sophisticated images of the animals they hunted or saw in their nomadic lifestyle.

The purpose of the paintings is unknown. They may have been part of rituals to ensure a good hunt, or to pass on knowledge. They could have been painted in honour of the animals killed, or simply for the joy of creating something that depicted life as they knew it.

inhabited by prehistoric humans. From the remains of a Neanderthal excavated in Le Moustier to the troglodyte caves, paintings and many other findings, it is rich in prehistoric artefacts.

With so much to see here you really have to take your pick – there are too many sites and museums to visit unless planning a long stay in the area. The two extremes of the area are clearly illustrated when 4 km further on, on the right-hand side you pass the Musée Fossiles et Préhistoire, complete with large model dinosaur on the outside and shortly after on your left the real and far more impressive Maison Forte de Reignac, a fortified château cleverly built into a rock-face.

This region isn't all about history, and shortly before entering Tursac you are invited to think about gastronomy as you pass Les Oies du Périgord Noir and its fields of geese on your right. Tursac itself has a restaurant and a shop selling *foie gras* and other local produce.

After Tursac, the road starts gently climbing away from the river, twisting its way through the beech trees for 3km, before descending again back toward the river. In another 2km when you reach the bridge follow signs for Toutes Direction over the bridge. The stage ends here, at the end of the bridge, and Les Eyzies is to your right if you are staying the night or wish to explore. To continue on to the next stage follow signs for Sarlat, D47.

Les Eyzies-de-Tayac

If you have an interest in prehistory then this really is a stop not to be missed. Whilst many come here to visit the Musée National de la Préhistoire and the many caves and grottos nearby, there are also quiet riverside spots where you can relax away from the crowds.

Tayac itself is a small village just on the outskirts of Les Eyzies-de-Tayac. It is 600 years older than Les Eyzies-de-Tayac and was founded by monks who were travelling between monasteries. One of their party was close to death so they camped near a water source at Tayac, and the water miraculously healed the seriously ill monk. This was taken as a sign to build a new monastery on the site.

The fortified church has little beauty but it served as a stronghold against attack as well as a place of worship. Few tourists venture down to the church and river bank, a 5-minute walk past the station, but there is a pleasant spot by the river that offers some space for quiet contemplation.

Sleep

Hotel
Le Cro Magnon

A golden coloured building smothered in ivy provides comfortable accommodation, pool and small library to relax in. It is worth staying here for the address alone.

54 Avenue de la Préhistoire, 24620 Les Eyzies-de-Tayac

00 33 (0) 5 53 06 97 06

www.hotel-cromagnon.com

Chambre d'Hôtes
Le Menestreln

By the river and just two minutes walk into the centre of town this allows you to visit all the key museums easily and have a quiet space with pool to return to.

1 Avenue de Laugerie, 24260 Les Eyzies-de-Tayac

00 33 (0)5 53 08 16 59

www.menestrel-perigord.com

Campsite
Camping Le Pech Charmant

2km outside of Les Eyzies in Le Bugue this is a more natural and rustic campsite than the 4 star options in Les Eyzies itself. For a glamping experience book one of the spacious safari tents for the night.

Le Pech, 24620 Les Eyzies-de-Tayac

00 33 (0) 5 53 35 97 08

www2.lepech.com

Supplies

Food
There are several boulangeries and specialist food shops. There is no shortage of *foie gras* here. For less decadent supplies there is a small supermarket.

Bike
Monti Bike

Behind the *office de tourisme* in Montignac this hire and repair shop will be able to deal with most eventualities.

Place Bertran de Born, 24290 Montignac

00 33 (0)7 77 08 29 63

Eat

Auberge de Layotte

Slightly out of town off the D47 north up a dirt track but worth seeking out. Paris trained chef Regis Gagnadre runs a cookery school and restaurant. There is a different set menu daily made with produce from his garden.

Layotte, 24620 Tursac, 00 33 (0)5 53 06 95 91

www.aubergelayotte.com

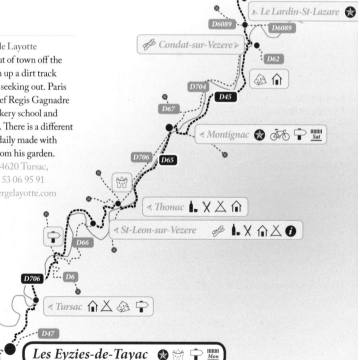

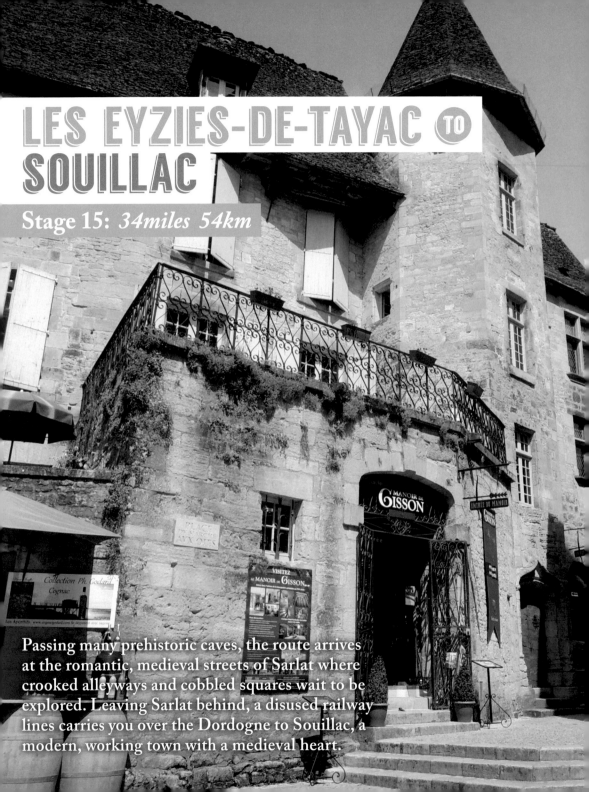

LES EYZIES-DE-TAYAC ⓉⓄ SOUILLAC

Stage 15: *34miles 54km*

Passing many prehistoric caves, the route arrives at the romantic, medieval streets of Sarlat where crooked alleyways and cobbled squares wait to be explored. Leaving Sarlat behind, a disused railway lines carries you over the Dordogne to Souillac, a modern, working town with a medieval heart.

Les Eyzies-de-Tayac to Sarlat-la-Canéda

Starting at the bridge, turn left for Sarlat 21km, D47. All along this road you will be passing signs to numerous grottos and châteaux. The first grotto you pass is Roc de Cazelle, off to your right. The cliff here has been inhabited since prehistoric times, and unbelievably, the last inhabitants only vacated in 1966.

Roc de Cazelle is a large museum with caves to explore that feature wax figures, used to create tableaux demonstrating different time periods in the caves' history. Whilst the collections of artefacts, the detailed descriptions and the homes laid out as they would have been at different points in its long history are very interesting, at times the figures can be a little strange and disturbing!

The next cave you pass, the Grotte de Bernifal, could not be more different. Visits are by appointment only and you will be shown round by the elderly gentleman whose land the cave is on, or by his son. A simple iron door leads you into the cave with no adverts, gift shop or elaborate display cases. There is no lighting but you will be provided with a torch to view the cave paintings. There are three rooms, the longest measuring 22 metres long by 8 metres wide. You will find 25 mammoths, 8 horses, 7 auroch or bison and two deer, plus many others that have not been identified.

Although you will need to have excellent French to fully understand the explanations, it will still be an atmospheric experience and very different to the other more commercial caves in the area. To make arrangements phone Gilbert: 00 33 (0)6 74 96 30 43 or 00 33 (0)5 53 29 66 39.

From here, the road climbs almost imperceptibly, requiring just a little extra effort. Rounding a bend you will see an unusual château very close to the road built upon a plinth of the honey-coloured limestone as if it had sprung organically from the rock itself.

Slightly further along, around 13km after leaving Les Eyzies, you will be able to make out a château perched high above the road to your left. This is the Château de Puymartin, built in the 12th-century, destroyed in the Hundred Years' War and rebuilt in 1450. It is now home to the de Montbrun family and is open to the public.

Sarlat-La-Canéda to Grolejac

Once you have taken the right for Cahors, there is a cycle path on your right – a narrow road, with car parking. Go straight over the mini-roundabout and at the larger second roundabout take the second exit signposted Cahors. At the next roundabout take the third exit, still following Cahors, and pass a giant supermarket on your left.

At the next roundabout take the second exit signposted Cahors, D704, and immediately turn right into a gravel car park. From here follow the cycle path on a disused railway line for the next 10km. The tarmac is beautifully smooth and the route, which is wide with no barriers to impede progress, keeps you away from the busy D704.

The cycle path takes you through a deep-sided cutting, where the trees arch cathedral-like high above your head and filter a greenish light. The track is quiet and tranquil, and, although well used, it is wide enough to prevent conflict with other users. Crossing the Dordogne on the old railway bridge, you will be able to see a wide expanse of river, with the woodland coming right down to the banks. Crossing the bridge there is a canoe-hire spot to your right which is popular with bathers as well as kayakers.

Where the *piste cyclable* ends it brings you up to merge onto a minor road; follow this to your right. After 500 metres you will arrive at a T-junction, turn left ignoring the *voie verte* sign for another cycle route. The road bends round to the left (do not go straight on as this is a No Entry). At the stop sign turn left, and in 200 metres at the roundabout turn right for Veyrignac, D50.

Grolejac to St-Julien-de-Lampon

Climbing up slightly, the quiet road surrounded simply by fields and trees, brings you into Veyrignac. There is little in the village but you will find public toilets and a picnic area to your left as you pass through. Shortly after leaving Veyrignac you will pass under overhanging rocks, leaning out from the bank at the road side.

After riding alongside the river for a short stretch, you enter the small hamlet St-Mondane, 3km from Veyrignac. Here you will be riding alongside walnut trees as once again you are on the *Route de la Noix* first seen as you were leaving Hautefort. The trees are planted in a precise geometric pattern and over the next few kilometres you will see trees of varying ages, from the newly planted through to mature. Walnuts have always been important to this region; traces of walnut shells were even found in the caves

At the height of the summer season there are illuminated night-time viewings. You can also stay there as the Comtesse de Montbrun offers *chambres d'hôtes*.

5km after the Château de Puymartin you will reach a large roundabout, follow signs for Sarlat, D6, third exit. The descent from here is fairly fast and on good tarmac, in 1km you will reach a stop sign; turn right for Sarlat. At the next roundabout, take the second exit signposted Cité Médiéval, at the next mini-roundabout turn right, continuing towards the *centre ville*. You will shortly come to another mini-roundabout. Directly ahead is a pedestrian area and the best way of gaining access to the medieval streets of Sarlat. The route continues to your right, steeply uphill, to traffic lights. Turn left here for Cahors. Continue down the hill then turn right for Cahors.

of Cro-Magnon man, our earliest modern human ancestor discovered in Les Eyzies. The nuts and the oil were highly prized and used to settle debts. In the middle ages, tenants paid their rent to their landlords in nut oil. It was used to clean skin and also as fuel for lamps. In the 17th-century, it became an important export trade for the area with walnuts sent all over France as well as to the UK.

Walnut farming covers areas of the Périgord, Dordogne, Corrèze and Lot, and the *Route de la Noix* links up the key areas of production. Four nut varieties are protected by *Appellation d'Origine Contrôlée* – *la Grandjean, la Marbot, la Corne* and *la Franquette*. Walnut trees like deep, well-drained, limey soils and they suffer from few diseases, making them a reliable crop. The only risk to the farmer is in early spring when, if bad weather prevents pollination, an entire crop can be lost even before the season has begun.

A further 3km takes you into the village of St-Julien-de-Lampon. A pizzeria and bar have set up their tables in the shadow of the church, making this a great place to stop for a drink or something more substantial. Despite its small size, there is a buzz of activity and a liveliness about it. Go straight on at the crossroads, staying on the D50.

St-Julien-de-Lampon to Souillac

After 1.5km you will pass the restaurant La Gabarre. This is a destination restaurant, busy every lunchtime and dinner serving traditional Périgord dishes using local produce. Immediately after, there is a switchback left that takes you down to river level. The riding now is flat, but although you are only a hundred metres away from the river you get only an occasional glimpse of the Dordogne through the trees.

3.5km later, the D50 seamlessly becomes the D43, where the D12 joins from the right in Mareuil. On your left is a slipway that takes you down to the water's edge, providing easy access for a paddle or a swim. Keep following signs for Souillac, D43. In a further 2.5km you will arrive in Le Roc, a tiny village mainly devoted to walnut farming. If you are interested in trying walnut oil you can buy direct from the farmer here – look for the sign *Vente Huile de Noix*. Walnut oil is increasing in popularity due to its many health benefits. It has been shown to help reduce the risk of cardiovascular disease, improve the function of blood vessels and balance cholesterol levels. Thanks to its high levels of antioxidants, it may combat the signs of ageing, whether rubbed on your wrinkles or splashed on your salad.

3km later you arrive at a narrow bridge over the river to

SARLAT-LA-CANEDA

It is worth parking your bike to wander the sunny squares and peer round the ancient alleyways of this often busy, yet incredibly well-preserved and evocative, medieval town. The warm ochre-coloured stone glows in evening sunlight and this is the best time of day to visit once the crowds have dispersed.

Sarlat was the first city in France to be given a protection order. It is now classified as a City of Art and History and has the highest density of historic monuments of any city in France. Starting life as a Gallo-Roman settlement, it grew in importance when Benedictine monks established an abbey here in the 8th-century. It has been developed and added to from the 11th century onwards, and particularly during the Renaissance period.

The town went into decline in the late 1700s, so by the mid 20th-century it was in a pretty poor state, but at least no modern building had infiltrated it walls.

Its importance was recognised by André Malraux, celebrated novelist, resistance hero and politician, who campaigned to preserve outstanding areas of architecture from post-war renovation and to ensure funds for their restoration.

reach the outskirts of Souillac, which, despite sitting on the Dordogne, is in the *département* of the Lot. At the T-junction turn right for Centre Ville.

As you approach the traffic-light controlled T-junction, you will see a church and *office de tourisme* on your left. The stage ends here.

Souillac

Souillac is very much a modern working town. It is the main gateway to the upper Dordogne bearing the brunt of the tourist traffic heading for Sarlat and the Périgord Noir. However, scratch beneath the surface you will be able to find tucked away squares and narrow medieval streets as well as the town's main attraction the Eglise Ste-Marie.

The Eglise St Martin in the Place St-Martin is a good starting point for finding the heart of old Souillac. The square has several restaurants where you can eat or enjoy a drink, feeling the calm of this ancient place despite only being a few hundred metres from a main road.

The imposing building of the Eglise Ste-Marie dominates the open area it is situated in. Its Byzantine domes are reminiscent of grander cathedrals in Périgueux and Cahors. Inside it is very simple and unadorned, giving it a sense of grace and nobility.

The first church was built on this site in the tenth century but was badly damaged during The Hundred Years' War and the Wars of Religion. It was restored in the 17th-century and then abandoned again during the French Revolution. Its Romanesque sculptures, though badly damaged, are still impressive.

The narrow streets away from the main modern shopping areas have the occasional interesting shop and there are some local crafts on display. If you are hungry, there are some excellent *charcuteries* and *boulangeries* that are worth a visit.

INDULGE

Château de Puymartin

Spend the night in the Château de Puymartin and risk an encounter with *Dame Blanche*, a white spirit said to reside there. The current Comtesse de Montbrun will be your host and you will stay in rooms that are every bit as elegant as they would have been in the 17th-century, allowing you to sample life in a château, if only for a night.

24200 Sarlat-la-Canéda
00 33 (0)5 53 59 29 97
www.chateau-de-puymartin.com

Sleep

Hotel

Le Pavillon Saint-Martin

A delightfully stylish hotel opposite the church of Saint-Martin in the older part of Souillac, exposed brick work and arched doorways reveals the age of the building and the individually designed rooms are comfortable and full of character.

5 Place Saint-Martin, 46200 Souillac

00 33 (0)5 65 32 63 45

www.hotel-saint-martin-souillac.com

Chambre d'Hôtes

Coeur de Souillac

In the heart of the medieval part of town and close to the Abbey this charming *chambre d'hôtes* has one family sized room tucked up under the beams on the top floor. It is light, airy and well decorated with a good breakfast to follow next morning.

Don Jones 8 rue de Juillet Souillac, 46200

00 33 (0)5 65 37 61 43

www.souillacchambredhote.com

Campsite

Domaine de la Paille Basse

An unusual campsite in a reconstructed medieval village surrounded by woodland. The three farms have been rebuilt to create accommodation and facilities for this five star campsite.

46200 Souillac

00 33 (0)5 65 37 85 48

www.lapaillebasse.com

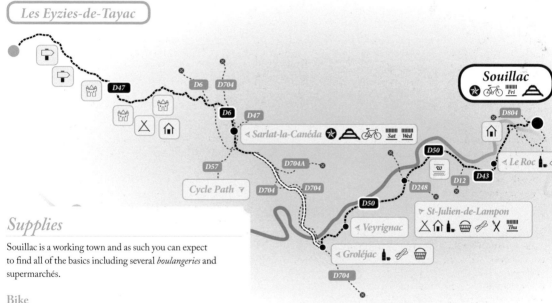

Supplies

Souillac is a working town and as such you can expect to find all of the basics including several *boulangeries* and supermarchés.

Bike

Veloland

Sarlat has one bike shop, Veloland, part of a national chain.

18 avenue Aristide Briand

00 33 (0)5 53 28 51 87

www.veloland.com

Cash Bike

Souillac has two very good bike shops almost directly opposite each other, if Cash Bike can't help Carrefour Cycle will.

18 avenue du Général de Gaulle, 46200 Souillac

00 33 (0)5 65 32 40 34

www.cashbike.fr

Eat

Le Beffroi

Perfectly positioned in the *place* in front of the church the wisteria covered outside terrace area is a delight to eat under of an evening. A good menu offering lots of local specialities at a reasonable price.

6 place Saint Martin, 46200 Souillac

00 (0)5 65 37 80 33

SOUILLAC TO GRAMAT

Stage 16: *28miles 45km*

A real cyclist's stage with the first climbs and descents of any length on the journey so far. The route rises out of the Dordogne valley to the top of the dramatic pilgrimage village of Rocamadour, clinging to the cliffs, before reaching the limestone plateau, which takes its name from the small town of Gramat.

Souillac to Château de la Treyne

With your back to the *office de tourisme*, turn right on the D820, signposted Cahors and Rocamadour. The first kilometre out of the town can be busy as road planners, unusually for this cycling-mad nation, momentarily forgot the needs of cyclists and constructed a traffic divider in the middle of the road, limiting the width of the carriageway!

Thankfully there is just a short section before you turn off left onto the much quieter D43, signed Rocamadour, just before the main road crosses the Dordogne river.

These upper reaches of the Dordogne river valley are actually in the Lot *département*. In common with many of rivers that shape France's landscape and its identity, they are too large to be confined by administrative borders.

The route tucks in alongside some small cliffs on the left and a row of fields separates you from being fully re-united with the Dordogne on your right.

You are back on the *route des noix*, referring to the old tradition of walnut production in this region. After 4km you pass through Pinsac with a campsite, small shop and *fromagerie*. The route descends very gradually for 2km before crossing the Dordogne river.

Look up to your right where the Château de la Treyne guards the single-track bridge over the river, peering out from the woods on the southern bank.

The château is both a highly recommended *chambre d'hôtes* and restaurant, and also overlooks a good spot for a splash in the river. Take the track through old white gates opposite the turning to the château. It's a short walk to a place where it's possible to get into the water, but you can swim to the road bridge for a view of the château.

The peaceful nature of the river before you, belies its chracter in a past life. During the 19th-century, before the railways came, two essential French ingredients – cheese and the wood used to make the barrels for the celebrated wines of Bordeaux – were transported on the river and carried downstream to where the Dordogne reaches the open sea.

Château de la Treyne to Calès

We now say *au revoir* to the Dordogne. The route climbs away from the river for 2km entering the Parc Naturel Régional des Causses du Quercy, the start of a limestone plateau region with a strong sheep-farming tradition. This area stretches 50km southwards to Figeac where it is bordered by the Lot river. The road abruptly swoops downwards passing a peach and *foie gras* seller.

After a 1km descent, on a sweeping left-hand switchback, take care to turn right signed Calès 4km, ignoring the road sign for Rocamadour. This alternative way is an infinitely more dramatic route, almost hand-built for cyclists. If you do miss the turning, after 1.5km you will find yourself at the Grottes de Lacave, a series of underground lakes and caverns indicated by an enormous hole behind the village of the same name. If you are interested you can take a highly organised guided tour through massive chambers of stalactites and stalagmites.

The road to Calès marks a significant moment in your journey, as you begin your longest climb of the trip so far. Admittedly at 4km, one of the first of two climbs to the dramatic village of Rocamadour is not the Col de Galibier, but the sensation of height gain is great as the minor road starts to peel away from the Ouysse, leaving the river looking like a trickle below. Indeed the Ouysse is a modest

tributary of the Dordogne but it is responsible for some dramatic scenery as soon will become apparent.

As you begin to climb up toward the Causses, you get a feeling of being in a more rugged and hillier landscape. This sensation of wilder terrain continues throughout the remainder of the route, whether you are riding through a narrow gorge or climbing a col in Provence. In many ways, this stage marks the dividing point from the green and placid countryside where we started, yet the road to Calès is perfectly manageable. As this area experiences some of the hottest summers in France outside of Provence, you will be grateful for the almost complete arch of oak and beech trees that shelter the climb.

After 3.5 km of climbing, keep to the left to continue upwards less steeply. After a further 500m you arrive in the village of Calès, which offers a great view of wooded hills to the west. In the village centre, by a hotel-restaurant, turn left signed Rocamadour 13km, D673.

Calès to Rocamadour l'Hospitalet

Calès lies at only 250m above sea level, but the view afforded over the Causses du Quercy are impressive as you ride on a flattish ridge for 1km, where you follow the road round a square left corner signed Rocamadour. What follows is a twisting, fun 3.5km descent through woodland to the valley bottom and a small bridge over the Ouysse river.

Immediately after the river a sign marks the head of a 2km side road to the Moulin de Cougnaguet, a 14th-century fortified mill. There is a river pool near the mill which makes for an excellent and invigorating swimming spot. The defences of the mill give you an insight into a more dangerous time in the history of this seemingly serene mini-gorge. The windmill has built-in slits so archers could aim at the enemy and a dam to release water rapidly on anybody tampering with the mill race. Churches, such as the fortified church of Rudelle near Gramat, were also protected from assault.

After 2km of flat in the valley, you can no longer follow the river in its mini-gorge. There is space only for the rugged river channel that cuts through the limestone and the GR6 long-distance walking route, which leads straight to the foot of Rocamadour. As a result, you are forced to pedal out of the valley. For centuries this area has been marked by the footsteps of those following long-distance routes. The GR6 points the way for pilgrims up the valley and here we cross paths with those on this ancient journey.

ROCAMADOUR

For nearly a thousand years, the narrow canyon of the Alzou river has sheltered the cluster of buildings that cling to its sheer cliff sides and make up the town of Rocamadour. The perfectly preserved body of Saint Amadour was discovered in a rock-covered tomb next to a small existing chapel in 1166, putting Rocamadour on the map as a destination for pilgrims.

Over the years, millions of pilgrims have journeyed here from all over the world, crawling up the *grand escalier* on their knees to visit the shrine of the Black Madonna, a small statue said to have healing powers. Today Rocmadour's visitors are often motivated less by religion and more by sight-seeing as evidenced by the accumulation of souvenir shops on the main artery of the old town.

Rocamadour in many ways is best viewed from afar. In particular, the viewpoint at the foot of the village is a great place to stop and take a picture, as is the cliff-edge *belvédère* just before leaving L'Hospitalet. Rocamadour does have a tourist 'Noddy' train but anywhere with such a theme-park accessory needs to be treated with caution!

Our route continues upwards and again the climb gives a sensation of ascent, in contrast to some of the pancake-flat landscape of northern France. Because of the views they offer, these changes in gradient feel greater than they actually are. The road climbs dramatically for 4km, with the occasional switchback offering views on to the serpentine route below. A flatter 2km, passing gaggles of geese and wandering sheep, leads you to a large car park and the Hôtel Bellaroc. Turn right just after the car park on the D200 for a view of Rocamadour from above as it clings to the cliffs.

Our route carries straight on at the car park and immediately after, you enter l'Hospitalet, a burgeoning service town for Rocamadour on the flat plateau above the cliffside village. It has all the amenities you expect from a tourist hotspot, including an *office de tourisme* and in this region the ubiquitous *foie gras* emporium.

If you're looking for something to put on your baguettes it is worth a stop at one of the *fromage de chèvre* sellers. Their cheese comes from the goats that forage on the limestone terraces of the plateau. The creamy AOC Rocmadour goat's cheese, which has been made since the 15th-century, is often served with a sprinkling of black pepper. Keep a lookout, as you cycle along through the region, for wooden notice boards; the cheese is often sold direct from the farm gate when it has reached maturity.

At a T-junction, amongst a cluster of hotel-restaurants in the centre of l' Hospitalet, turn right on the D32, signed Gramat. Then immediately after, at the next junction and taking care to avoid the left turn, carry straight on, signposted La Cité. There is an abundance of 2-star hotels here and Rocamadour village is tastefully lit up in the evening, but you will experience a more authentic French town if you continue on the mini-roller-coaster of a stage until you reach Gramat.

Rocamadour l'Hospitalet to Gramat

Immediately after the intersections, the road begins to descend but don't get up to speed too quickly because on the right is the most striking and possibly best view of Rocamadour. Time your ride to pass early in the morning or late in the evening for a peaceful photo opportunity. Shortly after the viewpoint, the road briefly enters an unlit tunnel followed by a sharp right-hand bend. Most of the 1.5km descent is on a slightly off-camber road.

At a sharp switchback to the left the *Porte de Figuier*, the gateway to the old town, stands straight ahead. One of the

main entrances, it is named after the fig tree to remind the pilgrim of the need for their spiritual journey to bear fruit. After the hairpin the route passes through a man-made concrete tunnel rather than the wildly blasted untamed rock of the previous tunnel. The descent can be great fun but take care – in summer you will be sharing the route with sightseers on all modes of transport.

At the bottom of the descent, turn left by the car park over a narrow stone bridge that takes you over the Alzou river, signposted Couzou 5km, D32. A 2km climb with a *chambre d'hôtes* at the top offers final glimpses of Rocamadour and its valley.

If tourist-ravaged Rocamadour is not your thing, the valley offers some great short technical climbs and descents that should be enough to satisfy any cycling purist. After undulating down for 1.5km, with great views of the wooded streamed lined valley and its classic interlocking spurs, the road then winds gradually upwards for 1.5km. This stage contains over 600m of cumulative climbing for the first time in the trip and your legs will begin to register them.

5km from Rocamadour you reach the village of Couzou. Keep left at the junctions signed Gramat, D32. 2km after the village carry straight on, signed Gramat 9km as the D32 becomes the D39. You follow this road to Gramat through a landscape of dry-stone walls and occasional hedges. This rugged territory and the occasional rhythmic tinkle of bells indicates you are firmly in sheep country. The sky feels distinctly bigger here on the *Causse de Gramat* in contrast to the closer confines of the valleys of Périgord.

Arriving in Gramat

On the outskirts of Gramat, passing a timber yard and catching sight of the prominent church, you arrive at a crossroads with a Renault and Elan garage opposite. If you are pedalling on to Figeac, carry straight across, signed Reilhac, D14. Gramat's outskirts look uninspiring but this working, pleasant market town may surprise you.

For the town, turn left onto the main road signed Centre Ville, D807, then immediately after, cross the railway line with the station on your right. After 1km turn left at a mini-roundabout and after 400m you reach the square.

Gramat's main square is dominated by the Lion d'Or hotel and the Maison Vigouroux Vin de Cahors, showcasing the renowned reds of Cahors, just south-west of here, as well as the products of the *Périgord Pourpre* to the north west.

The square houses one of the prettiest *offices de tourisme* in France, guarded by statues of sheep. If you venture off the main streets into the narrow medieval lanes, you'll find plenty of local independent shops.

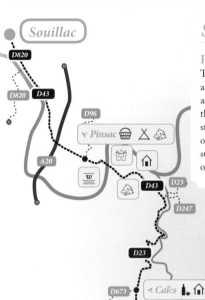

Supplies

Food

Two weekly markets are held on a Tuesday and Friday, illustrating Gramat's importance as a market town and a large settlement on the causses, an area where sheep farming is still crucial to the economy. There are plenty of boulangeries in the *centre ville*. There is a supermarket 1km north of town on the bypass on the road to Brive

Eat

Les Relais des Gourmands

Ignore the unusual location by the train station and indulge. Chef Gérard Curtet has a great reputation in the region and is in the club of the top 25 Bonnes Tables of the Lot department. Lots of local produce on offer such as Quercy Lamb. Also has rooms.

2 Avenue de La Gare, 46500 Gramat
00 33 (0)5 65 38 83 92
www.relais-des-gourmands.com

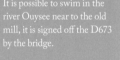

Swim

Château Le Treyne

Take the track opposite the entrance to the château. The water is mainly shallow and there is a lovely view of the château from the water below the road bridge.

Moulin de Cougnaguet

It is possible to swim in the river Ouysse near to the old mill, it is signed off the D673 by the bridge.

Sleep

Hotel

Le Lion d'Or

A large hotel, that belies the size of Gramat, with modern and comfortable rooms on the main square. Also boasts a popular restaurant which features in the Bonnes Tables du Lot.

8 Place de la République, 46500 Gramat
00 33 (0)5 65 10 46 10
www.liondorhotel.fr

Chambre d'hôtes

Aux Volets Blancs

An inviting guesthouse near the station 500m walk from the old town, with a pretty garden to relax in after a day's ride. The proprietor is a Québécoise who now hosts in this small town.

34 Avenue Louis Mazet, 46500 Gramat
00 33 (0)5 65 33 70 96
www.auxvoletsblancs.nuxit.net

Campsite

Camping de la Ferme en Paille

A working sheep farm, complete with 300 sheep, this place is a gem. A rarity in France, an authentic campsite with lots of eco-practices and a straw gîte, a world away from the mini-city formats some campsite take. located 1km south of town on the route followed in the next stage.

Chez Patrice Ravet, 46500 Gramat
00 33 (0)6 84 48 67 99
www.campingdelafermeenpaille.com

LOT

FILL your water bottles with little-known wines of the region from the friendly *cave* on the main street of Entraygues-sur-Truyère.

DODGE the jaws of the Beast of Gévaudan. Whilst the wolf may no longer roam the hills, the legend lives on.

CONQUER your first climb of over 1,000m and spot the names of riders painted on the road.

GLIDE through empty roads alongside serene river banks shaded by over-hanging trees and the sides of the valley.

VISIT three of France's *plus beaux villages* – Estaing, St-Côme d'Olt and Ste-Eulalie d'Olt.

MEANDER along quiet lanes over the limestone plateau of the historic Quercy region, with little to disturb you other than the tinkling of sheep bells.

145

GRAMAT (TO) FIGEAC

Stage 17: *28miles 45km*

Almost the entire stage is spent cycling through
the Parc Naturel Régional des Causses du Quercy,
a limestone plateau where flocks of sheep have
long grazed, segregated by the occasional dry-
stone wall. By the time you descend into Figeac,
with its medieval centre on the banks of the Célé
river, you will be closer to Nice than St-Malo for
the first time.

Gramat to St-Simon

If you stayed in Gramat, retrace your tracks back across the railway bridge on the western edge of town. At the crossroads by the Renault and Elan garages, take the road signed Reilhac 10km, D14. 1km after leaving Gramat you will pass a cheese-seller, campsite and the entrance to an animal park.

The smattering of houses when leaving town soon gives way to a quieter and significantly more rural road, where fields are edged with a combination of trees, crumbling old limestone walls and fences to contain flocks of sheep as they roam and graze the plateau.

Two thirds of the Lot department is dominated by limestone plateau or *causses*, much of it within the boundaries of the *Parc Naturel* which is dotted with traditional conical stone huts used by shepherds to tend their sheep.

Quercy farm lamb is known for its incomparable taste, flavoured by the short sparse grasses and wild herbs that thrive on the plateau. With few villages, only the sound of cicadas and sheep bells can be heard as you ride through the gently undulating scrubland, with close-cropped grass interspersed with low growing pines, oaks – and if you look closely, the occasional orchid.

Reilhac is a pretty hamlet with a *foie gras* seller where you can buy direct from the farm, but little else. 3km after Reilhac at a cluster of houses, turn left signed Flaujac-Gare 6km, D25. After 3km turn left at a crossroads where a small wooden sign marks Flaujac-Gare. Pass though the hamlet of Scelles with its small church before riding for a further 3km to Flaujac-Gare. There is no station actually in the village, but you will cross over the railway line just before entering it. Continue 1km past Flaujac-Gare to the small hamlet of Lalinié with an unmarked but distinctive T- junction, where there is a small triangular traffic island consisting of a patch of grass and three towering trees entwined with ivy. Turn right here. Immediately after at the crossroads, turn left signed St-Simon 4km, D25.

St-Simon to Assier

In St-Simon, ride straight through on the road which splices the small village green, ignoring minor road turnings to either side, before keeping to the left of a small triangular wooded

traffic island signed Assier, D25. The village buildings are briefly punctuated by a couple of fields. 0.5km later at another triangular traffic island, this time with a lone tree, turn right signed Assier 3km, D11. Leaving St-Simon there is a *chambre d'hôtes* on the right, then pass through a cluster of houses. Keep following the signs for Assier, ignoring minor turn-offs. The route arrives in Assier at a junction by the war memorial; turn left here towards the impressive church. Immediately after the church, turn right signed Reyrevignes 4.5km, D11.

Assier is a fairly isolated village but you may notice a few tourists' cars parked on the village square if the fortnightly Monday market isn't on. Many are coming to see the château built by Assier's most famous son, Galiot de Genouillac. The chief of French artillery made a name for himself in 1515 during a key French victory during the Italian Wars.

He returned home and built a château to celebrate, but now only the west wing remains, the rest having been sold off by the family over the years. He has left a more lasting impression on the church that he also built. A frieze runs round the building showing not scenes from the Bible, but cannons and guns being carried over the Alps.

Assier to Figeac

200m after the church, turn left on the edge of Assier signed Reyrevignes D11. It is 4.5km to Reyrevignes and the route climbs gradually, passing, after 3km, a small reservoir on your left before dropping down slightly into the village. At the T-junction in Reyrevignes, turn left signed Figeac 13 km D2. Moments later follow the main route round to the right signed Figeac. The route follows this road all the way to Figeac passing the small hamlets of Mouret and Lissac-et-Mouret, where the route continues straight on at the crossroads. After crossing a small river the road climbs for 2km before a series of sharp bends takes you down 2km to the edge of Figeac.

Arriving in Figeac

Speed bumps welcome you to Figeac. At a roundabout turn right signed Centre Ville D840 before following the road round as it bends left, again signed Centre Ville. Turn right at a mini-roundabout by café-bar Le Glacier, then left at the next mini-roundabout signed Decazeville D840. The road runs alongside the Célé river which is to the right at a mini-roundabout by Pont Gambetta bridge. You can either turn right over the bridge if you're pedalling on to the next stage, or hop off your bike and explore Figeac's pedestrianised medieval streets by turning left.

Surprisingly Figeac is not on many tourist itineraries, so you can wander its maze of medieval streets without tripping over camera-clad visitors. In peace, you will be able to admire its beautifully restored houses, made out of fine-grained local sandstone and half-timbered, many of which feature subtle carvings. Figeac grew up around a Benedictine House over 1,000 years ago and by the 13th-century was a thriving centre of trade and commerce. Two key trading areas were the Place Carnot with its market hall and neighbouring Place Champollion, which are great for a mid- or post-ride drink. The square is named after Jean-François Champollion, born in Figeac and the first to decipher Egyptian hieroglyphics.

THE ROSETTA STONE

The Rosetta Stone was carved in 196 BC and found in 1799 by French soldiers building a fort in Egypt at Rashid (Rosseta). The stone was written in three scripts: hieroglyphics (the language of the priests), demotic (the common script of Egypt) and Greek (then the language of the ruling class).

On the stone, Egyptian priests listed the deeds of the Pharoah. Jean-François Champollion, a student of Greek, cracked the code after years comparing the scripts, enabling ancient Egyptian hieroglyphics to be understood and opening up the world of the Pharoahs.

In Place Carnot you can go to the Sphinx café where the father of Jean-Francois Champollion had his bookshop. There is also an excellent museum in Figeac dedicated to the famed Egyptologist.

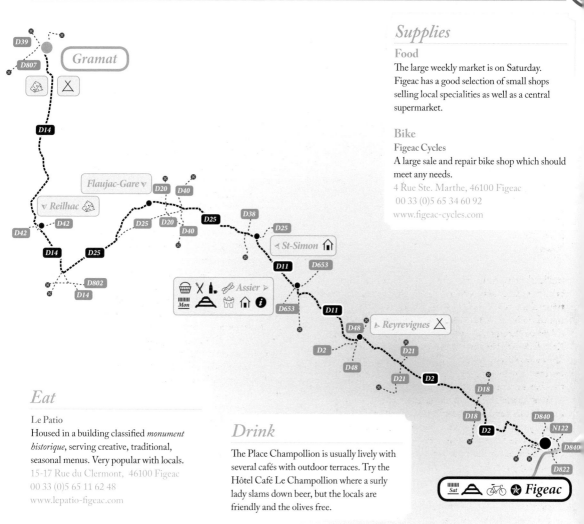

Supplies

Food
The large weekly market is on Saturday. Figeac has a good selection of small shops selling local specialities as well as a central supermarket.

Bike
Figeac Cycles
A large sale and repair bike shop which should meet any needs.
4 Rue Ste. Marthe, 46100 Figeac
00 33 (0)5 65 34 60 92
www.figeac-cycles.com

Eat

Le Patio
Housed in a building classified *monument historique*, serving creative, traditional, seasonal menus. Very popular with locals.
15-17 Rue du Clermont, 46100 Figeac
00 33 (0)5 65 11 62 48
www.lepatio-figeac.com

Drink

The Place Champollion is usually lively with several cafés with outdoor terraces. Try the Hôtel Café Le Champollion where a surly lady slams down beer, but the locals are friendly and the olives free.

Sleep

Hotel
Hôtel des Bains
Once part of the *Bains Publics* at the end of the 19th-century, now a tastefully renovated hotel. Relax on the terrace overlooking the river Célé.
1 Rue du Giffoul, 46100 Figeac
00 33 (0)5 65 34 10 89
www.hoteldesbains.fr

Chambre d'Hôte
Les Pratges
A 19th-century house, with a small swimming pool a stone's throw from the *centre ville*.
M et Mme Cournede,
6 Avenue Jean Jaurès, 46100 Figeac
00 33 (0)6 07 05 07 92
www.lesmaisonsdemarie.com

Campsite
Le Camping Domaine du Surgié
2 km outside Figeac, a large campsite with a hundred pitches and mobile homes to rent. Not exactly camping *sauvage*, but the site is by the river and has the pools and sports facilities one would expect in a large complex.
Domaine du Surgié, 46100 Figeac
00 33 (0)5 61 64 88 54
www.domainedesurgie.com

FIGEAC ⓣⓞ ENTRAYGUES-SUR-TRUYERE

Stage 18: *36miles 58km*

The stage gets off to a hilly start, climbing out of
the Célé valley past ancient chapels before plunging
down to meet the Lot river. The second part of the
stage is a flat, peaceful ride. Following the intricate
meanders of the Lot upstream, it crosses an ancient
medieval bridge into the perfectly positioned
small town of Entraygues, squeezed between the
confluence of the Lot and Truyère rivers.

Figeac to Montredon

From the *centre ville* side of the Célé river, leave Figeac, in the direction of Decazeville, by crossing the river towards the Hôtel Pont d'Or on the southern bank. Immediately after crossing the bridge, turn left at the mini-roundabout signed Decazeville, D840.

Climbing gradually, turn left off the main road 2km after leaving Figeac, signed Montredon 13 km, D2. The road ramps up for 2km, gaining height quickly to reward your efforts with views back to Figeac and the Célé valley over to your left. You will pass farmsteads and houses with square turrets, in contrast to the rounded features of the Loire buildings.

Reaching the *commune* de Lunan you are 200m above Figeac. The road now maintains its height on a ridge as you roll along for 11km to Montredon, descending and climbing slightly on occasions. The first 3km after the steep start are overall slightly downhill, as you cruise past the village of St-Jean-Mirabel slightly off-route to your left. You may see hikers and pilgrims trudging along the verges as the GR65 pilgrim route follows the roadside for a period.

Soon a welcome wooded section comes into sight. It is a godsend on a hot day as the first few kilometres of this stage are very open. Tucked next to the Ste-Marie-Madeleine chapel on the left in the small hamlet of Guirande is a fresh-water fountain.

This *monument historique* is a peaceful place to stop and listen to the chirping chorus of birdlife. Take a peak inside the chapel. It is often left open and still has an old wooden, double-sided confession box, so if you're riding in a pair you can both confess at once.

From the chapel it is a further 4km to the small village of Montredon. Butterflies dance in the breeze, fluttering out from the hedgerows as you ride along and the land becomes more wooded; there isn't a corn kernel in sight unlike earlier in the trip. The gradient and the woods obscure the small village of Montredon, except for its lofty church. The road kicks up a little again just before the village where you reach the highest point of the stage and can appreciate another refreshing water fountain by a picnic area on your right, which makes a convenient lunch or snack spot.

Montredon to Port d'Agrès

A 5km descent, the longest of the trip so far, is your reward for your early exertions leaving Figeac. Take care nearer the bottom as it gets twistier, with some switchbacks thrown in for good measure, after which you need to take a sharp, left turn signed Port d'Agrès 3km, D72. During the descent you will have left the Lot *département* and entered Aveyron, your 10th different *département* since leaving St-Malo. Ironically a few km after saying *au revoir* to the Lot department you say *bonjour* to the Lot, as the river is too long to be contained in one administrative area.

On the road to Port d'Agrès the Lot comes into view for the first time. Its little-visited upper valleys, and our relationship with them, govern the next three stages of our ride as we follow the Lot to its source deep in the Massif Central on the northern edge of the Cévennes, over 1,000 metres above sea level near the Col des Tribes. Whether side-by-side with the river or climbing up the valley sides, over the coming stages the Lot takes charge of the route and gradient. At times you enjoy its flat valley bottom, on other occasions the river has gouged out gorges, forcing the route away from the river and inevitably upwards, before being reunited after some exhilarating wooded descents.

For the rest of this stage the Lot is most definitely the cyclist's friend as the next 38km are flat, hugging the northern banks all the way to a medieval bridge upstream at Entraygues-sur-Truyère. Simply keep the river on your right. If you have a GPS switch it off. Sometimes it's good to escape the tyranny of watching the little screen and allow your eyes to roam around. Follow the river along its banks and enjoy this incredibly quiet road which has very little traffic, even in July or August, the only life being small communities of market farmers and a sprinkling of campsites occupied by those in search of a slower pace to their holiday. The water looks inviting, but check with the locals before wading in as it is dammed for hydro-electric further upstream, and when the water is released swimming is dangerous.

Pont d'Agrès to La Vieillevie

In Port d'Agrès turn right at the T-junction for a brief 200m on the D963 before turning left onto the road, signed Entraygues 35km, D42. On leaving Port d'Agrès, a church and a small château up on high guard the entrance as the valley becomes narrower, leaving behind the wide fertile farms that you rode past before the village. Now the valley becomes narrow with just enough space for the river, some trees and occasional parcel of farming land. The locals make use of these small strips of land squeezed between the road and river, cramming them full with vegetables in little smallholdings. Keep your eye out for boards announcing *fraises* (fresh strawberries), if you're passing in June.

6 kms after Port d'Agrès the route passes the entrance to St-Parthem village on the right, shortly after which you will pass Camping La Plaine, where they rent mountain bikes so may be able to help out in an emergency with some tools and spares. 3km further on at La Rondie, after a sweeping meander bend in the Lot that has almost been cut through, tomatoes and runner beans under covered sheets line the right-hand side of the road heading down to river. The quiet lane along the river is perfect for cycling and seems a world away from some of the honeypot sights of the Dordogne, such as Sarlat, that sometimes feel like they are swamped with tourists. When you reach a T-junction just after a café-brasserie on your right, turn left signed Entraygues 22km, D42. If you wish to visit medieval Conques, a UNESCO heritage site on the route to Santiago de Compostela, turn right at this T-junction. It's only 8km away but the Lot's steep valley sides will certainly get the legs pumping.

If you have been accustomed to the leisurely life by the Lot, and feel no need to interrupt it, continue with the river on your right for 1km. The route climbs very slightly, overlooking the

CONQUERING CONQUES

Listed as one of the *plus beaux villages de France*, pilgrims stopped at the abbey here to pay their respects to the relics of St-Foy. Much remains of the original medieval town, perhaps because, unlike London, the bread ovens were built outside the walls. As well as strolling round the remarkable old village, visit the abbey, with its Last Judgement tympanum over the entrance.

There is also Conques' famous treasure-trove –reliquaries made to house the bones of saints, dating from the first millennium, and finished in style by medieval goldsmiths. Their work is exquisite and the most famous piece, a small gold statue of St-Foy, contains part of the saint's skull. It's 8km extra riding, mostly climbing, to the south out of the Lot valley to reach Conques if the flat Lot side road is not challenging enough!

old river bridge, visible through the trees, before forking off the main road to the right, signed Entraygues, D141.

France's complicated regional picture persists as you enter the *département* of Cantal for the next part of the stage until after La Vieillevie, when you return to Aveyron, where the river briefly forms the border. Cheese-lovers will delight at the propspect of the tangy Cantal cheese, which has a vigorous taste reminiscent of a high-quality mature farmhouse cheddar, when well-ripened. Your first settlement in Cantal, 2km after the fork, is the small village of St-Projet with a *chambre d'hôtes* and, unusual in this rural valley, an internet café. It's 3km further to Vieillevie, the only village of any size on the whole stage, with a *place de multi-service*, a couple of cafés and a farm producer, specialising in *cabécou*, a regional goat's cheese.

La Vieillevie to Entraygues

It's a further 15km following the river to Entraygues, passing the occasional family who have found their own peaceful spot by the river, kids splashing around while parents read. Cycling under the shade of trees is perfect after a morning out in open. 4km after leaving La Vieillevie at *le port*, the point where canoe trips depart for river excursions, the road widens and the surface improves helping you pick up speed on the final straights of the stage, as the river cuts a more direct path and the road is less curved. 400 metres uphill on your left from *le port* is Ferme de Lavidalie if you wish to have a taste of their award-winning local cheese accompanied by wine.

The trees part briefly just before Entraygues, allowing a glimpse of the town over to your right, assuredly balanced between the confluence of the Lot and Truyère rivers, its

château taking centre stage where the rivers collide. When the road reaches a Stop sign turn right and go over the 13th-century bridge, the Pont Gothique. With the Hôtel La Rivière on your left immediately after the bridge follow the road as it turns square right and continue for 400m, with buildings, on either side until you reach the open Place de la Republique on your right where this stage ends. You will find the *office de tourisme* on the far side of the square and a cluster of bar-restaurants ready to offer post-ride refreshment or lunch.

Entraygues-sur-Truyère

It is worth exploring the small labyrinth of main streets that make up the old heart of Entraygues to the south of the square. Narrow lanes radiate off the central Place Castanie,

separating old houses adorned with colourful flowers emerging from wooden window boxes; the Rue Basse is a particularly picturesque 16th-century street.

Like the region itself, the vines of the region, cultivated here since the 1st-century BC, are little known but Entraygues-le-Fel was awarded an AOC in 2011. Only small quantities of the wine are made and you can seldom buy it outside of the region, so enjoy the distinctively scented and peppery flavours while you are here.

One of the best ways to appreciate Entraygues is to stroll along the river banks with your picnic supper. The stars shine bright at night out here with little light pollution – all the better to appreciate the quiet stillness by the river banks between the Pont Gothique and the château.

Sleep

Hotel
Hôtel la Rivière
A well-appointed hotel guarding the entrance to the town next to the Gothic bridge, with a nice pool out the back. The bar inside looks out over the bridge and across the river.
60 Avenue du Pont du Truyère, 12140 Entraygues-sur-Truyère
00 33 (0)5 65 66 16 83
www.hotellariviere.com

Chambre d'Hôtes
Le Clos St-Georges
Beautifully restored 17th-century mansion house full of character and just 600m from the *centre ville*.
19 Côteaux St. Georges, 12140 Entraygues-sur-Truyère
00 33 (0)5 65 48 68 22
www.leclosstgeorges.com

Campsite
Camping Le Val de Saures
A fantastic location on the far bank of the Lot from the *centre ville*, looking back across the water at the château. A pedestrian bridge links directly to the town making it a short hop to stroll around its streets.
12140 Entraygues-sur-Truyère
00 33 (0)5 65 44 56 92
www.camping-valdesaures.com

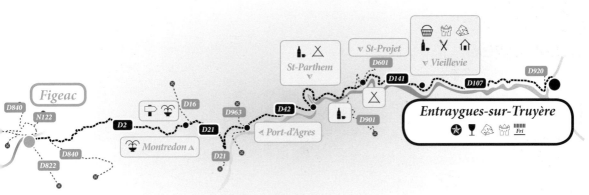

Supplies

Food
Entraygues holds a traditional market on Friday mornings and an additional one on Wednesday afternoons in July and August. On the main street, Tour de Ville, are two *boucheries/charcuteries* and an artisan *boulangerie*, specialising in local products – ideal for a picnic.

Eat

Restaurant Bar L'Indépendence
There are good restaurants attached to hotels such as La Rivière and Les Deux Vallées, and a variety of homely set menus are on offer on the Place de la République. If you prefer an establishment that just concentrates on cooking, L'Indépendence is situated on the main square.
5 Place de la République, 12140 Entraygues-sur-Truyère
00 33 (0)5 65 44 40 62

Drink

La Cave à Raymond
A unique wine wholesaler where you can fill your water bottle from a tap dispensing large vats of the local *vin rouge* should you wish! The wine is perfectly palatable and comes from the local Fel vineyards located at an altitude of between 200m and 400m.
33 Tour de Ville, 12140 Entraygues-sur-Truyère
0033 (0)5 65 44 22 52

ENTRAYGUES-SUR-TRUYERE ⓣⓞ ST-GENIEZ D'OLT

Stage 19: *33miles 53km*

The Lot river guides your ride, starting on your right and crossing it only once in St-Côme d'Olt, then taking you past Estaing's medieval bridge and through three of France's *plus beaux villages*. The road follows the river's course, only leaving its banks to climb into the wooded hillsides of this quiet corner of the Aveyron.

Entraygues-sur-Truyère to Estaing

The navigation for this stage is very simple. At the start of the ride the river is on your right until the route crosses over it at St-Côme d'Olt and then it remains on your left for the rest of the stage. Many of the villages on this stage end with d'Olt, which means Lot in the Occitan dialect. Starting with the Place de la République on your right, continue through the town.

As you reach the end of the rows of shops, the road makes a ninety degree left-hand turn where straight ahead you will see the river and a narrow bridge across it. This leads to a park with an activity trail and stone picnic benches.

After 300m you pass a bridge to your right, which signals the end of Entraygues. For the next 15km the road is accompanied only by the river and wild hillsides until reaching the next town, Estaing. The road closely hugs the river allowing you views into the deep rock-strewn gorge below. Little cascades tumble between the rocks and where large boulders sit mid-stream, you can see the river swirl and eddy as it separates to pass them. Overhanging trees are lush and green, even the stone wall you are riding alongside has the occasional vivid green fern or rogue sapling growing from it.

12km after leaving Entraygues you will pass the intriguing Chapelle del Dol on your right. The sad history of this mourning chapel, the *Légende d'Aveyron*, has captured many people's imaginations. Peter Woods, an English artist who had a studio nearby, worked with the Mayor of Le Nayrac to paint murals in the *commune's* chapel in a medieval style. These tell the story of two young lovers and their tragic fate. Often the chapel is open to visitors, but if it is locked the key is available from the *office de tourisme* in Estaing.

200 metres round the next bend the river widens and you can clearly see the magnificent meander, often featuring small boats tethered or floating mid-stream with fisherman out for their daily catch. Continuing alongside the river for another 3km you will reach Estaing. As you approach the town you will have a clear view across the river to the medieval bridge and rows of houses on the water's edge. As you follow the road through Estaing keeping the river on your right, you will pass the bridge; although the route does not go over it, the bridge offers a great vantage point.

Estaing to St-Côme d'Olt

Shortly after leaving Estaing the road moves away from the river so you are no longer such close companions. 4km after Estaing you will be able to see the Château de Calmont d'Olt on your right-hand side perched on top of the hill. From its vantage point at 500m it commands a view across the whole valley. A castle has been on the site since the 9th-century with a second wave of construction during The Hundred Years' War.

It was abandoned in the 16th-century and has been a site of archaeological exploration since the 1980s. Now a tourist attraction, Calmont d'Olt employs medieval military techniques and tools to stage re-enactments of life in a castle when under siege.

The outskirts of Espalion are slightly more commercial than anything you have seen so far but the road itself remains quiet. As you approach the town itself, turn left at the T-junction signposted St-Geniez d'Olt, then immediately after take the right fork to St-Côme d'Olt and St-Geniez d'Olt, D987.

Espalion itself is to the right at the T-junction. It has a medieval bridge similar to that at Estaing, but perhaps its most interesting attraction is the museum of scuba diving housed in a former church.

The inventors of scuba diving equipment were born near Espalion and the first attempts took place in the Lot river. Benedict Rouquayrol was a mining engineer who developed equipment used in the rescue of miners, including a regulator to control air-flow.

A naval officer, Auguste Denayrouze, then realised its potential for underwater rescue. Between them they developed the first pressurised gas cylinder with personal regulator and mouthpiece, similar to those used today.

4km after leaving Espalion turn right for St-Côme d'Olt village, signposted Lassouts, D6. To access the village itself take the second side-road to the left. St-Côme d'Olt is the first of the stage's *plus beaux villages*. Here you will find a pleasant square with several cafés and a water fountain. On market day, Fridays and Sundays, this whole street is lined with food stalls. A gourmet picnic can be put together with the fresh fruit and vegetables, local cheese, meats and breads on offer. The route by-passes the village taking you over the Lot, the river now remaining on your left for the rest of the day.

St-Côme d'Olt to Ste-Eulalie d'Olt

After crossing the bridge the road remains flat for 2km before beginning a gentle curve upwards. To your left is a view of St-Côme d'Olt, where the road begins to climb.

THE LEGEND OF AVEYRON

A tragic tale of young love haunts the Chapelle del Dol, with the same classic plot-line of star-crossed lovers that forms the basis of many fairy tales and plays.

The Lord of Estaing's young daughter has fallen in love with the youthful son of his neighbour, the Lord of Vallon.

However the Lord of Estaing has already promised his daughter to Baron de Thénières, an older man with an unpleasant and harsh character.

Vowing that they would remain faithful and would see each other again, the two young lovers are then separated.

When the Baron discovers plans for them to meet in secret, he destroys the middle arch of the bridge across the Lot that Lord Vallon would be crossing. In the dark, the young man falls into the river and is drowned.

At the request of his daughter, the Lord of Estaing buries the young man at the place where his body was found, and builds a chapel on top of his tomb. A hermit is then employed to pray for the two families.

The young girl, prostrate with grief, dies soon after her lover, and the pair are now said to haunt the chapel.

You can't see the river itself at this point but a line of bright-green birches marks its passage. The climb is a gentle one and on a sweeping right-hand bend you can see across to the opposite hillside and the village of Sonilhac. Cascading down the slopes, its narrow line of houses tumbles to the river.

8km after leaving St-Côme d'Olt the continual but gentle climbing takes you to the village of Lassouts. A hotel with ivy-covered terrace provides a good rest-point after the climb. A further 2.5km takes you to another small hamlet with a second hotel. From here the road flattens for 3km before the descent begins. As with the route up, the gradient is gentle allowing you to free-wheel round the bends, with time to enjoy the views of fields and chestnut trees that line the road-side. Between the trees you can see the rolling hills continuing on into the distance.

Near the start of the descent there is a section of flowing bends, then as the road straightens you will reach a crossroads

where you turn left, signed Ste-Eulalie d'Olt 5km, D988. Another series of flowing bends greets you, with the last one almost coming fully back on itself, then after this final bend the road straightens out for a final 3km of descending. Here it is possible to pick up some speed on the narrow roads. Steep-sided banks and more dense forestry obscures your view until you reach the bottom where you need to turn left into the medieval village of Ste-Eulalie d'Olt, D597. If you want to skip this village you can continue on the D988 but Ste-Eulalie d'Olt is listed as one of France's *plus beaux villages* so it is a worthwhile deviation.

Ste-Eualie d'Olt to St-Geniez d'Olt

Narrow twisty streets are bedecked with flowers and the many artists that live in the village have left their mark on the décor of the buildings. The community project, Ste-Eulalie d'Art, is designed to increase the importance of creativity within the village and make it a centre of artistic excellence. There is a small school of arts and one local artist, Marcel Boudou, has a museum and gallery to display his work. This, in addition to its 11th-century church, 15th-century château and water-mill make Ste-Eulalie a delightful place to explore.

The small village hosts many events throughout the year, with the most colourful and spectacular an enactment of the crucifixion on the second Sunday in July.

The church's reliquary holds a fragment of Christ's crown of thorns, which is the centrepiece of the event. There is a procession in period costume followed by a feast, entertainment and fireworks; everyone in the village takes part and the activities last the entire weekend.

The road meanders its way through the village, emerging again at a T-junction with the D988, where you turn left for St-Geniez d'Olt. The road drags up for 1km before you arrive on the outskirts. You approach the town through an avenue of trees, then keep right at the junction staying on the D988 signposted Centre Ville. After another 500m the stage ends at the crossroads outside the Hôtel de France.

St-Geniez d'Olt

While not as immediately attractive as other *d'Olt* villages, f you deviate from the route to go deeper into St-Geniez-d'Olt, more is revealed to you. The *terrain de boules* near to the *office de tourisme* and war memorial is a quiet restful spot beneath the trees, and there is an architecturally interesting mix of buildings surrounding it. St-Geniez d'Olt sits astride the Lot river with parts of the town on either side. It holds a privileged position between the Aubrac, a volcanic granite plateau, and the limestone plateau of the Grands Causses. If you look carefully this can be seen in the mix of building materials used in the older houses of the town. The emblem of St-Geniez d'Olt is the marmot, and local legend has it that two children of a fisherman caught a young marmot to keep as a pet. When a huge storm brewed the marmot ran away in fear and the children chased after it, only to find on returning a flood had washed away their home but the marmot had saved them from drowning with it.

Visit the bridge linking the two sides of the town and above you will see the white pillars of a mausoleum, commissioned by Marie Talabot, an orphan of the town to avenge herself of the humiliation she experienced there. The young Marie left St-Geniez d'Olt to live in Marseille where she met Paulin Talabot, noted railway engineer and pioneer who founded the Paris-Lyon-Méditerranée company. Once married she became an important member of Parisian society. After many years she returned to visit St-Geniez d'Olt but her vast entourage and grand ways did not go down well with the townspeople who remembered her as a starving orphan. For the real, or imagined, slights she received, she decided to buy the castle above the town, raze it to the ground and build an ornate mausoleum. She is alleged to have declared, ' You looked down on me in my life, but I shall look down on you in my death'.

Sleep

Hotel

Hôtel de France

A welcoming family-run, 3-star hotel within walking distance of all the main attractions of the town.

18 Place Du Général De Gaulle,
12130 St-Geniez d'Olt
00 33 (0)5 65 70 42 20
www.hotel-saint-geniez-dolt.com

Chambre d'Hôtes

Christiane et Claude Saleil

A small *chambre d'hôtes* where you will share the table with your hosts and enjoy a hearty breakfast of their homemade breads and jams.

58 Chemin du Séminaire,
12130 St-Geniez d'Olt
00 33 (0)5 65 47 52 00

Campsite

Camping Campéole La Boissière

Continue on the D988 and the site is sign posted to the left. A pretty spot surrounded by trees and close to the river.

Route de la Cascade, St-Geniez d'Olt
00 33(0)5 65 70 40 43

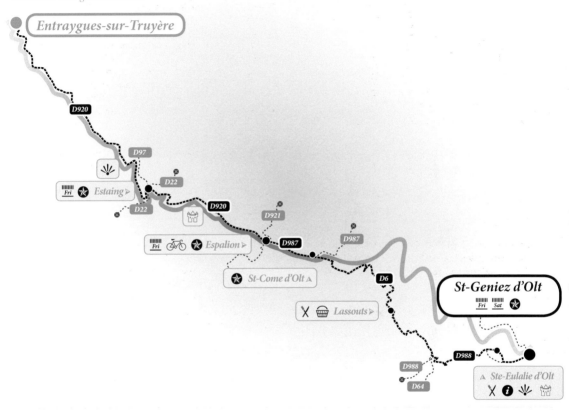

Supplies

Food

A reasonable size town, St-Geniez has everything you could want and there is a large supermarket on the road in from Ste-Eulalie d'Olt. There is a farmers' market every Saturday but you may see occasional small stalls in the car park outside the *mairie* on any day of the week.

Bike

Durao joaquim

Selling everything from tractors to high-end road bikes, this multi-purpose store will be able to solve any problems and sell you spares.

Durao joaquim
3 place pierre frontin
12500 Espalion
00 33 (0)5 65 48 02 36

Eat

Le Lion d'Or

A 2-star hotel with 2restaurants offering different atmospheres: one intimate with a huge 16th-century fireplace; the other a bigger more airy room. The food is regional but with an occasional imaginative twist from the chef.

Place de l'Hôtel de Ville,
12130 St-Geniez d'Olt
00 33 (0)5 65 47 43 32
www.leliondor-stgeniezdolt.com

ST-GENIEZ D'OLT TO MENDE

Stage 20: *41miles 66km*

Small tree-covered hills above St-Geniez d'Olt are a warm-up before the more testing roads above Marvejols, where they become small mountains. As you enter wolf country beware the 'Beast of Gévaudan' snapping at your heels as you conquer your first climb of the trip over 1,000 metres.

St-Geniez d'Olt to Banassac

Starting from outside the Hôtel de France, continue towards St-Laurent d'Olt on the D988. Here, the road begins to climb very gently and you exit the town via an avenue of trees. On leaving town the gradient increases slightly, and the climb winds its way up for 2km.

In the breaks in the trees you can see the rounded shapes of other similarly high hills dotted all around. After 2km of easy climbing the road takes a downward turn for 2km, snaking its way between the chestnut trees, before beginning to climb once again.

For the next 4 km you gradually gain height, and open fields interspersed with small outcrops of woodland are the only sights. Occasionally a field of cows might offer you some encouragement, but other than their mooing there is little to break the silence. After 4km of climbing you reach the tiny hamlet of La Crouzette, little more than a farmstead and a couple of buildings set back from the road. Whilst the countryside is idyllic, there is a sense of isolation – these small homes are surrounded by rolling fields and hillsides as far as you can see.

From here the road drops away again, a slightly longer and faster descent this time. Pale-green light from the sun shining on the canopy of leaves above and deep dense shadows pattern the road. Keep your eyes peeled for the old Suze advert painted onto the end wall of a building. This is another sign you are heading south; pastis becomes more popular the nearer you get to Provence. By the time you are in the true south you will spot pastis drinkers propping up the bar in every café from early morning onwards.

At the T-junction, turn left towards St-Laurent d'Olt 3km, D988. The road is wider here but traffic remains scarce. The trees disperse to give you a view of the river-valley below and the lumpy outlines of hillsides. A low wall separates you from the drop to the river beneath. Stay on the D988, passing the side roads that take you up into the village itself.

The road forms a loop, mirroring the meander of the river it runs parallel to. You feel almost as if you are coming back on yourself but, at the end of the loop, a stone bridge

163

takes you across the river. Once over the bridge a left-hand turn takes you down to a picnic area where an off-road path takes you under the bridge to a small beach, complete with brightly coloured changing huts to rival Brighton beach – a perfect place for a paddle or even a swim.

After crossing the bridge the route remains on the D988 and from here the valley flattens out. Open fields bordered with forest-covered hillsides line the valley floor. The road is predominantly straight and flat. Homes occasionally dot the roadside and for a short while the railway runs alongside the road. 8.5km after leaving St-Laurent d'Olt you approach the hamlet of Banassac where the road passes under the A75 *autoroute*. After riding under the A75 road-bridge, fork left signed St-Germain du Teil (the right fork is the slipway onto the A75). Immediately after the fork, at the T-junction, turn left onto the D809.

Banassac to Le Monastier

1.5km after leaving Banassac you will arrive at a roundabout, then continue on the D809 toward Monastier and Chanac. Immediately after the roundabout you will pass a sign announcing you are on the Route de Gévaudan. This was the old name for this region. The route covers the area that was once terrorised by a huge beast, most likely a wolf, that in the 1770s was responsible for over a hundred human deaths.

The road continues to follow the line of the river, although it is not always visible, for the next 7km. The railway is now on your right-hand side, sandwiched between the road and the river: three means of travel and communication running parallel. Shortly after entering the hamlet of Les Ajustons you cross over the railway line, and immediately at the next junction turn left on the D809 signed Monastier and Marvejols, then cross over the railway line again. The N88 to your right signed Mende will get you to the end of the stage more quickly but you will miss out on a beautiful quiet climb and you will have to contend with much more traffic.

This D809 was once the main road and the many disused buildings on the road sides attest to a time when it was a much busier route. Thanks to the N88 there is only a small amount of traffic but the road remains wide and the tarmac silky smooth. The N88 bridge, carries all the traffic, allowing you to pedal in peace, and it makes a dramatic silhouette as it straddles the skyline above. Beneath the bridge a sign tells you that your current height is 600 metres,

LA BETE DU GEVAUDAN

Between 1764 and 1770 the people of Gévaudan were terrorised by a wolf-like creature that ripped out the throats of its victims, drank their blood and left their partially eaten bodies behind. Far from being a mythic tale with no basis in reality, parish registers reveal that the beast was responsible for 113 deaths and 49 injuries.

The beast preyed on children when they were carrying out farming duties in isolated pastures. During one spate of attacks someone was killed everyday. Animals went untended, markets were cancelled and people stayed indoors. Such was the impact on the region that King Louis XV ordered the army to find and kill it but even they failed.

In January 1765, a story moved the entire country. A twelve-year-old shepherd boy, Jacques Portefaix, accompanied by four boys and two girls, was attacked whilst out in the fields. Though severely injured the boys held off attacks by the beast and survived. Word was passed to the king and each child was rewarded for their bravery and their education paid for by the state .

Despite the efforts of the army and wolf-hunters, attacks continued until a local man, Jean Chastel, finally managed to make the kill. When the beast was cut open they found in its belly the remains of a woman eaten the previous day. You will see images of the beast around the region, particularly in Marvejols. The subject of serious academic studies to fairy tales and children's books the beast is still used as a threat to naughty children who need to learn to behave!

between here and the highest point of the stage you will gain another 400metres in height.

The road begins to climb steadily in fairly undramatic fashion, but gradually the railway line to your right will begin to drop away as you start to gain height. 1km after passing under the N88 bridge you arrive at a roundabout, where you go straight across, signed Le Monastier, D809. Just as you enter Le Monastier there is a station on your right-hand side with connections to Mende.

Le Monastier to Marvejols

Stay on the D809 through Le Monastier, which blends into the pretty town of Chirac. As you emerge from Chirac the road once again picks up a river, the Colagne, a tributary of the Lot, following it as far as Marvejols. Rugged rock outcrops line the left side of the road whilst the river accompanies you on the right. 1km after leaving Chirac you will spot a lovely riverside picnic area – perfect if you need a rest to break up the climb.

3km after leaving Chirac you will arrive on the edge of Marvejols. At the roundabout follow signs for Centre Ville. As you continue towards the town, straight in front of you is the ancient fortified gateway to the town centre, the Porte de Chanelles. Marvejols once had status as the capital of the Gévaudan region and is twinned with Cockermouth in the English Lake District. Through this gateway you will find a selection of small shops, many of them selling books and maps, and in particular a second-hand book shop with many dusty but valuable finds for a determined browser. In the book shops you are likely to find many titles dedicated to *La Bête de Gévaudan*, the fearsome animal that once roamed the hillsides.

Marvejols to Mende

There are very few settlements on this stretch, so now is the time to stock up if you need supplies. Follow the road past the entrance gate until you get to a small roundabout, then turn right for Montrodat D999. Cross over the river and turn immediately right signed Montrodat D1.

Within 1.5km, just as you pass the sign denoting that you have left Marvejols, you will see La Domaine de Carrière, a former hunting lodge now a *chambre d'hôtes* and restaurant on your left. 1km after the lodge you arrive at a roundabout and turn right for Mende 19km, D1. The road is fairly flat as it passes between small farmsteads and fields dropping away to the river.

1.5 km after the roundabout turn right on the D42 signed Mende, now amazingly marked as 20km. The turning for the D42 is on the apex of the bend as the D1 sweeps round to the left. The D42 is a more minor road, narrower, with no road markings and a slightly rougher surface. Within 1km you cross over a narrow stone bridge with the river Coulagnet running beneath and then the climb begins.

The road surface is littered with the names of riders as this is part of Le Tour du Gévaudan that takes place in September every year. It's an important event locally with big-name teams, such as Crédit Agricole and Cofidis, sending their development squad or second-string riders to compete against the very best of regional French and Spanish teams. The climb lasts for just 2.5km, so it's not long but requires pacing. It is a lovely wooded climb but undeniably the toughest of the trip so far and the names on the road contribute to the sensation that you are now into the type of terrain beloved by serious cyclists. The sign at the viewpoint at the hamlet of Goudard provides a spot height of 1020m, the first time over 1000m on your journey.

In Goudard follow the sign for Mende 16km, D42. After Goudard the road kicks up slightly to the summit, with a cross marking the top. There is a clear view over the lower hills and mountains in the distance, so pause here to catch your breath and take stock of how high you have climbed before beginning the descent. This is where the payback arrives for your climbing and the reward is greater than the

effort you put in. Be careful if you are travelling with heavy panniers as less than 1km into the descent is a section of 12% gradient which feels very steep. When you reach the hamlet of Velcroze, 2km into the descent, remain on the D42.

5km from the summit you will reach a T-junction; turn left signed Mende D42, 2.5km of flat riding follows before a switchback signals the start of a new climb. This one is just under 1km and reaches only 890m at the top so it is not the beast the first climb was. Once the top is attained you begin the final 5km descent into Mende, remaining on the D42 the whole way.

Arriving in Mende

Mende has grown and developed in its role as the capital of the *département* of Lozère, with housing and business creeping up the sides of the valley from below as the town seeks space for expansion. From here you can see the spire of the cathedral poking up above the many buildings of this busy working town.

Following signs for Centre Ville, the road takes you over the river and toward a large roundabout; again follow signs for Centre Ville straight on. Bike shop Planète 2 Roues is to your right here and one of the best shops on the route. At the second roundabout follow signs for Centre Ville straight on, and you will start to see the spire of the cathedral ahead of you. Continue into the town, staying right to follow signs for Toutes Directions and Office de Tourisme for the next stage. This stage of the route ends here at the junction in front of the cathedral.

Mende is a small city nestled in the heart of remote mountainous countryside, making it a popular spot for those who want to experience both lifestyles. Its centre-piece is the 14th-century Gothic cathedral, Notre-Dame-et-St-Privat de Mende, which can be seen for miles from every approach to the city. Mende's real growth period was

during the middle ages, when it provided a gateway for trade and communications, but it suffered badly during the Wars of Religion and never recovered its previous status.

This is the biggest town used as a stage-end on this route, aside from Nice, but it is not crowded. It has a wide selection of bars, restaurants and cafés from the excellent restaurant in the Hôtel de France to basic pizza. The choice can be overwhelming when you have have become used to the simple facilities found in the villages.

It is easy to forget you are in the foothills of the mountains, but the air in Mende can be fresh, even chilly on a summer's morning, as the town sits at 700m.

INDULGE

Le Domaine de Carrière
A former hunting lodge in Marvejols has been transformed into a very chic *chambre d'hôtes* and restaurant. Decorated with sleek contemporary design to complement the original woodwork and floors, the overall effect is stunning simplicity with the occasional surprise.

Dotted throughout there are unusual pieces of modern Western and Japanese art. The grounds have been designed as a haven of tranquillity with secret gardens and walks. The restaurant is in the old stables and head chef, Ramón Carmona, brings a twist of Spanish cuisine to the traditional dishes of the Lozère region.

Quartier de l'Empéry, 48100 Marvejols
00 33 (0)4 66 32 47 05
www.domainedecarriere.com

Sleep

Hotel
Hôtel de France
Beautifully presented rooms and a fantastic restaurant, make this a relaxing place to stay. Great breakfasts set you up for your next ride.
9 Bd Lucien Arnault, 48000 Mende
00 33 (0)4 66 55 00 04
www.hoteldefrance-mende.com

Chambre d'Hôtes
Manoir de L'Esplanade
An elegant manor house, once a grand family home, with several large airy rooms, some with balconies. It is set in well-maintained gardens and there is a pool and spa area.
00 33 (0)4 66 32 40 27
14 Chemin de Mascoussel, 48100 Marvejols
www.manoir-esplanade.com

Campsite
Camping Sirvens
A lovely campsite set amongst the trees with a mountain backdrop. Facilities are basic but the site is peaceful and relaxing. There are no designated pitches so you can choose where to set up amongst the open fields and trees.
Route de Badaroux, 48000 Mende
00 33 (0)4 66 65 16 93

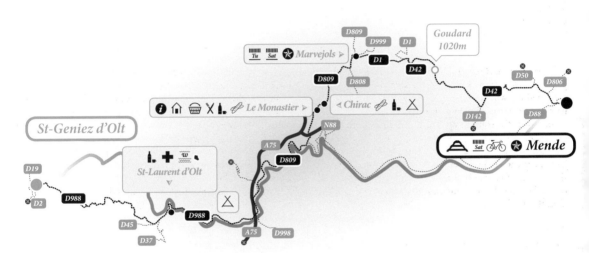

Supplies

Food
Mende has everything you might need from small *boulangeries* to larger supermarkets. There are excellent specialist food shops tucked into the narrow alleys and the farmers' market on Saturday is a real treat with fresh fruit, vegetables and local cheese.

Bike
Planète 2 Roues & Espace Bike
Mende has not one, but two of the best bike shops on the entire route. Any emergency will be catered for and browsing needs will be satified.

Planète 2 Roues,
5 Avenue du Pont Roupt, 48000 Mende
00 33 (0)4 66 49 17 00
www.planete2roues.com

Espace Bike
34 Route du Chapitre, 48000 Mende
00 33 (0)4 66 65 01 81

Eat

Les Voûtes
Within the vaults of a former convent, this family-run restaurant offers well-presented regional cuisine in an atmospheric setting.
13 rue Aigues Passes, 48000 Mende
00 33 (0)4 66 49 00 05
www.restaurant-les-voutes-mende.fr

Drink

Tucked away down a tunnel off Rue Basse, L'Osmoz is a lively small bar serving good quality, well-prepared food and highly recommended cocktails. It has an interesting mix of architecture: the exposed stonework of the roof and tunnel contrasts with the coloured lighting and modern bar décor.

CEVENNES - ARDECHE

TACKLE the wooded slopes of the Col des Tribes, the highest point of the journey outside Provence.

CYCLE in the tracks of the Tour de France as you head into the hills around bike-mad Mende.

DESCEND the seemingly never-ending road down to Villefort for a virtually pedal-free 25km.

SWIM under the iconic limestone arch of Pont d'Arc, the gateway to the Gorges de l'Ardèche.

ARRIVE in the south, and feel the warm air of the Ardèche washing over you as you descend from the cool Cévennes.

TWIST along the tight route through the limestone landscape above the Gorges du Chassezac.

MENDE ⓉⓄ VILLEFORT

Stage 21: *35miles 57km*

A stage of two halves. Leaving the capital of the *département* of Lozère, the route climbs gently following the Lot river virtually to its source at the Col des Tribes (1,130m). The route then descends gradually from the highest point of the trip outside Provence for a fantastic 25km. You rarely have to turn the pedals as the bike glides through the forest-clad slopes of the northern edge of the Parc National des Cévennes to the tree-lined main avenue of Villefort.

Mende to Col de la Tourette

Mende is easily navigated if treated as a big roundabout. Facing the square and cathedral, follow the road uphill to your right. This dual lane, one-way street keeps traffic flow encircling Mende's centre.

Follow the one-way system round until you see signs for Le Puy and Aubenas, fork to the right here at the second significant right turn. The route follows the N88 gradually upwards for 8km. In 2010 the Tour de France came down this road, finishing a gruelling 210km hilly stage in Mende.

The riders benefited from the luxury of a closed road, which you may be wishing for, as this stretch can be busy, but the route soon peels off south-east. With few villages or habitation the next few kilometres are amongst the most remote riding of the whole trip.

The first 3km along the N88 are relatively flat passing a string of sawmills, cutting the plentiful pine that covers the surrounding hillsides, before climbing gently for 2km to the village of Badaroux. If you have forgotten to stock up in Mende, Badaroux has a small supermarket and *boulangerie*. The road dips down for 1km then rises up for 2km to the top of the Col de la Tourette at 839m.

Col de la Tourette to Bagnols-les-Bains

At the col, turn right signed Le Bleymard, D901, a fantastic road that you will follow all the way to Villefort, alongside the river Lot. It then heads upwards to the Col des Tribes before following the river Altier down to the Lac du Villefort, just before the stage end. The road starts with a fairly steep 2km descent to the bottom of the Lot valley. Take care at a level crossing and then over the river.

From here the overall trend is up, with the Col des Tribes 20km away just after Le Bleymard. However, the are some flat meadow sections and even the odd bit of down, making the climbing very manageable, even if your pannier is laden with a guitar or the kitchen sink! The Tour rarely comes this way when it visits the region as the road isn't big enough, and the area too rural for its supporting commercial caravan. But the riders miss a treat on these relatively undiscovered roads.

From the valley bottom the road winds its way gently up

171

for 3km to the hamlet of Ste-Hélène through a wooded valley with the piercing scent of pine dominating its deciduous neighbours. After Ste-Hélène the route climbs slightly for a further 1km, before a suggestion of a descent into meadows with wooded hills either side of the valley. The road stays in the meadows which are dotted with contented cows gazing at their lush green surroundings.

There is a barely noticeable incline for 5km to Bagnols-les-Bains. The air is fresh and crisp providing clean refreshing gulps of oxygen as you pedal along. The various shades of green from fields and trees reflect the plentiful rainfall this area receives. After Brittany this stage is where you have the highest chance of getting wet on your ride, as the weather can be changeable

If you are unlucky enough to be caught in rain or simply would like a break, Bagnols-les Bains is a small spa town with a tempting *station thermale* though the Romans clearly weren't thinking of St-Malo to Nice cyclists when they founded the baths, as it interrupts your ascent of the Col des Tribes.

Bagnols-les-Bains to Col des Tribes

Leaving Bagnols-les-Bains you cross the Lot river and continue gently climbing alongside its northern banks. The Lot is now a more modest river but can still be heard babbling above the noise of the crickets. Frequent kilometre stones marking the altitude appear on the roadside, ticking off progress towards the Col des Tribes. After 3km you pass the village of St-Julien-du-Tournel, off to your right contained within a meander in the Lot. A further 1km later the road passes through a tunnel underneath the *Château du Tournel*, an austere and imposing castle despite its ruined state, which guards the entrance to the upper valley as the sides steepen.

In a further 5km beyond the tunnel, you arrive in Le Bleymard, marked by a large sawmill on the right-hand side. The residential area is off to the right, but you pass all the facilities on the main road. If riding past in the morning, it's worth a coffee stop at the Hôtel Restaurant La Remise on your left just before the small supermarket, if only to see the importance of such small towns as a hub, keeping this remote rural community of outlying hillside hamlets and farmsteads together. Usually a handful of local loggers chat at the bar over beer, *petits blancs* and coffee at all hours of the day.

Winters can be harsh up here in the shadow of Mont Lozère, which at 1,699m looms large to the south of the town, carpeted completely in pine forests. Mont Lozère is the highest point in the Massif Central, excluding the extinct

MENDE AND THE TOUR DE FRANCE

As you climb gradually out of Mende, imagine you were here on the 16th July 2010 as a peloton of hundreds of pro riders would be swooping towards you at over 50 miles an hour.

By this point the peloton had over 200km in their legs, as stage 12 of the Tour de France made its way to the finish in Mende with riders jostling for position. As with many stages of the Tour, there was a sting in the tail. The ride continued past the tight streets of Mende's centre and up the Croix Neuve, a 5km climb, gaining over 300m in height with pitches of 14% to Mende aerodrome at 1,050m on a small flat plateau south of the town. You may have caught a glimpse of it as you descended into Mende on the previous stage.

Alberto Contador had earlier attacked race leader Andy Schlek, taking 10 seconds off his main rival's time. He contested the sprint on the aerodrome with fellow Spaniard Joaquim Rodriquez, who won the stage in front of thousands high above this cycling-mad town. The cycling scene around Mende is not of the tourist variety like at Alpe d'Huez. It is a very well respected area amongst local teams and French riders for its quiet roads and range of long gentle climbs and descents, some fine examples of which you will ride on this stage.

volcanoes of the Auvergne, and warm southerly winds never quite reach Le Bleymard, which is often chilly even on the most glorious summer's day so it's worth having a layer handy for the descent. If you needed further indicators that you are in the mountains, note the signs to a small ski station nearby.

It's 3km beyond Le Bleymard to the Col des Tribes. After 2km you say goodbye to the Lot whose valley you have both loosely and intimately followed for over 200km. It is now a small stream that descends from your left with little fish darting about. Its source is just a few hundred metres above here on the Montagne du Goulet. The final 1km to the col at 1,130m is surprisingly gentle, as is the land, its high meadows some of the best pasture around. Drink in the awesome scenery and perhaps a bit from your water bottle as you will probably need it. Absorb the beauty of the northern edge of the Cévennes and celebrate your achievement of reaching the highest distinctive mountain pass of the whole route.

STATION THERMALE

Bagnols-les-Bains has been a spa town since Roman times. Its thermal waters are a constant 41 degrees and their healing properties are still recognised today. It is common for French doctors to prescribe *'une cure thermale'* for respiratory, arthritic and allergic conditions.

Under French health insurance schemes, patients are entitled to such a prescription and a stay at a *'centre thermal'*, such as Bagnols-les-Bains, totally free of charge.

It's also open to passing cyclists for massages without a prescription.

Col des Tribes to Lac du Villefort

What follows is one of the most exhilirating 25km of the whole trip as the road descends to the Lac du Villefort. A little pedalling will go a long way, enabling you to take in the scenery and enjoy a thrilling, twisting descent. It would seem rude to interrupt this section with any stops, but make sure you take in the wild yet secluded and intimate surroundings of the Altier valley. As you are flying along keep an eye out for roadworks. In winter, the road is susceptible to landslides, which local road crews often spend summer repairing.

If you wish to break up your flow down the valley for a breather there are a few diversions. 13km after the top, inside a large, sweeping right-hander, you will just notice the tower of the Château de Champ protruding above the trees. 1km further on, the village of Altier has camping facilities and a hotel. A further 7km is the Château de Castanet, spared from being submerged in the lake it overlooks by being designated a *monument historique* in the 1960s.

2km after the château are great views over the lake, back to the castle on the right. This is shortly before the route passes under the railway viaduct, which crosses the lake before the road. After crossing the lake it's just under 2km to some perfect picnic spots on the Lac du Villefort. The lake is well-stocked with trout and you may be sharing your spot with a fisherman trying to catch his supper.

Lac du Villefort to Villefort

At the mini-roundabout where the lake curves to your left, take the first exit signed Villefort 1.5km, D901. It is a quick 1.5km down.

Watch out for a sharp right-hander after crossing the river before the road becomes the Avenue de Cévennes, the main artery going uphill through the *centre ville*, each side lined with a perfect row of trees, where this stage ends. To carry on to the next stage, simply continue pedalling up the main street.

On your right there are many places to eat with dining terraces spilling onto the street. Villefort can be a hive of activity, with conversations echoing off the walls of the buildings that line the main avenue, as locals pass between the independently owned shops and cafés.

At night-time it is a quiet town, with just the sound of leaves rustling in the breeze. chatter and glasses chinking eminating from the street side cafes..

Few tourists visit this area which remains unfamiliar to all but a handful of walkers completing *randonnées* in the hills, and in-the-know mountain bikers raiding the steep wooded slopes that rise above the town.

Even though Villefort stands at only 575m, you have a real sense of being in a rural mountain town a world away from the more developed Alpine resorts.

Sleep

Hotel

Hôtel Balme

Villefort is not well endowed with hotels. For more choice pedal on to the next stage and Pont d'Arc. The Balme is the only 2-star option in town.

Place du Portalet, 48800 Villefort

00 33 (0)4 66 46 80 14

www.hotelbalme.online.fr

Chambre d'Hôte

Mas de l'Affenadou

If there's less than a dozen of you, head here for one of four individually styled rooms. A 16th-century former farmhouse, it captures the true nature of the area. The only things that might disturb you are the crickets!

Nelly Monifacier, La Vignette, 48800 Villefort

00 (0)4 66 46 97 23

www.gite-lozere.com

Campsite

Camping du Lac

Just under 3km north of Villefort on the shores of the lake, this large campsite has a wide range of facilities, including restaurant and laundry. There is a designated swimming area in the lake nearby.

48800 Villefort

00 33 (0)4 66 46 81 27

www.camping-lac-cevennes.com

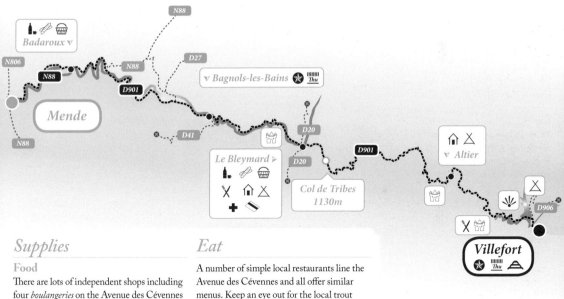

Supplies

Food

There are lots of independent shops including four *boulangeries* on the Avenue des Cévennes alone, and a well-stocked small supermarket. The market is held on Thursday mornings and specialises in local delicacies made with chestnuts and walnuts, such as *moelleux aux châtaignes* and *sables aux noisettes*.

Eat

A number of simple local restaurants line the Avenue des Cévennes and all offer similar menus. Keep an eye out for the local trout from the Lac de Villefort.

VILLEFORT ⓉⓄ PONT D'ARC

Stage 22: *40miles 64km*

A defining day when you truly arrive in the South of France, starting with the climb of the Col du Mas de l'Ayre before descending through the cool pine forests of the Cévennes to the warm valleys of the Ardèche crammed with vineyards and fruit orchards. The ride finishes at the stunning Pont d'Arc at the gateway to the Gorge d'Ardèche.

Villefort to Col du Mas de l'Ayre

The toughest part of the stage is the first 1km after Villefort. Continue up the main tree-lined Avenue des Cévennes, before climbing a further seven far more gentle kilometres through the wooded slopes to the Col du Mas de l'Ayre (846m).

On your right as you leave Villefort, inconspicuous above the public toilets in Place du Port, is a raised platform. On this platform on 13th July 1794 local priest Abbé Hilaire was executed for opposing the French Revolution of 1789 and voicing Villefort's royalist leanings.

As the road passes underneath the railway bridge on the edge of town, the route ramps up until it reaches possibly one of the most picturesquely located roundabouts in France. In a lofty position it affords great views of the slopes of the Cévennes to the south blanketed entirely in trees. Take the last exit at the roundabout signed Les Vans 23km, D901, the road continues climbing but significantly more gradually.

It's tempting to just get your head down and pedal to celebrate the relief of the friendlier gradient, but as the road winds up to the col ensure you look to the right occasionally to peer deep into the heart of central Cévennes, its banks of forest-clad mountain ridges with vibrant green sweet chestnuts shouting out from amongst the darker pines.

4km after the roundabout when entering the Forêt Domaniale du Mas de l'Ayre, you make a short visit to the département of Gard for 10km saying *au revoir* to the département of Lozère. Reflecting on the hilly last few stages, as you approach the summit, it is easy to understand why the Lozère is known as the 'département des sources'. In its mountains many of the significant rivers in this corner of France begin their journey as springs.

6km after the roundabout the road turns a sharp left-hander and the views of mountain ridges disappear, the forest becomes thicker and the verges of the road are littered with pine cones. When you pass a zip wire and activity park on your left you are only 1km away from the top.

The top of the climb is completely forested, with piles of logs stacked in lay-bys awaiting transportation. Take a lung full of the fresh, pine-scented air as you will soon be descending into warmer, Mediterranean-influenced, Ardèche.

177

LE PARC NATIONAL DES CEVENNES

The route skirts the northern edge of the Parc National which was created in 1970 and sits at the southern edge of the Massif Central. It is a mass of deep valleys with clear, winding rivers and hilltops covered in sweet chestnut, *châtaigniers*, known locally as *l'arbre à pain*. In the past they were the main source of food and trade, carrying the same importance as bread.

With renewed interest in traditional cuisine, the chestnut orchards are viable again. Not so the mulberry which is still visible and was planted in the 19th century to feed the silk worms bred in mills called *magnaneries*, another previous source of wealth. Today the Cévennes relies on a trickle of tourists – one of the less well-known and spectacularly wild national parks where wolves still roam.

The Cévennes has been attracting wanderers and those in search of solitude for years. Robert Louis Stevenson wrote a book about walking through them with a donkey named Modestine. This was *Travels with a Donkey in the Cévennes*, written in 1879, four years before his famous *Treasure Island*. Today you can retrace his footsteps on 'Le Chemin de Stevenson' part of the GR70. It covers 220km from Monastier-sur-Gazeille in the north of the Massif Central to St-Jean-du-Gard to the south. His path crossed the St-Malo to Nice route in Le Bleymard.

The name Cévennes is regularly used to describe a much wider area of mountains not just the National Park.

Col du Mas de l'Ayre to Les Vans

An enthralling 16km descent takes you from the top of the col into the small town of Les Vans in the *département* of Ardèche, as you lose nearly 700m in altitude that you have been gaining since leaving Entraygues. This is the biggest single height drop until you plunge towards the Mediterranean from the final summit on the last stage.

The descent is densely wooded on either side as it twists its way downwards tucked into the mountain side. Your brief stay in the Gard ends 5km after the summit.

Keep your eye out for the occasional glimpse of the cycling mecca Mont Ventoux, the *Géant de Provence*, in the distance as you descend. 10km into your descent it's worth stopping to gorge on cherries and juicy peaches, sold direct from the producer at roadside tables throughout the summer season. The lower slopes of the descent are less forested and occasionally terraced for fruit orchards.

To your left are glimpses of more gently sloping sandstone sundrenched hills, providing fertile soil for market gardens and occasional vineyards amongst dispersed hamlets housing generations of farmers. A cacophony of crickets provides a chorus to the lower part of your descent.

The warm air from the Ardèche battles with cool forest air as you descend gradually through the trees, until suddenly as you near Les Vans the wafts of warm air turn into waves and it feels like someone has turned the heating on. Welcome to the South!

Les Vans

Trees lining a straight avenue guide you on your last 1km into Les Vans and to the town square. At the square follow the one-way street keeping in the right-hand lane forking uphill signed St-Ambroix, D901, at the Bar des Sports. Keep in the left lane at this point if you wish to visit the old streets and the Place du Marché.

Les Vans is situated at a crossroads on the southern side of a flattish basin which is spliced by the Chassezac river – a subtle blend of the wooded Cévennes and the drier scrubland of the Ardèche surround the town.

To continue on the route climb the narrow one-way street. After 200m you pass Le Temple Rond, a rare Protestant church on your right similar to the unusual round church found in Bowmore, Islay, in Scotland.

Its circular construction meant there were no corners where the devil might lurk. Shortly after, at a roundabout, take the first exit signed Alès, Vallon-Pont-d'Arc, D901.

Les Vans to Chandolas

From the roundabout the road climbs steadily for 3km, then flattens for 2km, offering views of the fringes of the Gorge du Chassezac off to the left. 5km after leaving Les Vans turn left onto a smaller road to Casteljau, 5km D252. The landscape is markedly drier here than the Cévennes as the road twists downwards at a gentle gradient squeezing between mounds of limestone rocks on either side.

Take care as the road is only just over 2m wide in places, but thankfully caravans and campervans are banned in July and August. After just over 4km the road passes a small tarn on the left, ignore the sign to Casteljau immediately after and continue straight on.

The ride between Les Vans and Casteljau takes you through the *Pays de Lumière*, a land of limestone and light astoundingly different to the wooded hills of the Cévennes.

The air of this rugged and rocky land is filled with Mediterranean scents of rosemary and thyme, smells which will become more familiar as you head towards Nice. The surface is distinctly dry as water sinks to the depths through the limestone, meaning only goats and sheep can survive on the surface, evidenced by the dry stone walls and domed-shaped *capitelles*, shepherds' shelters.

Suddenly, after passing the turn-off to Casteljau, the landscape opens as the road spits you out on to the Chassezac valley floor. If you are here in summer you will be greeted by rows of astonishingly bright yellow sunflowers.

After 2.5km of flat pedalling past vineyards, fruit orchards and sunflowers, at a T-junction with a larger road, turn left signed Aubenas, D104. At this point, for a slightly more direct route, it is possible to turn right on the main road and then shortly after left on the D111 to Vallon-Pont-d'Arc. This D111 is lined with Vente Directe du Producteur signs seemingly every 1km, all selling a range of fruits direct from the farm. However this advantage is diminished by the road itself, which is often choked with campervans and cars full of tourists trying to speed past them.

The route described here is the quieter route. After turning left signposted Aubanas, D104, cross the river then turn right on a minor road signed Chandolas 2km, D208, and you spend only half a kilometre on the main road. If you need a bike shop continue straight on for 400m and surprisingly you will find one in the small hamlet of Maisonneuve. It is 2km along the narrow vineyard-lined D208 to the village of Chandolas with the Auberge Dolman, a nod to the ancient stone structures that dot the area.

Chandolas to Ruoms

The route now follows the Chassezac river more closely to Ruoms just north of its rendezvous with the Ardèche before attacking the limestone of the Gorge de l'Ardèche. The limestone that provides excellent sculpting material for water also provides good alkaline conditions for the many vineyards in the area. If you time it right you could forage for figs by the roadside, the Mediterranean climate usually affording them enough sunlight to crop twice a year.

5km after Chandolas the route passes through the village of St-Alban-Auriolles. Just under 2km after St-Alban-Auriolles. after a straight stretch of road surrounded by vineyards, the route passes the Musée Daudet on your left, not only honouring the works of the late-19th-century novelist born in nearby Nîmes, but also offering demonstrations of olive pressing and an insight into the lucrative silk trade built on the servitude of the humble silkworm.

After a further 2km the road crosses the Beaume river which is on its way to join the Ardèche. 1km later turn right onto a bridge crossing the Ardèche itself by an arch closely ressembling the Arc de Triomphe, signed Ruoms 0.5km.

Once over the bridge you are in the busy little tourist town of Ruoms. Follow the main road along a one-way system straight ahead through this small medieval town, founded in the 10th-century.

PONT D'ARC

Over the years the Ardèche river has carved a 30km- gorge through limestone, which you will be able to see from all angles on tomorrow's stage. But the jewel of the gorge is undoubtedly the 54m-high arc that guards the entrance.

Pont d'Arc is unique in France : the only example of a stone arch spanning a river that still flows. The arc was formed as the river sought a more direct channel than its previous long-winded meander as water eroded away at the rock. Eventually it forced a cut-through, which in time expanded into an arch.

The old river channel and meander bend, the former site of the resultant ox-bow lake, is indicated by a distinctively flat and fertile piece of land by the Auberge du Pont d'Arc. The majesty of the arc is best enjoyed in the soft evening light, after the crowds have dispersed, or floating on your back in the river gazing upwards.

By the Elan garage keep straight on signed Vallon-Pont-d'Arc. 2km after crossing the river on the edge of town you will see the enormous grey building of Vignerons Ardéchois the wholesaler and important *dégustation* representing local wine producers. The Vignerons Ardéchois is the largest wine cooperative in the whole of the Ardèche department.

The road swings round to the left, performing a hairpin bend round the back of the building, before reaching a roundabout where you take the first exit which is immediately to your right, signed Vallon-Pont-d'Arc 8km, D579.

Ruoms to Pont d'Arc

Just over 1km after leaving Ruoms, at a roundabout with vines growing on it, take the second exit signed Vallon-Pont-d'Arc, 7km. Shortly after you are united with the Ardèche river.

Carry straight on at the lights that control the flow in and out of the sprawling campsites on the far bank of the river. You are in summer-holiday country now. The road climbs slightly for 1km away from the river. As the first signs of a gorge begin to develop on your right, the road curves to the left onto a 3km flat straight section interrupted by a series of roundabouts.

Continue over the first 4 roundabouts, turning right at the 5th roundabout next to a small football stadium signed Gorges d'Ardèche, D579. For Vallon-Pont-d'Arc *centre ville*, the self-styled tourist gateway to the gorge and its facilities, carry straight on.

If you are likely to need any supplies for the next stage it's a good idea to head in to town to stock up as there are no shops in the next 40km of the ride. There are many overnight options in the town but, if you are looking for a quieter evening and the opportunity for a twilight swim underneath France's largest limestone arch, keep pedalling a further 6km to Pont d'Arc itself.

Continue straight on at the two roundabouts you come to as the route goes around the south of the town. This is camping and canoeing country: both are big business in the summer months and the *raison d'être* for the usually busy road. However, the gorge is popular for a reason and spectacular views are offered from the road, particularly in the next stage. After the ubiquitous canoe outfitters start to thin out, it's 4km to a viewpoint on your right which overlooks the arc itself.

Arriving at Pont d'Arc

The route is squeezed between a cliff and the river, including a series of short tunnels, before passing the Auberge du Pont d'Arc and a campsite shortly before you reach a viewpoint on your right overlooking the huge limestone arch as it straddles the river. To celebrate the completion of your stage head for a dip by retracing your tracks by 200m then following the *sentier pour piétons* sign down a 200m path to the stone beach nestled almost underneath Pont d'Arc. Avoid the short-cuts offered to the path as they are not designed for cycling shoes.

Sleep

Hotel

Le Belvédère
The only hotel actually near the Pont d'Arc. Just 200m beyond the end of the stage at the viewpoint. A refreshing surprise near a tourist hotspot, newly renovated with 3 star status and welcoming friendly staff.
Route des Gorges de l'Ardèche
07150 Vallon-Pont-d'Arc
00 33 (0)4 75 88 00 02
www.le-belvedere-hotel.com

Chambre d'Hôtes

Le Magnolia
An interesting house built of riverstones, offering 5 guestrooms, 7km before the end of the stage just off the straight stretch before Vallon-Pont-d'Arc. There are no *chambres d'hôtes* at Pont d'Arc itself.
Passera, 07150 Vallon-Pont-d'Arc
00 33 (0)4 75 88 10
www.lemagnolia.com

Campsite

Camping la Rouvière
With no fewer than 47 different campsites around Vallon-Pont-d'Arc you're not short of choice. La Rouvière is in a natural setting on the banks of the river 400m from the Pont d'Arc boasting a 300m-long river beach.
Route des Gorges, 07150 Vallon-Pont-d'Arc
00 33 (0)4 75 37 10 07
www.campinglarouviere.com

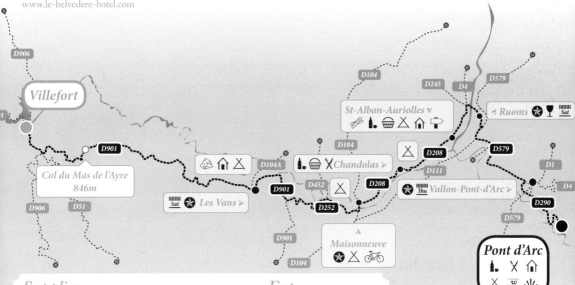

Supplies

Bike

Cycles Amc7
Just off the route after crossing the Chassezac river in the small hamlet of Maisonneuve. One of the most unusual places to find a bike shop, but a good range of supplies. There are some rental outfits in Vallon-Pont-d'Arc mostly mountain bikes, but they still might help out with a track pump or tube if needed.
Maisonneuve, 07230 Chandolas
00 33 (0)4 75 35 98 29
www.amc7.com

Food

If you need supplies be sure to stop in Vallon-Pont-d'Arc 6km before the end of the stage. As well as local speciality shops such as a *nougaterie* and *boulangeries* tucked in amongst the gift shops of the pedestrianised Rue Salengro there is also a small supermarket in the centre.

Eat

Auberge du Pont d'Arc
The only stand alone restaurant/café at Pont d'Arc so it's often busy. The restaurant at Le Belvédère listed above is a better option for dinner, superbly located and offers a variety of *menus prix fixes*, including a *menu terroir* you can eat on the pleasant outdoor terrace and enjoy the warm evening air.
Route des Gorges, 07150 Vallon-Pont-d'Arc
00 33 (0)4 75 88 01 57
www.ardeche-restauraunt.com

Swim

Follow the *sentier pour piétons* sign from the road 200m down to a stone beach below the arch at Pont d'Arc. This place is no secret and can be quite a scene, but take a towel and a picnic and once the crowds go home it's the perfect spot for an atmospheric evening swim.

PONT D'ARC TO AIGUEZE

Stage 23: *22miles 35km*

A meandering road follows the course of the river, offering views deep down into the steep-sided gorge where brightly coloured kayakers enjoy the long descent down the Ardéche. Panoramic views accompany the twists and turns of the road, whilst the scent of herbs and wild goats provides a heady concoction of smells. Arriving at the perched village of Aiguèze, there is an air of tranquillity and magnificent views from the ancient watch path toward the Rhône.

Pont d'Arc through tunnels

Starting from the viewpoint at Pont d'Arc with the arch itself on your right, the road remains flat for 2 kilometres, past a cluster of hotels and kayak rental spots, before you begin your ascent into the gorge. For this stage you remain on the D290 with no turnings until you exit the gorge.

The road starts to climb steeply, but don't be intimidated, this is not a taste of things to come. The hardest 2.5km of this section occurs right at the start, as you quickly gain height to enter the gorge and are treated to a dramatic view of the road you have just ridden, before shortly entering an unlit tunnel.

Once you emerge from the tunnel the first viewpoint is almost in sight, a welcome excuse for a breather. Stretched out beneath you is a meander of the river which more often than not will be speckled with bright oranges, yellows and greens, as the kayak day trippers begin their descent of the gorge. Whilst you will be winding your way up and down above the river, kayakers will be on a steady descent of the Ardèche, finishing shortly before it joins the Rhône.

Whilst the water has long calm sections, it also features 26 rapids to set the heart racing. Guided tours are easy to book from multiple locations in Vallon-Pont-d'Arc. They are one-way trips with a van returning you back to the start point.

CHAUVET CAVE PAINTINGS

Close to Vallon-Pont-d'Arc is the Grotte Chauvet, home to the oldest cave paintings in the world. Its exact location remains undisclosed. Discovered in 1994 by three adventurous cavers, its walls depict 425 individual animal drawings, painted 36,000 years ago. As well as the striking imagery, bones and footprints were also discovered, preserved in the soft clay floor.

The cave is currently undergoing review for UNESCO world heritage status, but the site will never be opened to the public for fear of damage to the unique paintings. Instead a faux cave will be created nearby and will attempt to recreate the images and sensations of entering the real cave.

Riding the gorge

The road, perched on the edge of the limestone cliffs that tower as much as 300m above the water, affords dramatic views down into the river. It mimics the river course, twisting and turning amongst the rock.

While the overall gradient is up, there is little sensation of climbing, as the ribbon of road almost pulls you along to its next curve of the river. The limestone cliffs are full of naturally formed caves. Humans have lived in the area for over 300,000 years and over 2,000 caves are found in the gorge, some of them painted.

Along the way you will see signs for the Grotte de la Madeleine, a slightly touristy attraction, but one that has scored three Michelin stars for its extravagant sound and light show and the stunning natural beauty of the caves with their numerous rock formations. If you are interested in learning more about the formation of the gorge and seeing inside its caves, it's definitely worth a quick visit.

You can see many of the cave entrances and wider depressions on the opposite cliff face. To primitive humans, struggling with the elements and the many dangers of wild animals, these caves must have once offered instant respite and shelter.

There is a distinct change in temperature over this and the next section, as we draw closer to Provence, and your senses will be challenged by the sudden changes. Firstly, your nose will be assaulted by a number of pungent smells. The waft of ripe goat's cheese will warn you that there is a nearby herd, useful forewarning as they often come cascading down the high banks and onto the road.

You'll also start to smell woody herbs, such as thyme and rosemary, a smell that becomes stronger once into the heart of Provence, where the sun-baked soil is home to a wide variety of herbs. A tinnitus ring of a thousand insects living amongst the roadside plants also accompanies you through this stage. Near the final viewpoint at the neck of the gorge, on the right-hand side, is a mature fig tree. In late summer it is heavy with fruit, well within picking distance of a peckish cyclist.

Exiting the Gorge

As you turn the corner after the final viewpoint you will see the river broaden and flatten out beneath you. The spikes of cypress trees, pointing up amongst medieval buildings on the opposite hill, show the end point of this section.

With the wind in the right direction, you'll be able to hear splashing and laughter from the kayakers reaching the end of their journey just outside St-Martin d'Ardèche.

Descending out of the gorge, turn right at La Camargue pizza restaurant up the road signed Aiguèze and St-Martin d'Ardèche. Far less picturesque than our final destination Aiguèze, St-Martin d'Ardèche does, however, offer a host of facilities. As you ride into the village the river will be on your right. This is the final stretch of the Ardèche and, for the first time since leaving Pont-d'Arc, you will be at virtually the same level as you ride along the Quai Pescadou. Here you will find kayaks for hire, easy access down to the river and numerous cafés overlooking the water. There is also Le Moulin campsite if you fancy staying at river level instead of above the river in Aiguèze.

St-Martin d'Ardèche to Aiguèze

The road takes you first under the huge bridge spanning the river, then, with a 180-degree hairpin, left up to it where the route crosses the river. Here you will see the Bellevue Logis Hôtel on your right and, if you carry straight on, you will also see the *office de tourisme*, again on your right. In this small square you will also be able to find a *boulangerie* and various gift and tourist shops.

Crossing the river provides a fantastic view both ways. However, it is very narrow and, although quiet with little traffic, it is not somewhere to hang around taking photos. After crossing the river stay on the D141 for 0.5km and then turn right onto the D901. After another 0.5km turn right on the D180 into Aiguèze.

Follow the road past the car park into the main square, where you will find two cafés overlooking a shady *terrain de boules*. The *office de tourisme* is directly next to the *boules* pitch, facing the entrance to the church.

Aiguèze has the honour of being one of the 156 *Plus Beaux Villages de France*, the fifth we visit on this route. It has plenty of accommodation and two charming, but very different, restaurants. Yet this small village, with a population of a little over 200, doesn't feel at all touristy.

You'll be congratulating yourself on finding such a peaceful, tranquil spot, where you can appreciate the atmosphere of not only a historic village, but also a real and active one, without hordes of other tourists.

Spend some time exploring the narrow cobbled streets and quirky, beautiful homes. Keep a particular lookout for the statues and grotesque gargoyles made by a local artist that feature on some of the houses.

At the end of the village is a 14th-century fort with a watch path providing fine views over the river with the distant silhouette of Mont Ventoux behind.

Sleep

Hotel
Le Castelas
Within one of the oldest and stateliest buildings in Aiguèze this small hotel offers apartments and studios. It has a secluded outdoor pool, within the old courtyard, and lovely lounge areas set beneath ancient arched ceilings.
Grande Rue, 30760 Aiguèze
00 33 (0)4 66 82 18 76
www.residencelecastelas.com

Chambre d'Hôtes
Les Mazets d' Aiguèze
Just 100 metres walk from the centre square, this spacious chambre d'hôtes has a pool and laundry service and welcomes cyclists.
Marlene et Patrick Vincent, 30760 Aiguèze
00 33 (0)4 66 82 34 28
www.mazets-aigueze.com

Campsite
Camping des Cigales
This campsite is on the edge of the village, 100 metres from the river. It has a bar, swimming pool and *dépôt de pain*, providing fresh bread every morning. Importantly for touring cyclists it also has several washing machines!
Quartier de la Blanchisserie, Route de Saint-Martin d'Ardèche, 30760 Aiguèze
00 33 (0)4 66 82 18 52

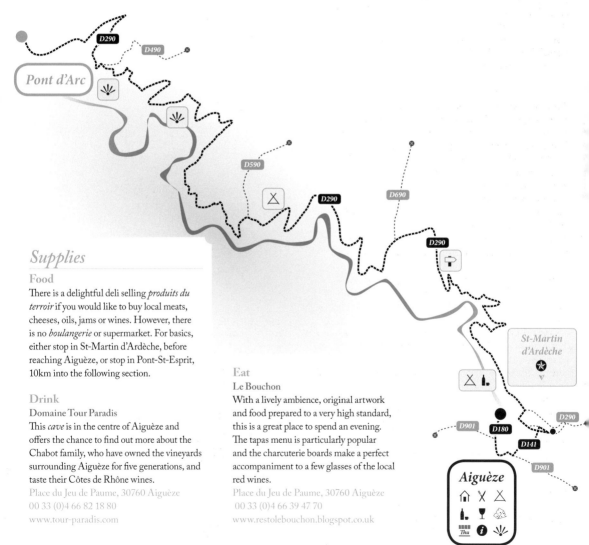

Supplies

Food
There is a delightful deli selling *produits du terroir* if you would like to buy local meats, cheeses, oils, jams or wines. However, there is no *boulangerie* or supermarket. For basics, either stop in St-Martin d'Ardèche, before reaching Aiguèze, or stop in Pont-St-Esprit, 10km into the following section.

Drink
Domaine Tour Paradis
This *cave* is in the centre of Aiguèze and offers the chance to find out more about the Chabot family, who have owned the vineyards surrounding Aiguèze for five generations, and taste their Côtes de Rhône wines.
Place du Jeu de Paume, 30760 Aiguèze
00 33 (0)4 66 82 18 80
www.tour-paradis.com

Eat
Le Bouchon
With a lively ambience, original artwork and food prepared to a very high standard, this is a great place to spend an evening. The tapas menu is particularly popular and the charcuterie boards make a perfect accompaniment to a few glasses of the local red wines.
Place du Jeu de Paume, 30760 Aiguèze
00 33 (0)4 66 39 47 70
www.restolebouchon.blogspot.co.uk

RHONE

PAUSE to watch a game of *boules* under the shade of plane trees in the ancient square of Aiguèze.

FREEWHEEL along the banks of the mighty Rhône as the tailwind of the Mistral propels you from Pont-St-Esprit to St-Étienne-des-Sorts.

DISCOVER the techniques and traditions that make the wines of Châteauneuf-du-Pape famous, at the Musée du Vin.

TASTE the wines entitled to the *appellation contrôlée* 'Châteauneuf-du-Pape' in the Place de la Fontaine in the centre of the village.

LEARN the skills of a sommelier at L'École de Dégustation in Châteauneuf-du-Pape.

WATCH olive oil extracted in the traditional way at the Moulin à Huile in Mazan.

AIGUEZE (TO) CHATEAUNEUF-DU-PAPE

Stage 24: *29miles 46km*

A picturesque ride thorough the vineyards, accompanied by the shadowy silhouette of Mont Ventoux, before you cross one of France's great rivers, the Rhône, helped on your way by the Mistral. Arriving in the most famous wine-producing village in the world, a large glass of fabulous red is the perfect way to end the stage.

Aiguèze to Pont-St-Esprit

To leave Aiguèze pass the *terrain de boules* in the central square, where you may be able to see a game being played beneath the trees, as it has been played for centuries, before you retrace your steps back to the D901.

When you reach the T-Junction with the D901 turn left; this takes you down a narrow avenue of trees. You will pass a campsite on your left and several *caves* for wine tasting but we suggest you hold back until you reach Châteauneuf-du-Pape, at the end of this section, for the best experience.

After 7 km you will reach another T-junction with the D6086, where you turn right toward Pont-St-Esprit. Even though you are approaching a more urban area, small vineyards still line the road all the way to the edge of the town. The road here can become a little busy as Pont-St-Esprit is very much a working town and also, as its name suggests, one of the key crossing- points of the Rhône.

2.5 km from the last junction you will arrive in Pont-St-Esprit at a roundabout with a large modern fountain in the centre. Your route takes you straight over the roundabout, but if you would like to see the crossing-point the town takes its name from, turn left here.

The first bridge was built in 1265 making Pont-St-Esprit an important town in the region, able to control traffic from one side of the Rhône to the other. The current bridge was completed in 1965.

If you cross to the middle of the bridge and look back toward Pont-St-Esprit you will see the domed roof of the Prieuré-St-Pierre, a *monument historique*, and also the Escaliers-St-Pierre, steps that would have led up to it from the riverside.

The Prieuré dates from the 12th-century and was home to Benedicitine monks. It has had a varied past, suffering serious damage during the 16th-century Wars of Religion before being restored in the late-17th century.

Since then it has operated as a church, a school and a military warehouse. Both are currently closed for renovation but, even from a distance, it is easy to imagine how impressive they must have appeared to those arriving from the other side of the river.

Leaving Pont-St-Esprit

After your short excursion to the bridge, return to the roundabout and turn left toward Nimes on the D6086, and then almost immediately left at the Banque Populaire into the parallel road, following it to your right. This smaller road is lined with car parking – in fact you could be forgiven for thinking it was the town car park. It has numerous cafés and small shops if you need refreshments or supplies. At the first roundabout with a fountain, head straight over, remaining within the confines of this parallel road. At the end you will see a small roundabout with a statue and traffic lights, where you exit left.

100m further on take a 90-degree right signed St-Etienne-des-Sorts, D138. You'll soon reach a roundabout with exits for the N86. Head straight over on the D138 and the road will become instantly quieter. Although you are riding parallel with the N86, the noise of road traffic is indiscernible above the noise of crickets in the long grass and in the vineyards that line the roadside.

Here the landscape begins to change. The road is flat and easy with various plantations of fruit trees and vines either side. Even with the heat haze that hangs over the vines at the height of summer, you'll be able to see the distant outline of Mont Ventoux on your left. Your constant companion over the next few sections of the route, its bulk is visible for many miles in this otherwise flat region.

St-Etienne-des-Sorts to the Rhône Crossing

In a further 6km from the roundabout, take the left at the T-junction signed St-Etienne-des-Sorts, D138. After 3km you enter the village. With a population of little over 500, it has been home to colourful riverside characters such as pirates and smugglers for centuries, but is now a stopping point on the *Route Touristique Côtes du Rhône* bringing an altogether more respectable traveller to the village.

At this point the full width of the river comes into view and you can fully appreciate the industrialised nature of the Rhône, the heavy river traffic and strings of pylons on the opposite bank contrasting with the pretty old church of the village. Be careful as you enter and exit the town as there are two tricky, off-set mini-roundabouts that are designed to slow down traffic.

As you exit the town you'll pass the village wine-producing co-operative. Here the musty smell of fermenting grapes contrasts strongly with the sharp tang of the river air. The road out of town continues straight on, with the river on your

left and vineyards stretching away to your right. You'll be rolling along now, pushed from behind by a strong tail wind, particularly if the Mistral is blowing. After a further 4km, just after your first sighting of the nuclear power station, turn left signposted Caderousse, D138A.

After another 3km turn left at the roundabout towards Caderousse and Orange. There is a lovely picnic stop on the right in amongst the trees on the bank of a small lake if you fancy a break. The road continues on until, after another 5km, you cross the full width of the Rhône, which you have

VALUABLE VINES

Châteauneuf-du-Pape can be crudely translated as 'the pope's new castle' and it is thanks to the wine-quaffing popes that viticulture was extended to this area. Châteauneuf-du-Pape is probably the best known of the Côtes-de-Rhône wines and its production and name is carefully controlled. Châteauneuf-du-Pape was the first wine to come under the rules of *appellation contrôlée*, which decrees the variety of grapes that can be grown as well as the percentage of alcohol, and ensures that all wine bearing the label is produced in that region.

Châteauneuf-du-Pape can be a red or white wine but rosé is not produced in the region. Wines are often high in alcohol, from 13% to 15% and must be a minimum of 12.5%. Until 2007, only 13 grape varieties were allowed, but that has since extended to 18, as white and black grapes of the same variety are now listed separately. Part of the success of wine-growing in this region is due to heaping *galets*, small rounded pebbles, typically quartzite, around the base of the vines. They retain the heat of the day and release it at night, which hastens the ripening of the grapes and also helps to retain moisture and protect the soil from erosion.

To learn more about viticulture, visit the *Musée du Vin – Maison Brotte*. Various displays explain everything from the history of wine-making to the geology of the area. Traditional tools are displayed and you can try various wines, including their own label *La Fiole du Pape*.

Brotte Musée du Vin
Ave. Pierre de Luxemburg,
84231 Châteauneuf-du-Pape
Tel: 00 33 (0)4 90 83 59 44
www.brotte.com

been pedalling alongside for so long. On a windy day you will feel the spray on your face and the smell of the river can be strong. You'll also be able to see the vast power-lines carrying electricity generated by the nuclear station to supply the heavily populated Rhône corridor.

The Rhône Crossing to Châteauneuf-du-Pape

A further 2km will see you cross the river again over a second smaller channel. Just under 0.5km after this you will come to a T-junction with a traffic island. The route heads right toward Caderousse, D237, but you can avoid this stretch of road by staying in the left lane and heading straight over to pick up a cycle lane opposite, partially hidden in the trees. This runs parallel with the route on the D237 for 2.5km, mainly hidden from the road by trees or high banks.

The cycle path ends at the entrance to Caderousse village and, although you are only a few kilometres away from your destination Châteauneuf-du-Pape, you may fancy a short detour into this bankside village where Hannibal was alleged to have crossed the Rhône with his elephants on his way to Rome in 218 BC. After centuries of flooding, in 1856 the village erected a dyke to surround the town with four entry points that can be shut off if waters threaten. If you fancy a break from pedalling you can walk the entire circumference of the village on top of the dyke. Here you will also find a range of amenities including a café, *boulangerie* and a supermarket.

After a further 3.5km you will pass under the motorway then turn left at the roundabout in the direction of

Châteauneuf-du-Pape, D976. After just 0.5km take the right on the D17 signposted Châteauneuf-du-Pape 6km. Along this road, after 2.5 km, you'll pass La Sommellerie, one of our recommended hotels and used by the Argos/Shimano team on their rest-day during the 2013 Tour de France.

Winding through the vineyards you start to have occasional glimpses of the now ruined Château des Papes to your left above the village. After 5.5km you'll arrive at the fountain in the centre of the village where you will often find a gathering of cyclists eating or drinking in the nearby cafés. The *office de tourisme* can also be found here in amongst the cafés and contains a wealth of information on Châteauneuf-du-Pape and the surrounding area.

Châteauneuf-du-Pape

Regardless of whether or not you are a serious wine aficionado, you shouldn't pass through Châteauneuf-du-Pape without sampling at least a small glass. The numerous *caves* in the small village offer tastings of their products and an opportunity to learn more about the Châteauneuf-du-Pape *appellation*. Once you know what you like order a glass – or a bottle – and relax in one of the three cafés near to the fountain and indulge in an afternoon of people-watching.

There are numerous cafés and hotel restaurants in the heart of the village. As you would expect, all of them offer extensive wine lists. Prices for meals can be high due to the high volume of tourist traffic but most restaurants still offer a good value *menu formule* at lunchtime.

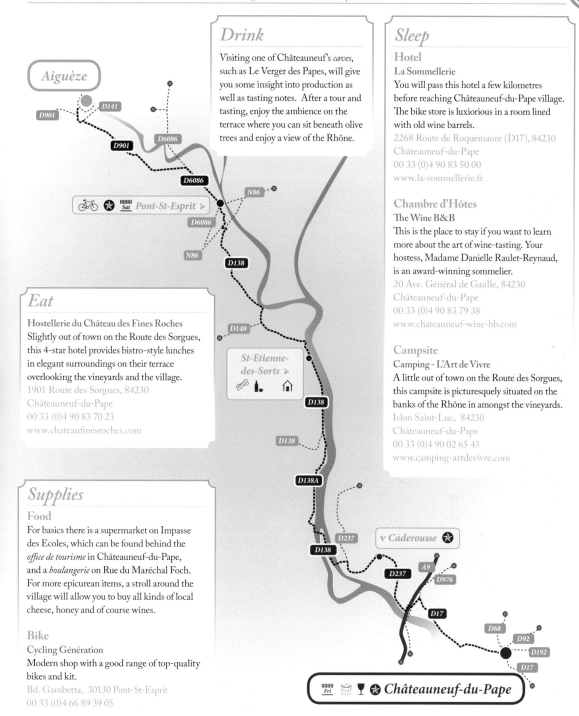

Drink

Visiting one of Châteauneuf's *caves*, such as Le Verger des Papes, will give you some insight into production as well as tasting notes. After a tour and tasting, enjoy the ambience on the terrace where you can sit beneath olive trees and enjoy a view of the Rhône.

Sleep

Hotel

La Sommellerie
You will pass this hotel a few kilometres before reaching Châteauneuf-du-Pape village. The bike store is luxiorious in a room lined with old wine barrels.
2268 Route de Roquemaure (D17), 84230 Châteauneuf-du-Pape
00 33 (0)4 90 83 50 00
www.la-sommellerie.fr

Chambre d'Hôtes

The Wine B&B
This is the place to stay if you want to learn more about the art of wine-tasting. Your hostess, Madame Danielle Raulet-Reynaud, is an award-winning sommelier.
20 Ave. Général de Gaulle, 84230 Châteauneuf-du-Pape
00 33 (0)4 90 83 79 38
www.chateauneuf-wine-bb.com

Campsite

Camping - L'Art de Vivre
A little out of town on the Route des Sorgues, this campsite is picturesquely situated on the banks of the Rhône in amongst the vineyards.
Islon Saint-Luc, 84230 Châteauneuf-du-Pape
00 33 (0)4 90 02 65 43
www.camping-artdevivre.com

Eat

Hostellerie du Château des Fines Roches
Slightly out of town on the Route des Sorgues, this 4-star hotel provides bistro-style lunches in elegant surroundings on their terrace overlooking the vineyards and the village.
1901 Route des Sorgues, 84230 Châteauneuf-du-Pape
00 33 (0)4 90 83 70 23
www.chateaufinesroches.com

Supplies

Food

For basics there is a supermarket on Impasse des Ecoles, which can be found behind the *office de tourisme* in Châteauneuf-du-Pape, and a *boulangerie* on Rue du Maréchal Foch. For more epicurean items, a stroll around the village will allow you to buy all kinds of local cheese, honey and of course wines.

Bike

Cycling Génération
Modern shop with a good range of top-quality bikes and kit.
Bd. Gambetta, 30130 Pont-St-Esprit
00 33 (0)4 66 89 39 05

CHATEAUNEUF-DU-PAPE ⓉⓄ VILLES-SUR-AUZON

Stage 25: *24miles 38km*

Wind your way through the quiet vineyards
outside Châteauneuf-du-Pape and a series of
small villages, before passing through the busy
market town of Carpentras. Leaving Carpentras
you regain your views of vineyards while heading
towards the ever more imposing outline of
Ventoux, the *Géant de Provence*.

Châteauneuf-du-Pape to Bédarrides

Starting from the Place de la Fontaine, the epicentre of Châteauneuf-du-Pape, take the Avenue Baron Le Roy which is to your left when facing the *office du tourisme*. Ride down this street until you reach the crossroads, then head straight over signed Bédarrides, D192.

As you climb up this gently rolling road, with acres of vines on either side, look back over your shoulder to appreciate the view of Châteauneuf-du-Pape and the ruins of the Château des Papes, perched above the village. To your right you can see evidence of modern wine production in the large industrial-looking sheds, which contrast strongly with the more romantic image of the 4-star Château des Fines Roches, a fabulous place to eat if you happen to be passing at an appropriate time. For a couple of kilometres the most dramatic views are behind you, so don't forget to turn round, but soon Ventoux appears on your left where it will loom large for most of this section.

Each division of vines is marked by the name of the producer. Look out for the famous *appellations* and well-known family names that have earned Châteauneuf-du-Pape global fame. A short but sweet, sweeping descent reveals a magnificent panorama with the slopes of Mont Ventoux standing out prominently from the low hills surrounding it. Below the *autoroute du soleil* slices through the landscape, carrying holidaymakers rushing toward the sun.

Bédarrides to Monteux

5km after leaving Châteauneuf-du-Pape, the road ends at a T-junction; take the left here, signed Bédarrides. The road carries you almost back on yourself. At the traffic lights go straight on, continuing to follow signs for Bédarrides. Be careful of the vicious speed bumps here.

After about 300m turn left underneath a railway bridge. You will shortly arrive at a water tower. Neoclassical in design, this *monument historique* was built in 1855 to supply water to the village and is one of three monuments in the town. To explore this pretty town, turn off to the right. To continue on the route, go straight on at the fountain, travelling along an avenue of trees until you reach one of the town's *monuments historiques*, the bridge over the Ouvèze river built in 1647.

197

At the end of the avenue of trees go straight over, crossing the bridge, then follow the road round to the left. Be careful here as it is a confusing junction with several minor roads joining together. After 1km turn left signposted Monteux D87.

This is a quieter road and, depending on the season, you'll see fields of sunflowers to the side and the tempting view of Mont Ventoux to lead you onwards. A raised bank of bullrushes on your right conceals a modest river, helping to irrigate the nearby fertile fields.

After 4km you will pass under the dual carriageway between Avignon and Carpentras, and after another 1.5km when you reach the junction, turn right toward Monteux. After crossing over the railway line turn left (do not be put off by the signpost for parkings), and pause to admire the elaborate gateway which would have formed the original entrance to the town. After a further 300m, the road bends round to the right and is signposted Carpentras. You'll pass the excellent Provence Cycles shop on your right – a good place to browse or stock up if you need anything.

Monteux to Carpentras

At the mini-roundabout head left, continuing to follow signs for Carpentras. You'll pass under a bridge through some traffic lights and then be free of the town. As you leave, Mont Ventoux once more comes into view. After 2km head straight across the roundabout toward Carpentras centre. In just over 1km you pass the *Hôtel-Dieu* (the old hospital)

At this point follow the signs for Mont Ventoux, D942. The *Hôtel-Dieu* was built in the mid-18th century and remained in use until 2006. Its *pharmacie* was at the cutting-edge of medical theory during the Age of Enlightenment and much of the original décor and drawers of herbal remedies still remain. At present you need to ask at the *office de tourisme* for a tour, but a huge restoration project is underway, the building will become a cultural hub for Carpentras.

Immediately after passing the *Hôtel-Dieu* on your right, keep left following signs for Mont Ventoux, passing the *office de tourisme* on your left. To explore Carpentras now would be a good point to duck off the route. There are many hidden gems down the narrow streets of the old town, including Europe's oldest synagogue. It would be unfair to judge the town simply on its traffic-choked, one-way system. Continue following signposts for Mont Ventoux until the roundabout just as you leave town where you head straight over, signed Mazan, D942. You remain on the D942 until Villes-sur-Auzon at the end of this stage.

INDULGE

Château de Mazan

Depending on your literary tastes, you may want to visit the Château de Mazan, former home of the Marquis de Sade and now a 4-star hotel and restaurant with outdoor pool. No doubt one of the most infamous residents of the region, de Sade was imprisoned and then later declared insane on account of his writings on gender, sexuality and philosophy. Sadism and sadistic, words that have entered our language, reflect his importance.

Rue Bernus , 84380 Mazan
00 33 (0)4 90 69 62 61
www.chateaudemazan.com

CARPENTRAS

On approaching Mont Ventoux, many cycling fans will be thinking about the death of Tom Simpson in 1967. Simpson had been the first British rider to wear the yellow jersey of the Tour de France leader, and had also been World Champion.

Adored by the British sports fans, he won Sports Personality of the Year.

Simpson collapsed just 2km from the summit of Mont Ventoux, a spot now marked by the Simpson Memorial.

The stage finished in Carpentras and the next morning the bells slowly tolled as the riders assembled on the starting line, led by the British team wearing black armbands. In homage to Simpson the peloton agreed a British rider should win the stage and team-mate Barry Hoban took the honours.

Carpentras to Villes-sur-Auzon

After 7km you reach the small town of Mazan and carry straight on over both roundabouts. If you need supplies, there is a supermarket and the excellent Boulangerie Cazalis off to the right at the first roundabout. There are occasionally hot-food sellers in the car park.

If you decide to turn off into Mazan itself, the Moulin à Huile, where olive oil is prepared traditionally and made into a wide range of local products, is worth visiting. After leaving Mazan the road becomes increasingly quiet. Vineyards begin to line the roadside again and once more Ventoux comes into view. This is a popular route with local and visiting cyclists so you may well have company on the road.

Lining the route you'll find several signs for châteaux offering wine tastings. One of the best is Château Pesquie, shortly after Mormoiron, a little way up the D184 in the direction of Flassan. Here you can walk amongst the vines, learn more about wine-tasting, and of course buy direct from the cellar door. There are also many fruit-and-vegetable sellers with roadside stalls.

Approaching Villes-sur-Auzon there are vineyards as far as the eye can see, with Mont Ventoux standing proud above them. As you enter the town you'll pass Terra Ventoux, one of the biggest local wine producers.

They offer several vintages marketed to cyclists, including the 2012 special edition *Maillot Jaune* which, as the name suggests, has a graphic of a cyclist in yellow on the label.

With the end of the section in sight, this may well be a good time to do some serious wine-tasting as the village centre is just a 500m wobble down the tree-lined avenue on which you entered the village. The stage finishes at the end of this avenue at the start of the one-way system opposite a fountain.

Villes-sur-Auzon is the base for many *cyclo-sportives*, including Le Défi du Ventoux, an event put on in the name of former pro rider Eric Caritoux who lives just outside Villes-sur-Auzon. There is no shortage of sportives in this area, most weekends of the summer months there is an event to take part in. There is also a bi-annual night time sportive to climb Ventoux, an eery sight as lights reflect off its white rocks.

Even if there is no event being held, you will see many cyclists gathering for a pre- or post-ride coffee, their bright Lycra and loud banter filling the outside tables at the small cafés.

Villes-sur-Auzon is a convenient stopping-off point on many of the popular routes around Ventoux and the fountain in the town is the last opportunity for filling up your water bottles before entering the dry Gorges de la Nesque, the subject of our next section.

Sleep

Hotel

Ferme Auberge du Couguieu
There is no hotel in Villes Sur Auzon. However, a short distance from the town toward Flassan, you will find the Ferme Auberge du Couguieu. Three bedrooms with their own terraces overlook the outdoor pool.
Chemin de Patey, Route de Flassan, 84570 Villes-sur-Auzon
00 33 (0)4 90 61 74 88
www.auberge-couguieu.com

Chambre d'Hôtes

La Sarrasine
One of the oldest houses in the village with frescos from the 17th-century. The vivid blue- and-green shutters and overhanging vines give the front of the house a typically Provençal look.
1 Place de l'Eglise, 84570 Villes-sur-Auzon
00 33 (0)4 90 61 93 78
www.lasarrasine.net

Campsite

Les Verguettes
A 4-star campsite within a couple of minutes walk of the village, with a pool and bar area. The 70 camping spots are well spread out to give privacy.
Route de Carpentras, 84570 Villes-sur-Auzon
00 33 (0)4 90 61 88 18
www.provence-camping.com

Supplies

Food

There is one *boulangerie* and a supermarket for any basic dry goods in Villes-sur-Auzon. The Wednesday market includes lots of local food, most grown on the fertile lower slopes of Mont Ventoux.

Bike

Vélo Relax
Very basic but offers spares and repairs.
No 2 Le Cour, 84570 Villes-sur-Auzon
00 33 (0)4 90 11 72 65
www.velorelaxduventoux.com

Provence Cycles
Top-end bike shop for browsing or buying spares.
20 bd Mar Foch, 84170 Monteux
00 33 (0)4 90 60 54 49

Vélo Center
A large well-stocked shop covering every discipline of cycling.
71, Boulevard Louis Giraud, 84200 Carpentras
00 33 (0)4 90 41 91 28

Eat

Les P'tits Bonheurs
A cosy indoor dining area and outside terrace make this the perfect restaurant for a long, lazy meal, whatever time of year you visit.
41 Avenue Jean Jaurès, 84570 Villes-sur-Auzon
00 33 (0)4 90 61 87 70
www.ptitsbonheurs.fr

PROVENCE:
PAYS DU VENTOUX

ABSORB the evocative scent of acres and acres of lavender and *lavandin* on the Valensole plateau.

MARVEL at the way Mont Ventoux dominates the landscape. Maybe even tackle the mountain yourself, not forgetting to pay respects to Tom Simpson as you pass.

MOUNT the many steps up to 12th-century chapel of Notre-Dame de Beauvoir in Moustiers-Ste-Marie, and be rewarded with a stunning view of the Gorge du Verdon.

BROWSE the labyrinthine bookshop, Le Bleuet, in the tiny village of Banon.
A must for any book lover, it draws visitors from all over Provence.

SAVOUR the unique honey lavender often sold by the roadside. As you ride past the fields of flowers, you will hear the constant hum of the bees at work.

WANDER the Wednesday street market in Sault, running since 1515, and find a variety of local foods, souvenirs and work by local artists.

VILLES-SUR-AUZON ⓽ SAULT

Stage 26: *19miles 30km*

Arguably the best 30km you can ride in the whole
of France. Leaving the vineyards behind, the route
winds through the spectacular Gorges de la Nesque
as it climbs gently at a perfect gradient for cyclists.
The stage ends at Sault, the atmospheric old centre
of the Provençal lavender trade.

Villes-sur-Auzon to Rocher du Cire

L inking the vine-covered lower slopes of Mont Ventoux that surround Villes-sur-Auzon and the Sault valley is a stunning ride up the Gorge de la Nesque. Starting where the last stage ended, facing the water fountain in Villes-sur-Auzon, follow the one-way system round to the right.

The sign reads Eau Non Potable but 100m round the one-way system on your right just before the *Point Info Tourisme* is a drinking fountain. Make sure you fill your water bottle as the Nesque is devoid of water sources. Shortly after the *Point Info Tourisme* fork off the one-way system to the right, signed Gorge de la Nesque D942, then after 100m turn right for the gorge, ignoring the road straight on to Sault.

The route climbs gradually from a height of 310m for the next 19km to reach a commanding viewpoint, Le Rocher du Cire, at an altitude of 750m. Gorge de La Nesque is initially a modest cutting in the landscape, created by a hydrological break through of the small Nesque river, which is invisible below. The ride becomes more spectacular as you climb, clinging to the side of the valley with the gorge to your right. The Nesque is not as instantly impressive as the larger Gorge du Verdon, in Provence, but it grows on you, with each turn unveiling another vista of wild beauty.

The Nesque is also an assault on the senses with its cocktail of colours, flavours and scents. You can almost taste the wild thyme and rosemary in places where the scrub that lines the road perfumes the air with aromas. It's like opening the Herbes de Provence jar in your spice rack.

3km after leaving Villes-sur-Auzon there is a picnic area offering good views. The road is strewn with fantastic *belvédères* after almost every curve, each offering a different perspective. The first section of the climb is lined with some inexplicably well-manicured topiary, where olive trees have been shaped by an enthusiastic resident. 10km after leaving Villes-sur-Auzon the landscape becomes a more enclosed, distinctive gorge as the hedges fade away to be replaced by wild olive and scrubland.

14 km into the stage, the road passes under a spectacular arch before 1km later you see the only sign of civilisation, a modest house tucked into the cliff-side selling honey.

The views get better as you look back on your progress through the gorge. 1km from the top the route looks almost improbable but two tunnels have been blasted through the rock to allow your passage to the Rocher du Cire viewpoint at the top.

Rocher du Cire to Sault

After the viewpoint, the route flattens out for 1km leaving the gorge behind. Across the surprisingly wide and open valley, Sault comes into view for the first time. The road descends the valley side for 3km to the village of Monieux, which is tucked into the hills just above the valley floor – a mosaic of golden spelt fields and purple hues of lavender. The route forks off to the left through Monieux before rejoining the main road, which by-passes the village.

The medieval village of Monieux guards the upland entrance to the Nesque canyon and is crowned by the remains of a watchtower. An authentic Provençal village, it hums with the atmospheric echo of people chattering on the outdoor restaurant terrace, as tourist and locals alike enjoy their long lunch.

On leaving Monieux the road flattens for 3 km as you ride through lavender fields. In June vibrant purple tones light up the landscape and, irrespective of the time of year, you can smell the lavender long after it has been cut as the scent is wafted around by the breeze. At the T-junction turn right, signed Sault 2.5km, D942. After 1km the road passes through the small hamlet of La Loge, where it is lined with small stalls selling lavender and honey, before crossing the modest trickle of the Nesque river, the cause of the stunning gorge you have just ridden up.

Arriving in Sault

After the flat plains of the Sault valley, the stage has a sting in the tail as the road curves back on itself round a switchback to the left, signed Sault 0.5km, D942. A sign welcomes you to this historic town, perched upon a limestone outcrop, announcing Sault's popular Wednesday market, one of the oldest in France and running since 1515.

The stage ends at a crossroads by a *nougaterie* and *boulangerie*. To explore the old streets and Place du Marché, turn left here. To continue onto the next stage turn up the hill to the right, signed Forcalquier, D950. Whatever your plans, make sure you continue straight on at the crossroads for 100m to a promenade area on your left. As well as offering an unrivalled view of Mont Ventoux and the

lavender fields below, the promenade can be quite a scene. Tourists sip wine in the sun at the southern end, heated games of *pétanque* take place under the shade of a handful of trees and cyclists gaze out at their nemesis, Ventoux. The observatory, protruding from the lunar-like upper slopes, seems like a lifetime of pedalling away. Cyclists who have conquered Ventoux always look elated, as they rehydrate from the water fountain outside the *office de tourisme*. Those that can't wait until dinner, head to the *feu de bois* (wood-fired) pizza wagon. Stay the night in Sault if you wish to attack Mont Ventoux as it is the highest of the three towns used by cyclists for an assault on the summit.

MAGICAL MIEL

Local honey is full of the scents of the land. Thyme gives the honey a robust flavour, whilst lavender gives it a more floral taste. Hives are located near wild flowers so bees can follow the calendar, whetting their appetite with rosemary and thyme on the scrubland in the spring, before indulging in a lavender feast in early summer. Lavender honey is one of the most potent symbols of Provence, the region's aromas and tastes captured in a jar.

Sleep

Hotel

Hôtel Le Louvre

A hotel full of Provençal charm, situated on La Place du Marché. Owner Antoine will make you feel at home, serving dinner and offering local knowledge on Mont Ventoux.

Place du Marché, 84390 Sault

00 33 (0)4 90 64 08 88

www.louvre-provence.com

Chambre d'Hôtes

Le Grand Jas

An old, restored farmhouse 5km out of town on the D30 towards St-Christol with a view over Mont Ventoux. Breakfast is included.

Mme. Chagnolleau, Route du St-Christol, 84390 Sault

00 33 (0)4 90 75 08 96

www.provence.guideweb.com/bb/grand-jas

Campsite

Camping Municipal - Le Défends

Shaded campsite 1.5km from the town centre next to the municipal swimming pool and tennis courts.

Route de St-Trinit, 83490 Sault

00 33 (0)4 90 64 07 18

Supplies

Food

There are many local specialist shops including the Andre Bouyer nougat factory.

Bike

Albion Cycles

A full range of bikes and accessories is offered, and a repair facility sure to keep you on the road. Up the hill on the way out of Sault on the next stage to Forcalquier.

Route de St-Trinit, 84390 Sault

00 33 (4) 90 64 09 32

www.albioncycles.com

Eat

Le Regain

A highly rated local restaurant with seasonal menus using regional produce, served in a peaceful garden.

Ancien Chemin d'Aurel, 84390 Sault

00 33 (0)4 90 64 01 41

Drink

Head to the terraces of the bars on the southern end of Sault's promenade to celebrate your ride of the Nesque, conquering of Ventoux, or to simply soak up the atmosphere.

LE MONT VENTOUX

16miles 26km

Sitting at an altitude of 1,912m, Mont Ventoux dominates western Provence. More than just a mountain, its fierce personality dictates the weather patterns and land uses of the region, and looms large in the psyche of tourists and locals alike. Mont Ventoux has humbled many a cyclist, pro and amateur, and though not part of the official St-Malo to Nice route, it is an unmissable challenge for Tour de France aficionados.

Sault to Chalet Reynard

Of the three routes to the top, Sault offers the easiest ascent as it is already over 700m above sea level and the gradient of its lower slopes from the east side is more forgiving. Cyclists completing all three ascents in a day from Sault, Malaucène and Bédoin, are entitled to join the 'Cinglés Club'.

Tackling Ventoux once in a day is an achievement in itself. It is a 52km return trip so before you set off on your 26km-journey to the top, be sure to head to the water fountain outside the *office de tourisme* to fill your bottles. The road descends briefly onto the Sault plateau before starting to climb gently.

For the first 19km the gradient is kind, and with the summit obscured behind a pine-covered hill, it is hard to gauge your progress. The road flattens for a kilometre before reaching Le Chalet Reynard where the steeper ascent, used by the Tour de France, joins from Bédoin. Here the white cap of the summit of Ventoux reveals itself again, the limestone scree giving the mountain a year-round appearance of snow cover.

Chalet Reynard to the summit

From Chalet Reynard it's only 6km to the top but, with nearly 500m of altitude still to gain, this section can be brutal. It is with a sense of foreboding that you pass the last stubby pine trees and enter a lunar landscape. The gradient ramps up to 13% in places – much higher than the 4.5% average for the climb overall. You can mark your slow progress with the poles that line the final stretch, testament to the winter snows that cover the mountain.

1km from the summit, as you gasp for air, you will pass the Tom Simpson memorial dedicated to the revered British cyclist. He died of exhaustion and heart failure at this very spot on the 13th July 1967 during the Tour de France. In December 2013, part of the stone memorial was damaged by the howling Mistral winds that can buffet the summit unannounced. If the trees are gently swaying on the promenade in Sault, the winds are guaranteed to be whipping across the summit and are more than sufficient

to unseat even the most stubborn cyclist, leaving them humbled by the powers of Mont Ventoux. The same strong winds dry the moisture in the air, often leading to spectacularly clear and serene deep-blue skies.

As you round the final switchback up to the summit from the observatory car park, the view over Provence is sublime. Catch your breath and visit the overpriced Haribo man at the top, who will be happy to help you part with sweaty euros from your back pocket for a sugar fix. For a quieter Mont Ventoux experience visit in the late afternoon when golden light reflects off the rocks.

Be sure to bring layers, though. It can be 20 degrees colder at the summit than in Sault and receives twice as much rainfall. If you're admiring a spectacular sunset you've left it too late to descend in daylight, as it's a long way down.

The descent is exhilarating but take care to keep left at Chalet Reynard so as not to finish in Bédoin. It's a long way back up!

BEYOND THE BIKE

Mont Ventoux is not only revered by cyclists but has been classified by UNESCO as a biosphere reserve with a uniquely diverse flora and fauna. This diversity is due in part to the wide range in temperature between the peak and lower slopes.

The peach orchards and lavender fields on the plains surrounding Ventoux's lower slopes give way to beech, oak and conifer woodland, whilst arctic flowers such as the Greenland poppy are one of the few signs of life near the summit. Ventoux is also home to 120 different species of bird and wild Corsican sheep and boar also forage on its slopes.

LE TOUR'S TOUGHEST CLIMB

Marcel Bidot, former manager of the French National Road Cycling Team once proclaimed 'Le Mont Ventoux ne tolère pas le surrégime' (Mont Ventoux takes orders from no one). Ventoux has both humbled and overawed many of cycling's biggest stars.

It plays a decisive role in the final outcome of the race whenever it appears in the *parcours*. Fans endlessly debate their favourite Ventoux moments but Marco Pantani's sprint to the line in 2000, where he was barely able to celebrate, and Chris Froome's elation after mounting a stinging attack in the final stretch in 2013, are arguably two of the most memorable in recent times.

Beware of how much effort you put into Ventoux as it can linger in cyclists' legs for days – whether riding Le Tour de France or St-Malo to Nice.

SAULT ⓣⓞ FORCALQUIER

Stage 27: *33miles 53km*

This stage presents a full range of Provençal scenery from the lavender fields above Sault, with the ever present shape of Ventoux on the horizon, to a long valley filled with rocky outcrops and small pine forests. Purples, greens and blues form the colour palette of the ride and the air is rich with the scents of lavender and pine.

Sault to Revest-du-Bion

Starting from the crossroads as you entered Sault, follow signs for St-Trinit and Forcalquier, D950. The road starts to climb gently as you pass a car park on your left and older-style houses on your right.

Once the buildings thin out the road starts to climb a little more in earnest, beginning with a sweeping left-hand bend. At the roundabout go straight on, signed St-Trinit 5km and Forcalquier 53km, D950. To your left as you leave Sault you will find Albion Cycles on a small *centre commercial*.

Before the ride enters a short stretch of pine forest, you will be able to see, and sense, the presence of Mont Ventoux over your left shoulder. You glimpse its white peak against the skyline all along this road, receding as you leave it behind. As you enter the woodland you will pass a sign to the *hippodrome* on your left and a campsite on your right.

After the woodland the road opens out again, twisting and curving its way between stubby oak trees and the occasional pine. The gradient is barely identifiable to the eye but noticeable to the legs – just enough to make you feel you are going slow in relation to the effort you are putting in. If you climbed Ventoux as well, you will probably just put this down to feeling heavy-legged, but reassure yourself that there is a continuous drag to this first section.

After 6km you pass the turning for St-Trinit; to enter the small village, surrounded by pine, oak and beech forest, swing off to the right. There is a pretty picnic area near to a lavender oil distillery and the church and abbey are typical of Roman design in Provence – very simple and square.

Lavender fields are plentiful throughout this stretch, the parallel lines of the plants accenting the curve of the Albion Plateau that you are riding across. Groups of bee hives are often placed in the corner of fields so that the bees can make good use of the sweet pollen when the lavender is in flower; a constant hum emanates from the roadside as they work. You will still be able to see the white summit of Ventoux, framed by the lavender in the foreground and one of the classic images of this region.

8km after St-Trinit you will pass through Revest-du-Bion, which is surrounded by chestnut forests. The trees are

celebrated with a large fair, *fête de la châtaigne* each autumn.
As you enter the village there is a green on the right planted
with trees, many a hundred years old. This shady space is
popular with people just sitting and watching the world go
by, so you may get a friendly wave as you pass.

Part of the old fortified walls still remain and you will be
able to see the Portissol gateway as you ride through. Follow
the main route through the town, ignoring narrower side
roads, signed Banon 13km D950.

As you exit the village you reach an unsigned crossroad,
where you have the right of way to continue straight on.

Revest-du-Bion to Banon

The road continues on its very gradual ascent across the
false flat of the plateau. Occasional wide bends steer you
round the crevices and crenulations of the landscape. One
particular bend does a roller-coaster, 180-degree curve
down to a narrow stream, before crossing over it and back
up the other side.

The fields of lavender continue sporadically with
small patches of woodland at the fields' edges. 8km after
leaving Revest-du-Bion the road makes a dramatic plunge
downward, and a steep, fast, hairpin approaches rapidly.

The scenery also changes in an instant; the steep-sided
valley sides are covered in gnarled, stunted trees with a
stone wall stopping the edges from collapsing onto the road.

4km of descending takes you into Banon, then you
climb again to reach the centre of the village. Banon is
an attractive and lively place with stone-paved streets and
archways dating back to the 14th-century. Many homes still
have their ancient, solid-wood front doors.

There is a real mix of shops. You can buy deliciously
scented lavender soaps and toiletries in one store and
second-hand books in another. Book-selling is a particular
theme in Banon: its internationally famous bookshop, Le
Bleuet, draws in visitors from all over France.

Market day is Tuesday. Look out for the stall selling
Banon's tasty goat's cheese, matured in chestnut leaves and
hand-tied with raffia. Banon is a a real town and you sense
that it has a life of its own once the tourist traffic has passed
through. The cafés are always alive with people gossiping
and exchanging news.

When you stop in the cafés you will see old men at the
bars sipping pastis and exchanging gossip at any hour of the
day. The community life of the town seems vibrant
and varied.

LE BLEUET

Owned by Joël Gattefossé, a former carpenter
who bought his first bookshop in 1990, Le Bleuet
stretches over three floors and offers 150,000
different titles. It is already the 7th largest book
shop in France, though its ultimate goal is to
be the biggest. There is also a thriving internet
business that has created many jobs for this small
village. In a place with just over 1,000 inhabitants
an average of 1,600 books are sold per day.

This book-lover's paradise has floor to ceiling
shelves, lots of dead-end corridors and hidden
corners. The owner's passion for books shines
through in the wide range and choice of titles,
and in the atmosphere he has created. One author
who gets pride of place is Jean Giono, born in
Manosque. His award-winning fiction is set in his
home region of Provence and Banon is mentioned
in his book *The Man who Planted Trees*.

Banon to Le Rocher d'Ongles

As you exit the town the road starts to descend again. As it curves to the left there is a good view of the village, now above you, to your right, . You can clearly see the strong position it holds on top of the hill. At the bottom of the descent you will reach a staggered crossroads, requiring you to turn left then right, signposted Forcalquier 24km.

The scenery here is dramatically different. Gone are the rows of purple lavender, to be replaced by small oak trees, interspersed with occasional pines and outcrops of rock. The road descends for 4km, flattening out again after the hamlet of La Largue where fields make a re-appearance either side of the road. After the long, flat straight the road begins to climb amongst the trees and rocks again.

5km after passing La Largue you reach Le Rocher d'Ongles. You will notice on the right an impressive rock formation jutting out from the hillside with wide, open caves. On your left the village itself sits astride another big rocky outcrop.

Le Rocher d'Ongles to Forcalquier

After passing the entrance to Le Rocher d'Ongles, the scenery opens out again with fields edging the roadside and hills rolling into the distance.

The road undulates slightly for the next 10km but the overall trend is downwards. The kilometres click off rapidly as you ride down the valley, crossing the tributaries feeding into the Laye river and eventually terminate in a reservoir.

At the bottom you cross over the bright blue-green waters of the reservoir and then immediately start to climb. As you climb parallel with the reservoir for 2.5km you soon see the full extent of it stretching away into the distance. As you turn away from the reservoir, after the left-hand bend on a straight section, you will see an ancient dwelling called a *borie*. These domed, dry-stone buildings are made from white limestone slabs, called *lauzes*.

They date from around 2000 BC and were regularly re-built using traditional methods. The walls are as much as 4-ft thick, creating a solid and stable structure. Around 3,000 *bories* are still standing but few are in use. 2.5km after the *borie* you will arrive at a roundabout.

You will be able to see Forcalquier directly ahead, go straight on at the roundabout signed Forcalquier 0.2, D4100. Cross the bridge, as you continue along you can see the ruined castle of Forcalquier above you, directly ahead.

Keep following signs for Centre Ville, going straight on at the roundabout and up a tree-lined avenue with cafés and shops on either side. The stage ends in front of the 12th-century cathedral opposite Place Le Bourguet, the café-filled main square where the market is held.

Forcalquier

Built around the slopes of a conical hill, Forcalquier is topped by an octagonal chapel with panoramic views. This was constructed on top of the former citadel destroyed in 1601.

The oldest parts of the town can be found around the Place St-Michel with its 15th-century fountain, but the liveliest is Place Le Bourguet where we finish the stage.

To the south of the city there is an observatory. Its position was determined by a research study in the 1930s to find the town with the cleanest air. The *Centre d'Astronomie* has an interesting exhibition and at certain times the observatory itself is open to the public for star-gazing.

Sleep

Hotel

Charembeau

Built within the walls of an imposing farm-house, this small 3-star hotel has light, spacious rooms and a beautiful garden with swimming pool to relax in.

Route de Niozelles, 04300 Forcalquier

00 33 (0)4 92 70 91 70

www.charembeau.com

Chambre d'Hôtes

A simple but large Provençal-style farmhouse with generous rooms and gardens. Use of a sauna and massage can be arranged.

Route de Limans, 04300 Forcalquier

00 33 (0)4 92 75 01 52

www.gite-labeaudine.com

Campsite

Indigo Camping

An old-fashioned campsite with lots of space. Pitches determined by the layout of the trees and natural features give it a relaxed feel.

Route de Sigonce, 04300 Forcalquier

00 33 (0)4 92 75 27 94

www.camping-indigo.com

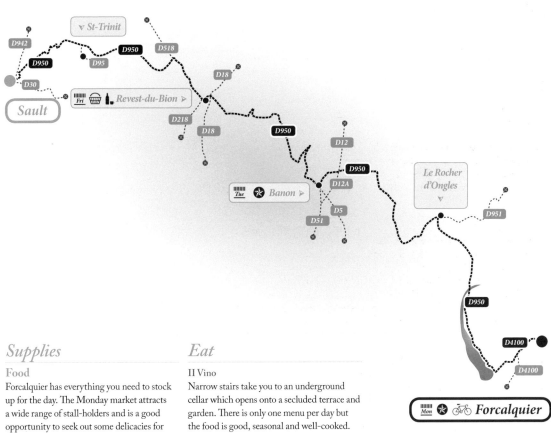

Supplies

Food

Forcalquier has everything you need to stock up for the day. The Monday market attracts a wide range of stall-holders and is a good opportunity to seek out some delicacies for your next picnic.

Bike

Forcalquier Motos Cycles

500m before the end of the stage as you approach the *centre ville*, this small but comprehensive shop is on your right.

5 Boulevard, 04300 Forcalquier

00 33 (0)4 92 75 12 47

www.bachelas-cycles.com

Eat

Il Vino

Narrow stairs take you to an underground cellar which opens onto a secluded terrace and garden. There is only one menu per day but the food is good, seasonal and well-cooked. As you would expect from the name, the wine list is exceptional.

10 Ave. St. Promasse, 04300 Forcalquier

00 33 (0)6 87 10 43 42

FORCALQUIER ⊕ MOUSTIERS-STE-MARIE

Stage 28: *37miles 60km*

Starting with a descent, the route reaches the
Durance river valley, which divides Provence in
two, before climbing to the Plateau de Valensole.
The plateau is a sea of lavender surrounding the
town of the same name and is the number-one
production area in France. The route rolls on to
Riez with its ancient roman ruins, before arriving
in Moustiers-Ste-Marie precariously perched on
a cliff-face and guarded by a star chained high
above the town.

Forcalquier to Valensole

From the *centre ville* with the church on your right and main square on the left, follow the main road, signed Digne. At the first roundabout you come to take the first exit, signed A51. Shortly after, at a second larger roundabout, take the first main exit, signed A51 and Oraison 12km.

For the majority of the ride to Oraison the road descends past open fields, which are noticeably more fertile than the classic Mediterranean vegetation of the previous stage. After crossing a small river, climb slightly to La Brillanne. At the crossroads in La Brillanne turn right, signed Oraison 3.5km, D4096. 400m later, after passing a bike shop on your right, at the roundabout take the final exit signed Oraison, D4b.

The route almost doubles back on itself briefly but the road drops down to cross the A51 *autoroute* then the Durance river before reaching Oraison. The Durance can sometimes seem like a channel of boulders rather than a water course, but in late spring it fills with the snow melt of the high Alps to the north as it makes it way south to the Mediterranean.

In Oraison follow the main road through the town as it bends right and cuts through a leafy pedestrianised central plaza. Oraison is a small but busy town at the gateway to the Parc Naturel et Régional du Verdon. 4 flat kilometres after the *centre ville* the road crosses the Asse river.

Turn left after the river, signed Brunet D15; the road then forks immediately and you take the right-hand fork, signed Valensole.

The road climbs steadily for 5km, with deciduous woods on either side, gaining 300m in height before the landscape opens out. Shortly after, the road descends for 0.5km into the small, wooded Ravin des Cognets before climbing again for 1.5km. The route flattens out for 4km and cuts across the Plateau de Valensole, before reaching the town of the same name, with a mixture of golden spelt and aromatic lavender delighting the senses along the way.

As you enter Valensole, at a crossroads carry straight on signed Centre Ville and Riez, D8. The road descends

a little through this small town which is capped by the tower of a Gothic church at its highest point. When you reach a T-junction, turn right if you need any facilities in the *centre ville*, or left to continue on the route signed Riez D6. Admiral Villeneuve who fought against Nelson in the Battle of Trafalgar is perhaps Valensole's most famous citizen, but even he plays second fiddle to lavender here.

Sault may claim to be the historical centre of the lavender trade but it is the Plateau de Valensole that is now France's most important lavender-growing area. The plateau can be prone to sudden and dramatic storms in the late afternoon, when an angry purple sky echoes the deep purples of the lavender below.

Valensole to Moustiers-Ste-Marie

From Valensole, it is 13km along the D6 to Riez. The route climbs a little and affords great views back to the town. The route between Valensole and Riez is fairly remote save for a *Camp Naturiste* but it is fun – a series of short twisting climbs and brief corkscrew-like descents.

The route flattens out for the last kilometre before Riez. At the T-junction turn right signed Centre Ville. 200m after the T-junction the road bends left then sharp right. Turn left after the bends onto the main street, which is unsigned but distinctive, and lined with large plane trees, cafés and restaurants.

After the main street keep on the left-hand fork signed Moustiers-Ste-Marie, D952. The park by the river in Riez, offers not only a good picnic spot, but four impressive Roman columns standing rather nonchalantly in a field – the remains of a temple built in the first century.

3km after Riez the route passes the small village of Roumoules. From here, it is a further 11km to the stage end in Moustiers-Ste-Marie. The road climbs gradually for 6km to just over 700m before losing height on a series of three tight switchbacks. As the route levels out you can see Moustiers-Ste-Marie embedded proudly in its rock face backed by orange-hued cliffs above.

Arriving in Moustiers-Ste-Marie

At the roundabout turn left signed Moustiers-Ste-Marie, whih is built into the side of the hill at height of 634m. It's 1km uphill to the stage finish by a stone bridge over the rushing torrent of the narrow but lively Rioul river, its ravine slashing the village in half.

The last 1km can seem tough on the legs if you have done

LAVANDE OR LAVANDIN ?

There are in fact two species of lavender (*lavande*). One, sometimes called 'true lavender' is *Lavandula angustifolia* ; the other is *Lavandula* x *intermedia* (in French, *lavandin*).

Locals have always gathered the wild lavender growing on the mountainsides, but began to cultivate *lavande* almost a century ago at over 700m on the plateau, as an alternative to cereal production. *Lavandin*, a hybrid form that was introduced later, gives a greater yield, smells less floral and can be grown at a lower altitude between 400 and 700m. On the vast Plateau de Valensole, averaging just under 600m it is technically *lavandin* that you see and smell rather than *lavande*.

'True' lavender oil is valued for its soothing properties as well as its fragrance, and is used in aromatherapy, skincare and the quality perfumes produced in nearby Grasse. *Lavandin* oil has a different chemical profile containing 10–12% camphor, and is used in insect repellent, candles and less-expensive perfumes.

Lavandin has three flowering stalks compared to *lavande*, which has one, so the plant yields three times as many blossoms. Local farmers are in dispute with EU commissioners who want to classify *lavandin* production under chemicals, as the oil distilled from the plant contains many potential allergens. The resulting regulations and taxation could threatening this unique landscape as well as local livelihoods. Head for the *Musée Vivante de l'Abeille* in Valensole to find out how the local lavender honey is made.

multiple stages in one go, so reward yourself with a drink and watch the coming and goings of this popular but pretty village. From the bridge looking up along the river towards the towering rocks, you can see a series of stone bridges which unite the two parts of Moustiers.

Make sure you take a glance at the famous star that hangs on a 227 metre chain between two cliffs above the village. Legend has it that a knight taken prisoner during the Crusades vowed that if he ever returned to Moustiers he would hang a silver star above the village. The current star was put in place in 1882.

Moustiers was established in the 5th-century by monks who lived in the caves hollowed out of the cliff walls, and it has been a stopping place for pilgrims since the 13th-century. There are several chapels and religious artefacts dotted through the small village. If you still have strength in your legs, walk up, guided by the star, to the 12th-century chapel of Notre-Dame de Beauvoir perched on a ledge above the village, with a waterfall cascading past and breathtaking panoramic views.

INDULGE

La Bastide de Moustiers
Owner Alain Ducasse discovered this 17th-century property while touring Provence on his motorbike in 1994. Enlisting local artisans he has restored it to its former glory.

The restaurant's location is stunning, set in a beautiful garden with views of the surrounding mountains. The Provençal menu chnges daily, according to season and the local produce available. For the sights, sounds, smells and taste of Provence, this is the place to be.

Chemin des Quinson, 04360
Moustiers-Ste-Marie
00 33 (0)4 92 70 47 47
www.bastide-moustiers.com

Sleep

Hotel

La Bonne Auberge
Simple, airy rooms, a swimming pool and tasty cooking make this hotel a good choice. It is within walking distance of the local restaurants and cafés.
Rue Principale 'Le Village', 04360 Moustiers-Ste-Marie
00 33 (0)4 92 74 66 18
www.bonne-auberge-moustiers

Chambre d'Hôtes

L'Oldalyre
Two rooms with private entry and patio, with breakfast and wifi included, situated 600 metres from the village centre.
Florence Delorme, Chemin de Quinson, 04360 Moustiers-Ste-Marie
00 33 (0)4 92 74 61 04
www.lodalyrechambresdhotes.com

Campsite

Camping Manaysse,
Only 500m from the village centre with its shops, cafés and restaurants, this is a practical location for Moustiers, although there are other sites on the way to Ste-Croix should you prefer a more rural location.
04360 Moustiers-Ste-Marie
00 33 (0)4 92 74 66 71
www.camping-manaysse.com

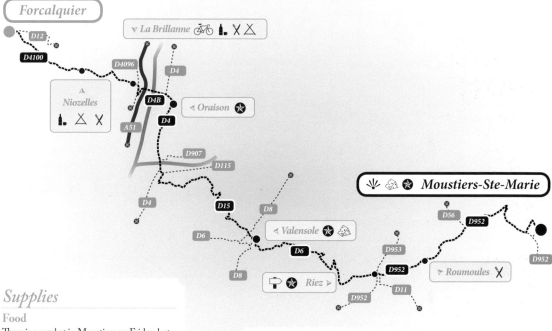

Supplies

Food

There is a market in Moustiers on Friday, but you can enjoy the local produce available in the village stores, including the star-shaped *biscuits de Moustiers*, at any time.

Bike

Cycles Da Silva
A small shop in an unlikely place 11km after leaving Forcalquier. This is the last shop until you reach Nice, as the route heads for the mountains of the Alpes Martimes. Stock up with a couple of tubes if you're running low.
24 Route des Alpes, 04700 Brillanne
00 33 (0)4 92 74 34 47
www.cyclesdasiva.fr

Eat

La Treille Muscate
A lovely bistro, serving local fare, in the main square overlooking the small but fast-flowing stream. Alfresco dining and good choice of menu and wines.
Place de l'Eglise, 04360 Moustiers-Ste-Marie
00 33 (0)4 92 74 64 31
www. la-treille-muscate.com

PROVENCE:
ALPES-MARITIMES

KAYAK the emerald-green waters of the Gorge du Verdon, Europe's largest canyon.

BATHE in the natural pools and waterfalls in the Gorge du Loup, and picnic on the rocks.

FLY with your head in the clouds on a tandem *parapente* flight at the École Cumulus in Gréolières, or at least stop to admire the bright colours as the gliders drift above the mountains.

RIDE a *vélobleu*, the hire bikes on offer in Nice. The perfect vehicles for getting around town, these are just the job for cruising the Promenade des Anglais.

BRAVE the tunnels cut into the edge of the Gorge du Verdon. These short but unlit tunnels through solid rock, take you high above the river.

CELEBRATE with a dip in the sparkling blue waters of the Med. There is no better way to commemorate your ride across France.

MOUSTIERS-STE-MARIE ⓉⓄ
BALCONS DE LA MESCLA

Stage 29: *25miles 40km*

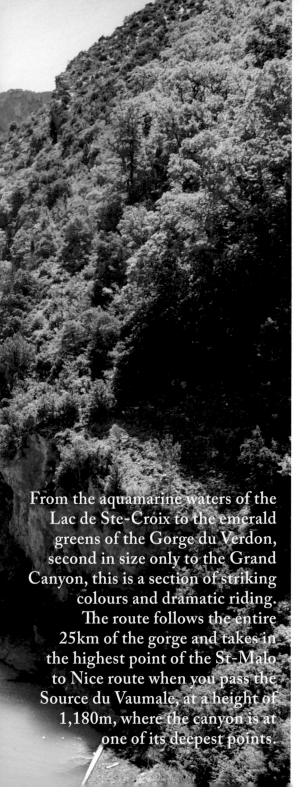

From the aquamarine waters of the Lac de Ste-Croix to the emerald greens of the Gorge du Verdon, second in size only to the Grand Canyon, this is a section of striking colours and dramatic riding. The route follows the entire 25km of the gorge and takes in the highest point of the St-Malo to Nice route when you pass the Source du Vaumale, at a height of 1,180m, where the canyon is at one of its deepest points.

Moustiers -Ste-Marie to Aiguine

The next two stages are best ridden together as one ride in order to fully appreciate the drama of the Gorge du Verdon and descent towards Castellane. However, if you want to split your day up, at 34 km from Moustiers-Ste-Marie you will find the Hôtel du Grand Canyon, with elevated views of the gorge, and on the next stage Comps-sur-Artuby has camping options as well as the Grand Hotel.

Leave Moustiers-Ste-Marie down a one-way street that becomes a tree-lined avenue which, if you happen to be in Moustiers-Ste-Marie on a Friday, takes you past the market, an ideal place to pick up some fresh local produce for your lunch. When you reach the first roundabout go straight over, but be careful at the second roundabout, 2km out of town, to go straight on. Do not take the route signposted Gorge du Verdon. Your route instead follows the Corniche Sublime, a winding route offering many far-reaching viewpoints and is far more dramatic than the recommended tourist route.

A sweeping descent through meadows takes you down to the level of the Lac de Ste-Croix and your first view of the famous emerald waters of the gorge. As the view of the lake emerges on your right-hand side, the road starts to ascend and is a pleasant warm-up for what is to come. As you crest this short climb you are rewarded with a spectacular view of the mouth of the Gorge du Verdon. Limestone deposits in the water create an opaque surface that reflects the colour of the sky, so expect to see anything from deepest emerald green to bright turquoise.

Descending from the viewpoint you cross the bridge over the mouth of the gorge, where you will see rafters and kayakers on the waters beneath you. The road then rises up slightly until you reach a crossroads, then take the left turn signposted Gorges du Verdon and Aiguines D19. This is a category-one climb and is both one of the most challenging but also rewarding climbs of the route.

The 7km climb to Aiguines takes you up the south side of the gorge through verdant meadows and low-growing oak trees. The gradient is easy and the curving road offers occasional glimpses of the lake through the trees. The final sweeping bend into the village gives a fantastic view of the lake before you climb up through the narrow street to an area

PARC NATIONAL REGIONAL DE VERDON

The *Parc Naturel Régional de Verdon* covers 180,000 hectares and offers myriad leisure opportunities. If you fancy a break from cycling, Castellane would be a good choice for an extra night stopover. With many of the activities being highly energetic, we wouldn't go as far as calling it a rest day but it would give your legs a break from pedalling. Rafting, canyoning and kayaking would allow you to experience the gorge from an entirely different perspective, whilst gliding and paragliding would give you a view from above. For the truly adventurous there are 993 rock- climbing routes and even the possibility of bungee jumping from the Pont de l'Artuby.

with multiple cafés and a water fountain. Sit with a coffee on the terrace of the Hotel du Vieux Château and listen to the way voices echo through the narrow streets. Although the fountain has a sign indicating *non potable,* locals will tell you the water is good, so this is a perfect opportunity to fill your bottle before the next stage of the climb. If you don't fancy risking it the café will oblige.

Aiguines to Hôtel du Grand Canyon.

As you leave Aiguines you will pass a church and château. On your right, slightly further up, you will see an ivy-covered *chambre d'hôte,* opposite a left fork in the road signposted Gorge du Verdon, which is the beginning of the second part of the climb. Within a couple of hundred metres you will find yourself above the village and looking down on the brightly coloured tiles of the roof of the Château d'Aiguines.

The castle was first established on this site in the 12th-century with many additions and alterations being made by successive owners. The distinctive mosaic-tiled roof was added in the 1600s. Its flamboyance is unusual for the area and an eye-catching sight against the aquamarine setting of Lac de Ste-Croix.

The road keeps ascending with increasingly open views to the lake and, on a clear day, even as far as the snow-capped Alps and Mont Ventoux. Col d'Illoire at 967m is rather deceptively named as a pass, as immediately after you have taken in the view the road will continue to carry you upwards. From this point you will be able to see into the gorge and spot the lower road that would take you up the northern side of the gorge. The Source de Vaumale at 1,180m is a welcome sight on a hot Provençal summer's day and an opportunity to splash your face or fill your bottle. At this point you are virtually at the top of the climb, the highest point of the entire journey.

From the top of the gorge 5km of descent treats you to sweeping bends and far-reaching views of the gorge itself. The Hôtel du Grand Canyon is a great place for coffee, especially if you can find space on the terrace at the rear. From there you will be able to see deep into the bottom of the gorge and spot the road you will be taking above, as it passes through tunnels cut into the limestone cliff.

Hôtel du Grand Canyon to Balcons de la Mescla

From the hotel there is 3km of gentle climbing until you reach the tunnels. Although short they are unlit and the third tunnel has a kink in it, which means for a brief moment you are in almost pitch darkness.

Have the confidence to keep going straight ahead and almost instantly you will see the piercing Provençal light at the end of the tunnel. From the tunnels the road descends again and at the bottom you will see Pont de l'Artuby spanning a tributary gorge, which is impressive in its own right and well worth a photo stop. Just don't look down if you're not a fan of heights.

A further 2km of climbing takes you up to the Balcons de la Mescla. There is a café on the right if you missed out on a coffee at the Hôtel du Grand Canyon. However, the best thing to do at this point is leave your bike on the roadside and walk down the stone steps on your left to the viewing point that overhangs an impressive meander, a 180-degree switchback that any road would be envious of. Impossible to see from the road, this lofty position allows a bird's-eye view and you can look directly down into the canyon.

D952

Moustiers-Ste-Marie

D952

D952

D957

D957   **D19**

D71

▽ *Aiguines*

D19   **D71**

Source du Vaumale 1180m

Balcons de la Mescla

D71

Hôtel du Grand Canyon ▷

229

BALCONS DE LA MESCLA ⓣⓞ CASTELLANE

Stage 30: *25miles 41km*

Cruise along a welcome flat stretch to Comps-sur-Artuby before plunging into the depths of the upper reaches of the gorge alongside the Verdon river, hugging the over-curving walls as your enter the intimate depths of the canyon. Alternatively, tackle a cracker of a climb that rewards you with an exhilarating descent of the tight little Canyon du Rayaup.

Balcons de la Mescla to Comps-sur-Artuby

Leaving the Balcons you have your last sight of the gorge until the Pont de Soleils, just outside Castellane, where you re-enter the gorge riding low down just above the river, shaded by the narrow rock walls. From the Balcons the road steadily climbs upwards between bushes of yellow broom and wild flowers.

On a hot day you will get the scent of thyme wafting up from the verge. Flatter and more open as you move away from the gorge, the plateau Tels de Fayet is an unusual feature for the top of a Provençal climb. The grazing goats and flat green expanse create an impression of pastoral peace in contrast to the tumultuous waters of the gorge below.

The final part of the climb passes the hamlet of Le Petit St-Maymes, from this point it is a fast gradually descending road through a mixture of open land and small clumps of pine forest. For the next 10km it requires only the occasional turn of the pedal to maintain your speed, so sit back and appreciate the views as reward for your efforts on the climb.

At the T-junction the route takes you to the left but, if you have the time and inclination, Comps-sur-Artuby is a pretty village with a chapel built by the Knights Templar. Another chapel, dedicated to St-André, perched on a hill above, is a miniature version of Castellane's Notre-Dame du Roc. There is an artisan baker with an unusual mural on the wall, several options for cold drinks or coffee and a collection of craft shops.

Comps-Sur-Artuby to Castellane

If you have ducked into Comps-sur-Artuby, rejoin the route and turn left just out of town where it is signposted Castellane. The road climbs slightly for 1km before descending fairly quickly. After a few turns in the trees, the road spits you out into the open on a sweeping left-hand bend. If you chance to glance back over your shoulder you will have a view towards the chapel on the hill at Comps-sur-Artuby, where it stands aloft the surrounding hazy hillsides.

4km after Comps-sur-Artuby, the routs splits in the small village of Jabron. Now is the time to decide between the 6km

shorter but more challenging route to your right, or the easier 23km to your left that takes you down to the Pont de Soleils and along the river to Castellane. From Jabron to Pont de Soleils it is a gradual descent, which is most welcome to the legs. Turn right at the T-junction after the Pont de Soleils, keep an eye out for rafters returning from a day in the canyon.

From Pont de Soleils you re-enter the gorge, the road tightly hugs the turns of the river, climbing almost imperceptibly. The steep-sided walls tower above you and reinforce the impression of being within the gorge, offering cool respite on a hot day. Overhanging rock shades the road and if it has been wet you may see water splashing down the rock walls or feel it dripping from above. The river is broader at this point with occasional small stony bays giving way to inviting-looking pools but take care to seek safety advice from locals before swimming.

Arriving in Castellane

At Castellane, the road brings you almost directly to the Place du Marché where the stage ends. Many bars border the square if you fancy a post-ride beer but, if you need food, you are in luck as there is a *boulangerie* that stays open unusually late into the evening and is a good choice for a quick food fix.

The most striking aspect of Castellane is the Chapelle Notre-Dame du Roc, built in 1703, sat high above the town on its own rock plinth dominating the skyline.

It is a brisk 30-minute walk from behind the church in the town to reach the top but if you have the energy the views are worth it.

In its earliest manifestations, Castellane was spread over three sites; the top of the rock, the middle and the bottom in the valley where the town currently is.

The original Roman town was lost when it crumbled and fell into the Verdon river. Rebuilt in the 1400s, Castellane

became a sturdy fortress and withstood many sieges during the Wars of Religion, although little remains.

One of the most famous seiges came in 1586 when local villager Judith Andrau gained notoriety and hero status by pouring boiling tar from the town gates onto the captain of an advancing army. The people of Castellane celebrate her efforts every 31st January by letting of firecrackers.

The town walls are now mostly gone and the welcome much warmer today. Castellane is perfectly placed for those wanting to explore the canyon. During the summer months the town is lively with bars and restaurants busy with families swapping tales of adventure from their day hiking, climbing, or kayaking in the gorge.

If you wish to prolong your holiday a little longer as your arrival in Nice draws closer you could always switch pedalling for paddling on a rafting trip down the Verdon river.

CHALLENGE ROUTE

If your legs are feeling strong then the shorter, hillier route from Jabron is well worth doing for the descent into Castellane, which takes you through a mini-gorge over several stone bridges. If you enjoy the sensation of fast hairpin bends and the challenge of a technical descent, this is not to be missed.

As you come into Jabron look out for a right-hand turn to Brenon and Le Bourget. From this point it is 17km to Castellane but, although the end is in sight, before the final treat of the descent you have 11km of mostly gradual

climbing to tackle. This final climb takes you up another 300m to a height of 1,060m before the dramatic plunge to Castellane.

After Jabron you begin climb in the minor road through quiet grazing land before entering woodland on the outskirts of Le Bourget.

The village of Le Bourget is only 10km from the end of the ride but, if you need refreshment to get you through the final 4km of the climb, there is an *auberge* and water fountain.

The climb from Le Bourget is steep in places and will create

some leg burn when taken on top of the climbing in the last stage. The top is clearly apparent and once crested you can give yourself over to the joy of flying down the descent.

Look out for the sculptural shapes in the gorge walls, caused by centuries of water action, and the small stone bridges that hop you across the deep but narrow tributaries.

As you approach the bottom, Castellane comes into view on the left-hand side and straight ahead is the iconic Notre-Dame du Roc perched high above the town on an outcrop of rock.

Sleep

Hotel

Hôtel du Commerce

An inviting 3-star, family-run hotel between the Place du Marché and the bridge over the river. Lots of lounge areas well-endowed with comfy chairs, both inside and out, to enjoy that post-ride beer.

Place Marcel Sauvaire, 04120 Castellane
00 33 (0)4 92 83 61 00
www.hotel-du-commerce-verdon.com

Chambre d'Hôtes

Castellane-Aqui Sian Ben

A traditional Provençal style bed and breakfast, each room with its own character and just a short walk from the main square.

30 Boulevard Saint Michel, 04120 Castellane
00 33 (0)4 92 83 37 85
www.location-castellane.com

Campsite

Camping Provençal

A well-equipped site 1.5km from the town centre. Bread is delivered daily and there is *pain au chocolat* in the morning on request.

Route de Digne, 04120 Castellane
00 33 (0)4 92 83 65 50
www.camping-provencal.com

Eat

La Voûte

The main square and the Rue Saint Victor boast a range of restaurants. La Voûte is highly recommended for its cosy interior and delicious Mediterranean cooking.

3 Rue du Mitan, 04120 Castellane
00 33 (0)4 92 83 10 59

Supplies

Food

For supplies, there is a supermarket just off the main square and at the opposite corner, an excellent *boulangerie*.

Bike

There is no bike shop in Castellane but in an emergency, there are several mountain-bike rental places that may be able to help.

Aqua Viva Est Veló Vtt
12 Boulevard de la République, 04120 Castellane
00 33 (0)6 82 06 92 92

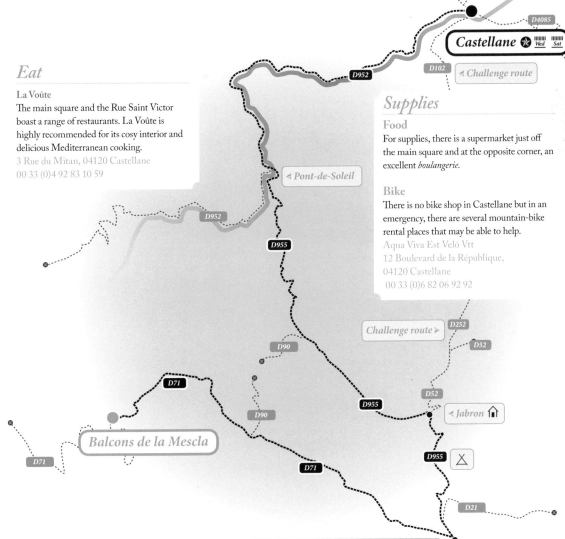

235

CASTELLANE ⊤o GREOLIERES

Stage 31: *29miles 46km*

Two climbs take you above 1,000m to a long, flat meadow-filled plateau, then towards the end of the stage the route plunges through a tight limestone gorge. It finishes by spectacularly clinging to the cliffs and weaving through arches blasted through the rock to the precariously perched village of Gréolières.

Castellane to Col de Luens

By now you will have discovered the rugged mountainous nature of Provence. You still have two more climbs to go on the journey to Nice – the first a gradual 7km to the Col de Luens, the second a shorter 3km.

From the mini-roundabout by the Place du Marché at the centre of Castellane, follow the sign for Grasse and Cannes, D4085. There is a great *boulangerie* on the right before you cross the bridge over the Verdon river on your way out of town. It might be worth stocking up as the facilities in this part of rural Provence have sporadic opening hours.

To the right as you cross the river, you may see rafters setting off down the river. To your left see a different angle on the Notre-Dame du Roc chapel where it presides over Castellane, looking as if the faintest flick would tumble it from its lofty cliff- top position.

The route follows the main road to Grasse, the D4085, for 18km. The first 1.5km are flat until Les Framboiseilles *gîte rural et camping* where the route begins the gradual 7.5km climb though pine forests and the occasional pasture to the top of the Col de Luens (1,054m).

The climb includes a 1km flat section, 5km from Castellane in the small village of La Garde, which has a hotel and a local organic food store. The top can be breezy if the Mistral is blowing so watch out for pine cones flying from the trees.

Col de Luens to Malamaire

Unfortunately the Col de Luens is a false summit. The road descends for a short but twisty 2km before climbing a further 3km to the top of a second unnamed but slightly higher Col, at just over 1,100m. Put a fist in the air to celebrate conquering the last climb of any significance on your trip to Nice. Near the end of the descent you pass a sign welcoming you to the Alpes Maritimes, your 19th and final French *département* of the trip. Shortly after, turn left off the main road at Restaurant Le Grand Saule, signed St Auban, D2211.

This first section can be busy. The main road continues straight on to perfume capital Grasse, then Cannes, famous for its film festival, on the Côte d'Azur, but our route turns left to along a high valley to enjoy the solitude of Provence's rugged interior for just a little longer.

The road climbs very slightly for 2.5 km, where the route forks right signed Gréolières, D2. Shortly after turning right, you pass round the small hamlet of Malamaire. Follow this road for the remaining 26km of the stage to Gréolières. The road maintains its height, hovering just above 1,000m for the next 20km along the valley floor.

Meadows and fields are farmed, where possible, before giving way to scrubland and then higher mountain ridges, particularly on the northern side to your left. You pass various clusters of houses and farmsteads which dot the valley, some named, some unsigned. The relatively wide valley floor, unusual in Provence, is covered in wheat fields with bright red poppies piercing the crop, and there is also grazing land as you ride past kilometre markers counting down to Gréolières.

Malamaire to Clue de Gréolières

Just under 5km after Malamaire you pass the entrance to the small village of Valderoure, visible off-route to your left. Turn off if you need a *boulangerie*, otherwise continue straight on the principal road passing the Chez Valle et Fred *gîte rural*. It is 2km to La Ferrière with a café-bar and small supermarket. All the old villages of the valley were intelligently built. Tucked

into the ridge of mountains running along its north edge, they are sheltered from northerly winds and face the sun, as well as maximising the rare fertile farmland of the valley floor.

5km after La Ferrière you pass a turning on your right for Lac de Thorenc. 1km further will bring you to Les Chasseurs, a sporadically open locals' café. You may be in luck if they see you lurking outside looking for a fix in this caffeine-scarce valley. A further 1.5km on, an unassuming junction with a turning to your left and right marks the point St-Malo to Nice crosses the historical Raid Alpine route, which links Thonon-les-Bains to Antibes on the Côte d'Azur, tackling some significant undulations and high alpine passes along the way.

You continue straight on, following the main road as it rises slightly for 2.5km to a kilometre marker reading 1,170m, the highest point of the stage and the watershed between the small Lane and Bouisse rivers.

The road then descends gradually for 1km to a roundabout at the entrance to Gréolières les Neiges, the closest ski resort to the sea in the whole of France, sitting on the northern slopes of the Cime du Cheiron (1,770m) up to your left. In early spring it's possible to ski in late-season snow in the morning and be in the warm sunshine of the Côte d'Azur in the afternoon! Carry straight on at the roundabout signed Gréolières. It's 7km to the village and 1km until limestone walls close in on both sides and the road twists alongside the Clue de Gréolières.

Clue de Gréolières to Gréolières

With a limestone cliff to your left, to your right you will see a small almost bleached-white canyon beginning to form the Clue de Gréolières with the Bouisse river at the bottom. Clues are deep-cut canyons with barely room for a stream as the ferocious power of the water has channelled its energy at weaknesses in the limestone.

The rocks in the bottom of the clue often feel silky to the touch, smoothed by the water flow. It is a popular area for canyoning, but take care because of the narrow nature of the clues. They can turn from a sedate near-dry stream into a ranging torrent that rapidly fills with water, especially during summer-afternoon storms. However, with common sense and an eye for the weather, clues can be exhilarating places to explore.

THE MIGHTY MISTRAL

In the *langue d'Oc* mistral means 'masterly' and when this north-westerly blows it can whip across the high plateaus and passes of Provence with tremendous power, sometimes reaching gusts of 100km/h.

It is generated by a high-pressure system from Central France funneling towards a low over the Mediterranean. The Mistral can be felt on the Col de Luens out of Castellane, if blowing, but you are most likely to have encountered its benefits along the Rhône, pushing you southwards. The mountains on either side form a corridor encouraging the winds to greater speeds.

It can blow for a day or a week but thankfully, it is at its fiercest outside the main cycling season in winter and spring. Life has been designed with respect to the Mistral for centuries. Iron bell towers on churches are open so the wind can blow through them sounding for miles.

Houses face south, not towards the strong Provençal sun but with their backs to the wind, with no windows on the north side that may be susceptible to the Mistral's assault. Roofs are kept at low angles so not to loose tiles. Hopefully, the only hint of this powerful wind will be a friendly, cool breeze at your back helping you southwards!

Arriving in Gréolières

5km before Gréolières one of the most dramatic 10 minutes of riding in the whole of France opens out before you as the clue plunges to create a dramatic gorge, dropping away to your right to join the Loup river valley over 400m below. The road is left in its wake, clinging to the rock face high above the river on the north side of the valley as it descends towards Gréolières. The road snakes downwards urging you onwards through a series of short tunnels blasted through the rock with a combination of tight left- and right-handers sweeping you towards Gréolières. Peugeot have used this twisty corniche with its amazing rock formations in many of their TV adverts.

The road offers a great view of the *village perché* of Gréolières and the ruins of its castle sit in a commanding position at the pinnacle of the village. You may notice the remains of an even older village on your left near the end of the descent. A very tight, abrupt right-hand switchback,

followed by a more gracefully curved left-hander, welcomes you to Gréolières. At the mini-roundabout continue straight ahead to carry on to the final stage signed Nice, 42km, D402, or turn right signed Centre Village to explore the small maze of narrow tightly knit streets that make up this fine example of a Provencal *village perché*, some barely wide enough for a bike.

With the Mediterranean within touching distance and 800m of descent enticing you onwards to Nice, it is likely you will be pressing on to the final stage, however, Gréolières is a great place to relax for lunch or stay over. The enviously slow life of the village goes on, untouched by the hustle and bustle of the Mediterranean below. Head for Place Pierre Merle where there are a couple of great spots for a coffee or bite to eat on the terrace. Gréolières is popular with parapenters who fill the sky above the village on weekends, taking advantage of the warm thermals rising up from the Côte d'Azur. You can watch them land just below the town on the start of the next stage.

Sleep

Hotel

Le Foulon

A Provençal country house 4km below Gréolières on the final stage towards Nice. Extensive garden and a yoga retreat. Best to check ahead as it is occasionally block-booked by groups.

4220 Route de Grasse, 06620 Gréolières

00 33 (0)4 93 24 41 38

www.le-foulon.com

Chambre d'Hôtes

Villa Regain

Just before the last switchback on your descent to Gréolières, a warm welcome with three rooms available. A *table d'hôte'* menu is an option in the evening.

M. Daniel Stas,

440 Route de Gentelly, 06620 Gréolières

0033 (0)4 89 24 66 94

www.villa-regain.vpweb.fr

Campsite

There are no campsites in the immediate area, so head down the Gorges du Loup on the next section where you will find a handful popular with Côte d'Azur holidaymakers.

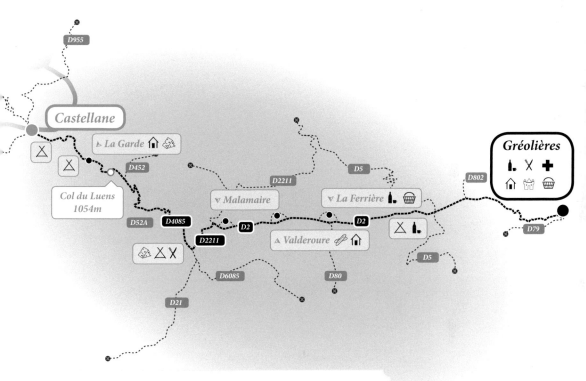

Supplies

Food

With a population of under 500, the village punches above its weight in restaurant offerings but supplies are thin on the ground so head to the small supermarket on the way out on the next stage. They also sell baguettes and pastries in the morning as there is no *boulangerie*, so get there early to avoid a duel over the last *pain au chocolat*!

Eat

Restaurant le Cheiron

Traditional restaurant and pizzeria with a warm welcome, serving local cuisine alongside home-made pizza and pasta.

130 Grande Rue, 06620 Gréolières

00 33 (0)4 93 59 98 89

GRÉOLIÈRES TO NICE

Stage 32: *28miles 45km*

This final stage is one to be savoured; your journey is nearly at an end and it really is all downhill to the finish. Despite the temptation to enjoy the speed and rush toward the glamour of Nice, take your time to appreciate the drama of the stunning Gorge du Loup, maybe even stopping for a quick dip in the waterfall.

Gréolières to the Gorge du Loup

From the roundabout where you ended the last stage, follow the D2 out of town signed Vence and Nice. Immediately you start on a gradual descent and you will now be descending all the way to the sea.

Just as you leave town you will see a small supermarket on your left, if you need supplies for the day, and on your right is the large, flat, landing site of Gréolière's parapenting club. If the weather is right you'll see the bright specks dangling high above the peaks of the mountains, and if you stay awhile you'll be able to marvel at the skill that allows them to land with careful control from such a great height.

1km after leaving town you will come into a tight right-hand hairpin that immediately flicks into a left-hand hairpin; the top section offers plenty of fast fun descending. A further 2.5km will bring you to a roundabout. Our recommended route is to follow the D3 down the Gorge du Loup, the second exit. However, you can take the third exit for the D2 and cross over the Col de Vence.

Climbing the Col de Vence is no mean feat. It is a tough ascent but gives you an early view of the Mediterranean and Nice stretched out below. Descending the Gorge du Loup means it is all downhill to the finish, a pleasantly relaxing way to end your journey, but the Mediterranean remains hidden from you, only revealing itself as you make your final turn.

Entering the Gorge du Loup

5km into the descent you will cross a tributary of the Loup river, from which the gorge gets its name. The river itself is on your right. At the small hamlet of Bramafan cross the river, then immediately take the left fork for the D6.

Shortly after, depending on your speed of descent, you will see the Cascades du Saut du Loup. Open from the start of July to the end of October, this popular tourist attraction allows you to walk behind and above the dramatic waterfalls. There is also a snack bar and souvenir shop.

However, if you don't want to stop or pay for a tourist attraction, there is a superb waterfall to come. 1km after a rock tunnel you head back over the river, the bridge offering a tremendous view of the gorge in both directions.

As you emerge from the next rock tunnel you will see a waterfall, the Cascade de Courmes, immediately on your left. Plunging 40 metres over the edge of the cliff, this dramatic waterfall looks almost exotic in appearance.

There is a deep splash pool for bathing in and you can change discreetly behind the low wall. The wall is designed to discourage bathers but it is easily climbed and popular with those in-the-know.

300m after the waterfall is a long but well-illuminated tunnel with car-parking spaces on the right before you enter. From here, a footpath to your right leads to a popular cliff jump and whirlpool – a last chance for a freshwater swim before reaching the sea.

Pont du Loup to La Colle-sur-Loup

2km after exiting the tunnel you will reach a crossroads. Our route continues straight on the D6. However, if you want to visit Tourrettes-sur-Loup or Vence, turn left on the D2210.

At this point of the ride you will probably start to notice many more cyclists. The route through the Gorge du Loup is popular ride with local riders escaping the suburbs of Nice.

The road descends more gradually for the next 12km, and whilst still far from the busy hubbub of Nice and the Côte d'Azur, the houses become more frequent as the mountains slowly give way to the suburbs, their groomed front gardens contrasting with the rugged terrain visible above.

At the T-junction turn left on D6, signed Nice and La Colle-sur-Loup. A simple check is to remember is that the route you are following is consistently downhill. In this area there are numerous campsites and snack bars but they look slightly tacky and rundown.

They are neither near enough the coast to benefit from the money and the glamour, nor far enough away to have rural charm. With less than 20km of riding left to go we recommend you wait until Nice and stop for a coffee with a view of the Mediterranean.

2km after this junction you reach La Colle-sur-Loup, the first real urban area you will have cycled through in some time, days even. Take care as the nearer you get to Nice, the faster and more urgent the flow of traffic becomes.

After so much riding on quiet roads it can take a while for your senses and reactions to get back up to the speed of a bustling town. Another 1km on, continue on the D6 straight over the roundabout. At this point ignore the signs to Nice as you will actually be greeting the beautiful blue Mediterranean at Cagnes-sur-Mer.

COL DE VENCE

For an alternative finish to your journey, consider going over the Col de Vence. It is significantly harder – the Gorges du Loup being almost entirely downhill – but its rewards are far-reaching views of the sparkling Mediterranean. Vence itself is a beautiful, medieval walled town famous for its springs.

There are many fountains around the town offering delicious fresh water.
Vence is also famous for the Chapelle du Rosaire, often referd to as the Matisse Chapel. It was designed and decorated by Henri Matisse from 1949-51 to thank Dominican nuns who nursed him through an illness.

It contains many examples of his work from the stained-glass windows to the ceramic decorations. Its plain white exterior with blue-and- white tiled roof is stunning in its simplicity.

Continuing straight on, to your left is a drainage channel and as the road follows round to the right the cycle path restarts. At the next set of lights continue straight on into a 30 kph zone. The green cycle path is still travelling alongside the drainage channel and, as this is a one-way street, you will need to use the cycle path. Then, seemingly out of nowhere, at the end of the street you hit the sea! Cross the road to join the cycle path that runs parallel with the sea and follow it for 11km.

Cagnes-sur-Mer to St-Laurent-du-Var

Whilst it is tempting to see the sight of the Mediterranean as the end of the journey, there is a little more to come. Riding along this cycle path with the sea to your right is an experience in itself, but the end point outside the old town of Nice gives a much more ceremonial and special experience than simply stopping on the outskirts.

There is much to see as you ride toward Nice. You'll be sharing the cycle path with any number of other cyclists: *vélobleu* riders, strange four-seat tourist bikes, joggers and skaters. Using the cycle paths is an important part of Nice life, and users are of all ages and walks of life, from the most fashionable young women to sporty old guys.

They will all be whizzing up and down this path. There is a 20km an hour speed restriction and police on bikes to make sure you keep to it! You will need to keep your wits about you, particularly at junctions, but this lively environment is what Nice is all about.

Soon you will be able to see the airport built on its spit of reclaimed land. Landing in Nice is always a nerve-racking experience. As you peer out the window it looks as if the plane will be landing in the sea until, at the very last moment, its wheels find the runway. Rock groynes often have lone fisherman casting out to sea whilst the beaches are filled with families, perma-tanned ex-pats and glamorous women clad in tiny, brightly-coloured bikinis. It's hard to keep your eyes on the cycle path! Whilst the stone beach does not look that comfortable for sunbathing, the bright sunlight and sparkling azure water are a lot more inviting than the greys and sea mist of St-Malo – even though St-Malo has sand.

This section is busy with bars and restaurants, often with their own private beaches. The traffic is normally slow-moving or at a standstill, so as you cruise past you'll hear the booming of car stereos and the occasional waft of expensive perfume or aftershave from a top-down sports car. There is a definite smell of wealth in the air.

La Colle-sur-Loup to Cagnes-sur-Mer.

Around a kilometre after entering La Colle-sur-Loup, the town becomes Villeneuve-Loubet. You can see Vence up on the hill to your left. This area is definitely becoming more of a suburb of Nice than a town in its own right. The route continues on the D6. Take a left at the first roundabout signposted Nice Vence, A8 then right at the second signed Nice and Cagnes-sur-Mer, A8.

There is a cycle path on the pavement to the right if you prefer to use it, but watch for the side roads. After a further 2km you reach another roundabout where you need to turn right following the white sign to Antibes and Nice. If you make a mistake here you will be heading towards the *autoroute*.

Less than a kilometre after this, at the traffic lights, take the road directly ahead of you passing under the motorway then ducking under a railway bridge. Go straight across the small light-controlled junction and on the left you will spot the first *vélobleu* stand. This is Nice's bike-hire system, it is definitely one of the best ways of getting around Nice and an experience not to be missed.

There is a short section not on the shoreline as you go past basketball and volleyball courts just before you leave Cagnes-sur-Mer and enter St-Laurent-du-Var. You might see some slack-liners bouncing up and down on their tightropes stretched between the palm trees. There is a sporty outdoor feel to the area with so many people jogging or cycling.

St-Laurent-du-Var to Nice

After entering St-Laurent-du-Var you'll come across some tricky sections on the cycle path that have the potential to be dangerous. Be aware, slow down and observe the road markings as there are a large number of 'give way' lines on the cycle path, particularly near the marina.

After another 1.5km you'll cross the Var river and see the airport drawing closer. You are now only 7km from the old town and just 2km from the start of the Promenade des Anglais. Nice was a popular destination for many English aristocrats in the 1800s who escaped their winter on the sunny French Riviera. The idea for the promenade was conceived by a member of the English clergy in 1821 with the purpose of providing employment for the numerous beggars of Nice, it was built with funds raised from the English community.

Initially just a 2-metre wide path, it has undergone many developments. It now stretches from the airport around the whole of La Baie des Anges. Its striking Art Deco facades, distinctive white lamp posts and ornate pergolas make it one of the finest promenades in Europe, especially when combined with the backdrop of luxury hotels such as Le Negresco with its impressive dome. Many of the buildings on the sea front, such as Le Negresco, date from the glamorous days of the *belle époque*. Don't neglect to come back and see this section at night; the illuminated hotels and spot-lit palm trees are a spectacular sight.

Finally, the beautiful journey comes to an end on the Quai des Etats-Unis, opposite the arched entrance to the Cours Saleya. A palm tree and squared-off corner of the promenade jutting out over the beach make the perfect backdrop for photographs with space to pop a champagne cork to celebrate. Secure your bike and ease your saddle-sore limbs with a reviving dip in the sea.

There is no better way of marking the achievement of having ridden across France from the misty atmospheric bay of St-Malo to the sparkling blue of the Côte d'Azur than a swim in the sun-warmed waters of the Med.

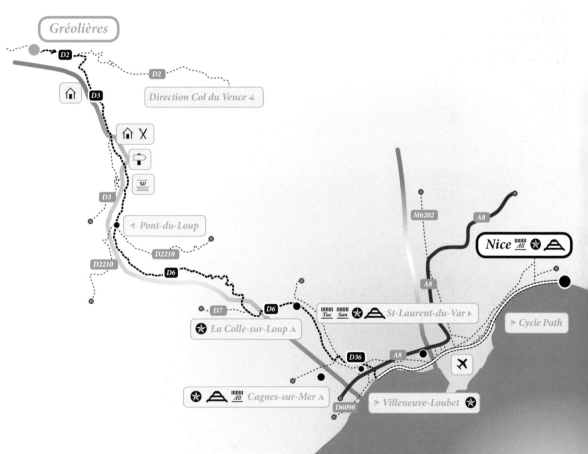

Gréolières

D2

D2

Direction Col du Vence ◄

D3

D3

◄ Pont-du-Loup

D2210

D2210

D6

D7

D6

La Colle-sur-Loup ▲

Tue Sun ★ ▲ St-Laurent-du-Var ▶

M6202

A8

Nice ▲ ★ ▲

A8

▶ Cycle Path

D36

A8

★ ▲ Cagnes-sur-Mer ▲

D6098

▶ Villeneuve-Loubet ★

NICE:
L'ARRIVEE

After the many small villages and quiet towns passed through on the route, Nice feels lively, busy and frenetic, although in reality the pace is relaxed. Nice is a large living city not just a tourist destination and both locals and visitors alike have fun here.

Nice: L'Arrivée

Nice is France's fifth biggest city and is hugely popular with tourists thanks to the diversity of activities it offers. Take a refreshing dip in the sparkling waters of the Côte d'Azur, enjoy a relaxing stroll through the many lanes and alleyways of the old town, or go in search of culture. Nice is the only city in France with more art galleries and museums is Paris.

On arrival you will have already discovered the Promenade des Anglais and the clean but uncomfortably pebbly beaches. From the end-point of the route, it is only a few hundred metres before you step into the old part of Nice, crossing over the busy main road behind you and entering through one of the arches on the Quai des Etats-Unis. The unusual-looking, low white buildings here were once used by fisherman, but now house art galleries and restaurants.

As you enter the town through the arches you will find the Cours Saleya, a flower market from Tuesday to Sunday and a fantastic place to shop in the daytime. Come the evening, however, the tables of the restaurants that line the street take over, creating a vibrant and lively outdoor terrace, albeit a little touristy.

There are many dining and drinking options in Nice, including a restaurant with two Michelin stars, Le Chantecler in the Hôtel Negresco. Nice has many of its own cuisines and flavours: look out for *socca*, chickpea pancakes that are tastier than they sound, and *pissaladière* similar to a pizza with anchovies, black olives and cheese but without the tomato.

Of the many museums and galleries the Musée Matisse is one of the best. Matisse came to live in Nice in 1916, moving around the city before finally settling in the fashionable Cimiez district on the hill overlooking the old town, which is where the museum can be found.

It features many of his paintings and personal belongings, plus a unique collection of photographs, including some by famed war photographer Robert Capa, that offers fascinating insights into his work.

Many pro riders base themselves here, its a perfect training ground with mountains that rise up to the the north of the city and a warm climate all year round.

Nice is an easy city to explore on foot but the best way of getting around quickly is a *vélobleu*, one of the city's hire bikes and the perfect way to nip around. All you need is a credit card and a mobile phone; the simple instructions are displayed on each stand and journeys of less than 30 minutes are free.

Onward Travel

Nice is very well connected. Its international airport is France's second busiest, with direct flights to America and worldwide connections via Dubai. High-speed train services mean you can reach Paris in under 6 hours, and you can also travel directly to Italy with Trenitalia. Ferries run daily to Corsica, a beautiful island to explore by bike. If you don't have to head home and want to continue your journey there are plenty of tempting options!

Boat

Nice ferry port is easy to find; follow the Promenade des Anglais toward Villefranche-sur-Mer and the docks become visible. The passenger ferries depart from the far side of the port. Two ferry companies run from here, Corsica Ferries (www.corsica-ferries.co.uk) and SNCM (www.sncm.fr). From Corsica it is possible to catch another ferry to Sardinia if you want to extend your cycling odyssey.

Plane

Nice Côte d'Azur International Airport is built on reclaimed land jutting out into the sea on the western side of the city. Nice St-Augustin train station is a ten-minute walk from the terminal buildings and can be reached from the main Nice-Ville station. Airport buses also run from Nice-Ville station every 30 minutes, but allow at least 30 minutes travel time to the airport.

Nice is served by many different airlines with a wide range of flights to the UK and the rest of Europe. Budget airline

Easyjet (www.easyjet.com) flies to eight UK airports as well as many other European destinations. For international transfers Delta Airlines (www.delta.com) run direct flights to New York, and Emirates (www.emirates.com) flies to Dubai, from where you can connect to Australia or New Zealand.

Train

Nice-Ville station is on Avenue Thiers within walking distance of the city centre. It is a major national and international station, well served by the high-speed TGV service to the rest of France and Europe. Nice to London takes just over 15 hours with one change in Paris or Lille. If you are travelling with a bike bag, it is easier to go via Lille as you won't have to change stations. All TGV tickets must be booked in advance and always ensure that you are able to take your bike on the train before making your booking.

Check out www.voyages-sncf.com for tickets and timetables. For useful information on how to get your bike on the train look at www.bikes.sncf.com or call Voyages SNCF on 0844 848 5 848.

Car

Many car hire options are available. Most companies have two branches – one at the airport and one at Nice-Ville station.

INDULGE

Hôtel la Pérouse

Built on a promontory looking over the bay and the Promenade des Anglais, la Pérouse is set in the green lushness of a cliff-top garden. It is a perfectly positioned hotel to rest and recuperate after your long journey.

With access to a private beach, pool and within walking distance of the hanging gardens and old town of Nice, you can choose between putting your feet up and sunbathing or exploring the city you pedalled so far to reach. The highest floors have the best views, so remember to check availability when booking.

11 Quai Rauba Capeu, 06300 Nice
0033 (0)4 93 62 34 63
www.leshotelsduroy.com

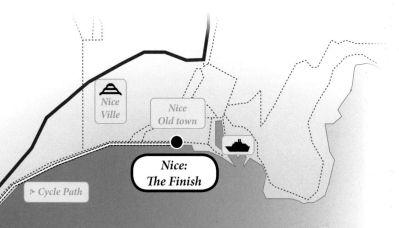

Swim

There is no better way to celebrate your arival in Nice than a swim in the Mediterranean. The beach is pebbly and uncomfortable underfoot, but the water is clear and warm. There are showers on the public beaches and some hotels and cafés have their own private beaches.

Nice Ville

Nice Old town

▷ Cycle Path

Nice: The Finish

Nice St-Augustin

Nice Côte d'Azur International Airport

Sleep

Hotel

Nice Garden Hotel
Within walking distance of the beach as well as culture in the old town, this hotel is a haven of tranquillity, its beautiful gardens offering shade and calm. The rooms are all tastefully decorated in traditional style, but their finest feature is the view of the Mediterranean.
11 Rue du Congrès, 06000 Nice
00 33 (0)4 93 87 35 62
www.nicegardenhotel.com

Chambre d'Hôtes

Villa L'Aimée
A stylish but comfortable B&B overlooking the Parc Chambrun. Close to many of Nice's attractions, it is situated in the St-Maurice area, which has many restaurants and covered markets, and within walking distance of the tram for access to the whole of Nice.
5 Avenue Piatti, 06100 Nice
00 33 (0)4 93 52 34 13
www.villa-aimee.co.uk

Camping

Le Val Fleuri
There is little camping close to Nice, although there are sites in the Gorges-du-Loup. Le Val Fleuri is in Cagnes-sur-Mer, close to the beach. All the attractions of Nice are within easy reach, either by bus or *vélobleu*.
139 Vallon des Vaux, 06800 Cagnes-sur-Mer
00 33 (0)4 93 31 21 74
www.campingvalfleuri.fr

Supplies

Bike

Culture Vélo
If you need a bike shop before you return home or continue your journey, there is a Culture Vélo store. The well-stocked store is part of a national chain and situated just off the M6202, Route de Grenoble.
23 Avenue Auguste Vérola, Hibiscus Park 06200 Nice St-Isidore
00 33 (0)4 93 18 59 60
www.culturevelo.com

Eat

Oliviera

This little restaurant is an off-shoot of a business selling hand-picked Provençal olives and olive oils. The daily menu is not extensive but all the food is fresh and locally grown. You will be able to sample the wide range of olive oils as well as admire their creative use in the various dishes.
8 Rue du Collet, 06300 Nice
00 33 (0)4 93 13 06 45
www.oliviera.com

Drink

Les Distilleries Idéales

Unusually this bar seems as popular with locals as it is with visitors, possibly because of its great position for people-watching, with lots of small tables lined up against its outside walls. Go for happy hour and watch the world go by.
24 Rue de la Préfecture, 06300 Nice
00 33 (0)4 93 62 10 66
www.lesdistilleriesideales.fr

PACKING AND PREPARATION

Before embarking on this epic journey it's worth taking time to think about how you will get yourself ready for your trip.

A 1,000 mile journey may seem daunting but, broken down into sections, it is well within the reach of even the most casual cyclist. A little bit of preparation before you go can make all the difference to your enjoyment.

It is not neccesary to be at the peak of physical fitness to undertake the journey, it is more important to be comfortable in the saddle for several hours every day, without feeling tired, so you can fully enjoy the experience of the ride.

Your posture on the bike plays a huge part in feeling comfortable. A bike that doesn't fit you can lead to all sorts of problems from backache to saddle sores.

Many bike shops offer a bike-fitting service so consider doing this before you go, allowing yourself plenty of time to get used to any changes in your position.

If you aren't a regular cyclist, build up to your trip by gradually increasing the lengths of your rides and try riding back-to-back days, so your body gets used to riding two days in a row.

One of the joys of a long trip is that it gets easier as the trip progresses and your fitness increases. A small amount of aches and niggles are inevitable, particularly in the early part of the trip, but taking some breaks during your ride to stretch and walk around will help.

Whether you are going for five days or five weeks; whether you are camping or staying in hotels, self-sufficient or fully supported, there are some essentials every cyclist needs, starting with a good pair of padded cycling shorts. You might want to go for brightly coloured Lycra or cover them with baggy shorts for a casual look; it's entirely up to you.

It's easy to take too much casual wear for a long tour – remember a large part of your day will be spent on your bike. When you are cycle touring it helps if your clothes can do double-duty, and there are plenty of brands making clothes that look as good in the café or bar as they do on the bike. Café du Cycliste is a Nice-based brand making clothes that are both functional and stylish.

Generally, cyclists are welcome anywhere and there are so many people enjoying cycling in France you are unlikely to get funny looks or be turned away from any but the smartest of restaurants, even if you turn up in full Lycra.

There are bike shops along the route but they are infrequent in rural areas, so be prepared to deal with basic problems yourself.

Carry spares with you, and if you are travelling unsupported make sure you know a few simple skills, such as how to change an inner tube, to keep yourself on the road.

Packing for cycle touring needs careful consideration and even a practice trip to make sure you have got it right. In addition to our 'essentials' list you will need a lightweight tent, a sleeping mat, sleeping bag, bike light or torch. There is a simple equation to consider for every item you wish to pack – how much do you want it versus how much does it weigh?

Essential Cycling Kit

On the bike

- 2 x padded shorts
- 2 x cycling socks
- 2 x jerseys
- arm warmers (thin tubes of Lycra that convert your short sleeve jersey into a long sleeve)
- leg warmers (thin tubes of Lycra that convert your shorts into full leggings)
- windproof jacket
- gloves
- cycling shoes
- helmet (helmet use is not compulsory in France but is recommended)

Tools and spares

- multi-tool including chain splitter
- puncture repair kit
- spare inner tubes
- chain links
- cables
- spare foldable tyre

Hygiene

- wash kit
- basic first aid kit
- chamois cream or Vaseline

Off the bike

- casual clothes for evenings and sightseeing

Picnic Essentials

Corkscrew - essential if you enjoy a glass of wine with your picnic.
Pen knife - useful for slicing cheese, buttering your bread and peeling fruit.
Swimming gear - leave this near the top of your bag; there are lots of spots to go for a dip.
Lightweight towel - a microfibre towel or thin sarong to dry off after your swim or to use as a picnic blanket.
Hand gel - for before you eat.

ESSENTIALS

Planning is part of the pleasure and anticipation of a trip; here you will find some helpful tips on how to get the most out of using this book. Pour a glass of wine, open the map and begin your journey.

Regions and Stages

The route is divided into 9 regions outlined on pages 8-9. Many reflect official names for regions, although for the purposes of this journey they have been classified based on their landscape, change of riding and sense of identity. For example, Pays du Ventoux is not an official region but the *géant de Provence* looms large over the route and determines land use, *terroir* and riding in the area. Ardent geographers need not be offended as the French often refer to regions with little respect for the official boundaries, preferring to take into account a sense of place, identity and landscape.

The route is also divided into 32 stages. The stages are the building blocks of your journey and have been chosen to end in an interesting place, usually with a range of facilities. Stage lengths vary as the route is predominantly rural, so distances between stage towns or villages differ. For statisticians, a 'metres climbed' figure is included for each stage on page 10 to help you construct your journey. For armchair cyclists, each stage gives an insight into different aspects of France.

Maps and the Route

Each stage map provides an overview of the riding. They are all in proportion but not all the same scale. When approaching or leaving a town, consult the relevant section of the text to help guide you through urban areas. Arriving in a town following the Centre Ville signs is usually straightforward. When leaving town, it is important to follow the written directions as the routes require some attention. However they ensure that you are quickly rewarded with hidden lanes and country roads that are perfect for cycling

As France's landscape varies, so does the level of attention to navigation needed to complete the route. On the lanes of Brittany, you need to stay alert, whilst Provence has much fewer roads. If a road changes its number, this is because it enters a different administrative department.

Whether guided or on your own, poring over traditional maps offers a great perspective on the route (see franceenvelo.cc for details of Michelin maps). The key on the front inside flap denotes the symbols used for facilities you may need on the way. Fountains, ATMs and signed attractions are only marked when specifically mentioned in the text, or when in a rural area where you may not expect to find them.

Eat, Sleep, Supplies

Nearly every stage town lists a hotel, *chambre d'hôtes* and campsite. Lists are not exhaustive but offer suggestions across a range of accommodation. A restaurant is also listed and places for a drink are included where there are good watering holes. Occasionally there are directions to an area with a number of restaurants so you can take your pick, depending on what looks good that evening.

Wherever there is a bike shop along the route, information can be found in the boxes around the map. Most places have direct websites listed, but bike shops are often the last bastions of the internet illiterate (or cling to traditional values, depending on your point of view) so not all have websites. Bike shops are usually closed Sunday and Monday and there is a growing trend for them to be located on the outskirts of towns.

Guided Rides

With limited holidays and busy lives, not everyone has time to painstakingly plan their route or book multiple nights' accommodation. Travelling with Saddle Skedaddle makes preparation for your holiday effortless, and on arrival your guide will help ensure everything runs smoothly giving you more time to enjoy riding your bike, exploring and relaxing.

A Final Thought

The information and map symbols are by no means comprehensive, you will discover your own special places. An impromptu café stop or wild swimming opportunity can form memorable moments of a journey. Follow your whims, make this journey your own; duck down interesting looking roads and climb up hills to see what the view is like. It was from such a sense of curiosity, the occasional detour, and an eye for an interesting road that this route was developed.

Further Information

www.franceenvelo.cc

For added details on each stage use the following method to create a URL. Type **www.franceenvelo.com** followed by **/route** then the first letter of the departing stage and the last letter of the stage end. For example:
/route-sn is St-Malo to Pontorson
/route-fe is Fougerés to Vitré

This will take you directly to the correct page. Here you will find PDFs of the map to print, other route information and updates.

Log onto the website to share your experiences about your journey with us and fellow cyclists.

Important Cycling Phrases

1 *J'ai un problème avec ...*
I've got a problem with...
e.g *J'ai un problème avec les freins.*
I've got a problem with the brakes.

2 *Vous pouvez régler... ?*
Could you adjust... ?
e.g *Vous pouvez régler les freins?*
Could you adjust the brakes?

3 *Vous avez... ?*
Do you have...?
e.g. *Vous avez une chambre à l'air?*
Do you have an inner tube?

4 *...est cassée.*
is broken.
e.g. *La chaîne est cassée.*
The chain is broken.

5 *J'ai un pneu crevé/ une crevaison.*
I've got a flat tyre/ puncture.

Components

English	(the/a) French
bolt	*le/un boulon*
brakes	*les freins*
cable	*le/un câble*
chain	*la/une chaîne*
cog	*la/une roue dentée*
frame	*le/un cadre*
gears	*le dérailleur*
	les vitesses
gear lever	*le/un lévier de vitesses*
helmet	*le/un casque*
Allen key	*la/une clé allen*
inner tube	*la/une chambre à l'air*
lock	*l'/un antivol*
lubricate	*lubrifier*
oil	*l' huile*
patch	*la/une rustine*
pump	*la/une pompe*
puncture repair kit	*le/un kit crevaison*
saddle	*la/une selle*
screw	*la/une vis*
screwdriver	*le/un tournevis*
brake pad	*le/un patin*
spanner	*la/une clé*
spoke	*le/un rayon*
strap	*la/une courroie*
tyre	*le/un pneu*
tyre lever	*le/un démonte-pneu*
tube	*la/une tube*
water bottle	*la/une bouteille d'eau*
wheel	*la/une roue*

Other Useful Phrases

Pour aller à... s.v.p?
Please can you tell me how to get to.....?
e.g. *Pour aller à Mende s.v.p?*
Please could you tell me how to get to Mende?

à droite / à gauche / tout droit
Right / left / straight on

Je vais à...
I'm going to.....

Je vais de St-Malo à Nice
I'm going from St-Malo to Nice.

Pouvez-vous remplir ma bouteille avec de l'eau / du vin rouge s.v.p?
Could you fill my bottle with water / red wine please?

Je peux passer avec mon vélo?
Can I get through with my bike?

Cycling Slang

ne pas passer un pont de chemin de fer
to be terrible at cycling uphill (unable to cross a railway bridge)

finir sur la jante
to be completely knackered on arrival (to end up on the rim)

In an emergency, dial 112 for emergency services.

Au secours!   Help!
J'ai eu un accident et j'ai besoin d'aide s.v.p.
I've had an accident and need help please.

Important Signage

Déviation	Diversion	*Sens Unique*	One Way
Route barrée	Road Closed	*Sans Issue*	Dead End
Travaux	Roadworks	*Vous n'avez pas la priorité*	Give Way
Chaussée Déformée	Uneven Surface		

France en Vélo
The ultimate cycle journey from the Channel to the Med.

Words
Hannah Reynolds and John Walsh

Photos
Hannah Reynolds and John Walsh – except those listed below.

Cover illustrations:
Neil Stevens – crayonfire.co.uk

Design and layout:
Jim Clarkson – gauge-studio.com

Maps: Jim Clarkson

Proof readers:
Anna Kruger, Sylvia Walsh and Chris Walsh

Distributed by:
Central Books Ltd
99 Wallis Road
London, E9 5LN
Tel +44 (0)845 458 9911
orders@centralbooks.com

Published by:
Wild Things Publishing Ltd.
Freshford, Bath,
BA2 7WG, United Kingdom

hello@wildthingspublishing.com

Copyright
First edition published in the United Kingdom in 2014 by Wild Things Publishing Ltd, Bath, United Kingdom.
Copyright © 2014 Hannah Reynolds and John Walsh.

Photographs
All photographs © Hannah Reynolds and John Walsh except:

© Rob Sharp 9 mid-left, 14 top, 15- top left, 17 top right, 22, 27 top right and bottom right, 29 top and bottom, 142, 146-147, 150-151, 160 top left, 162-163, 168-169, 174, 204-205, 208-209, 210-211, 253 bottom right, inside back cover left.

© Chris Davison 2-3, 6, 18, 24-25, 238 top left 239 top right, 240 242-243, 248-249, 250, inside front cover mid and bottom

© Daniel Gould 11, 31, 252 © Daniel Start 8, 27, 64-65, 245 © Fougères Office de Tourisme 49 ©Mont St-Michel Office de Tourisme 44 © Brittany Ferries 36 top right

Acknowledgements
Many thanks to Chris and Sylvia Walsh for tireless reading, correcting and large doses of patience. Thanks to James for his creative observations. Thanks to Lillian for her advice on photography. Thank you to those who appear in our pictures. Thanks to Jo Munden for being part of the journey, despite a few route barrée we got there in the end. Thanks to Sophie and Will for a memorable time in Nice and all our friends who supported us in this project whilst we were immersed in writing. Thanks to Liz and Dom for giving us somewhere inspirational to write and thanks to Bryony for allowing us to monopolise her kitchen. Many thanks to Chris Jones at Brittany Ferries. Thanks also to www.skedaddle.co.uk and www.cafeducycliste.com.

Finally many thanks to those who made this book possible. Thanks to Daniel Start for his support, ideas and the backing of Wild Publishing. Thank you to Neil Stevens for the eye-catching illustration and Anna Kruger for her careful proof reading. Many thanks to Jim Clarkson for the huge amount of time and effort that has gone into making this book look good.

Health and Safety
Like any outdoor activity cycling has its risks. Always obey the rules of the road and ensure your bike is carefully maintained and suitable for purpose. Helmet use in France is not mandatory at present but it is highly recommended. Swimming locations are changeable, it is up to you to assess conditions and exercise due caution. Authors and publisher will not be held legally or financially responsible for any accident, injury, loss or inconvenience sustained as a result of the information or advice contained in this book.

Every effort has been made to ensure the information in this book is accurate at time of press businesses may change ownership, and road lay outs may be altered.